Praise for

THE GREY DANCE OF LOVE

"This is a helpful, uplifting book, full of good ideas for you to start and build loving relationships with other people in your life."

—Brian Tracy, author of *Stay in Love Forever*

"George Araman has taken the leading names in therapy and distilled their advice down into a book that will make you look at your relationships in a fresh light."

—Andrew G. Marshall, marital therapist and author of
the international bestseller *I Love You, but I'm Not in Love with You*

"A rewarding love potion for the broken-hearted."

—Nicholas Boothman, author of *How to Make People
Like You in 90 Seconds or Less*

"It is easy to be lost in the maze of relationship confusion, hurt, disappointment and heartbreak. Author George Araman has brought light to the relationship darkness so many people experience. Through his accessible and profound personality analysis, insightful understandings of partner dynamics, and his loving, thorough advice, George takes us on a journey guaranteed to reveal hidden treasures we can use to enjoy relationship fulfillment, perhaps even for a lifetime. Read this book, find yourself in it, and bask in your newfound confidence, personal power, compassion, and love."

— Bruce Cryer, Founder, Renaissance Human, former CEO - HeartMath,
singer, dancer, photographer, writer, artist and lover of life

NURTURE

MS. FRIEND
AMORE

MR. FRIEND
AMORE

MASCULINE

FEMININE

MS. NICE
MIRROR

MR. NICE
MIRROR

MR.&MS.
GREY
DANCE

NATURE

MR. BAD SPARKS

MS. BAD SPARKS

Which of the 8 characters are you? Take the test and discover your
"Relationship Character Type" at: www.greydanceoflove.com

THE GREY DANCE OF LOVE

Step-by-Step Guide to

Finding Love that Lasts

GEORGE ARAMAN

Published by
Hasmark Publishing
www.hasmarkpublishing.com

The Grey Dance of Love

Disclaimer

Permission should be addressed in writing to
George Araman at connection@greydanceoflove.com

The fabulous team that helped the author prepare this book:
Cover Designers: Amjad Shahzad & Nailia Minnebaeva
Interior Book Designer: Darlene Swanson
Illustrations and Characters Designer: Zhivko Zhelev
Masculine & Feminine Energy Editors: Justin Spizman & Sandy Draper
Proofreader: Sean Sabo
Indexer: Maria Sosnowski

ISBN 13: 978-1-989161-68-5

www.greydanceoflove.com

DEDICATION

I DEDICATE MY WORK TO all who, just like me, have tried to decipher what we call the mystery of the heart and tried to understand the different phases of love. Whether you are Mr. or Ms. Bad and want a stable relationship; whether you are Mr. or Ms. Nice and want a passionate romance; whether you are Mr. or Ms. Friend and are friend-zoned constantly or find yourself on the other side trying to understand how to create sparks; or even if you have experienced a wonderful love story but time has changed your relationship dynamic … I wrote this book for you.

To my friends and family, to my parents, to my sister, and to myself: Thank you for all of your love and support as I partook in this amazing journey through love.

To my ex-best friend: You were my motivation and inspiration; you started a fire in me. Thank you for motivating me to search for a solution I could offer to a society constantly searching for love.

To my readers: I am honored and humbled to join in on your love journey, even if momentarily. I hope our time together will bring you all the answers you are seeking and that love will be a beacon of light in your life. In my journey of love I found that there is a solution for any problem if you find the strength to stay on it long enough. So don't give up too soon and let us sparkle some love.

PREFACE

JUST LIKE THE JOURNEY OF love, the resources within this book are truly endless. In the appendices at the end of the book, you will find a series of resources that helped start me on this journey. *The Grey Dance of Love* is simply the next logical step along the way. It is the culmination and highlight of many works that came before and should lay the groundwork for much of what's to come.

And while the list is unexhaustive of wonderful authors, therapists and scientists who contributed, the below are those who impacted the most my research:

Physical Chemistry is based on Dr. John Gray, Don Miguel Ruiz, Renee Wade, Liz Rave, Evolution Male, Corey Wayne, and Jennifer Nielsen's work.

Intellectual Chemistry is based on Dr. Carol S. Dweck, Louise L. Hay, and Dr. Leslie Becker-Phelps and Megan Kaye's work.

Emotional Chemistry is based on Liz Rave, Christina Antonyan, Shelly Bullard, and Renee Wade's work.

The Biology and Chemistry section is based on Dr. Helen Fisher, Dr. Leslie Becker-Phelps and Megan Kaye, Allan and Barbara Pease, and Jed Diamond.

What women want is based on Neil Strauss, Hot Alpha Female, and Corey Wayne.

Some additional notable mentions mainly in Part II: Dr. John Gottman, Esther Perel, Arielle Ford, Drs. Katie and Gay Hendricks, Andrew G Marshall, Nicholas Boothman, Annie Lalla, Kyle Benson, and Hannah Fry.

Their work is truly remarkable. I encourage you to read their books and claim their materials, as I am not going in-depth (since they have already done so tremendously well). The purpose of my book is to link them all together in order to have one solution for a happy forever after once and for all. Each ingredient of the Love Formula alone is incomplete. Physical Chemistry is based on biology and nature, Intellectual Chemistry is based on society and nurture. It is time to embrace both nature and nurture in order to be complete (from within).

TABLE OF CONTENTS

Part II: The Step-By-Step Solution for Each Love Problem to Get You from Where You Are to Where You Want to Be

Part III: Afterthoughts

A Note from the Author

We have been told that love is a fairytale

We have been told that love is magical

And yet we have also been told that love is not in our hands.

What if I tell you that love *is* a fairytale

What if I tell you that love *is* magical

And yet I am also telling you that love *is* in your hands.

However, to have your fairytale and live in magic,
you have some work to do

Some fun home passion since it is all about discovering
the underdeveloped ingredient of your love potion
and balancing your chemistry equation.

Wishing You a Happy Forever After

PART I

A Conversation of Love

MOST OF US WILL AGREE that there is no force more polarizing than love. It has been the topic of books, movies, studies, and pretty much anything and everything in-between. From the beginning of our lives, we hope to receive a pure and unconditional type of love and total reliance on our parents or caretakers to offer us the essentials we need to grow and develop. However, along the way, we discover different facets of love and interpret love in different ways, which leads it to transform into something much different. Love is just as important as ever, if not more so, but it seems to be more elusive and difficult to comprehend and locate fully, and yet it can be so simple once we demystify it. We meet man after man or woman after woman and begin interacting with them in the hope that we will form a strong bond based on the very essence of love.

Along with the great joy we find with being in love, we often see an equally painful side of the same coin when our counterparts break our hearts or we are faced with love lost. However, lost love is not forever. We mend our heart, brush off the dirt, and, eventually, recover so we can once again continue our journey to find endless love.

This book begins with a conversation on love, focusing on discussing the different love problems we often face, discovering the magical formula that will solve most relationship problems, uncovering the first love ingredient, and then helping you to evaluate the type of partner you might be.

We will then discuss the three stages of a relationship and move through intellectual and emotional chemistry, eventually progressing to a conversation on the biology of love. Finally, we will close this section with outlining the difference between what women and men want versus what they need.

Antoine de Saint-Exupéry, the author of *The Little Prince*, wrote: *"I then drew the inside of the snake, so that the grown-ups can understand. They always need explanations. Grown-ups never understand anything on their own."* If you, like me, became a grown-up and eventually lost your understanding of relationships, then this book will help you. I wrote it so that you can regain and improve your understanding of relationships.

CHAPTER 1

IDENTIFYING THE DIFFERENT LOVE PROBLEMS AND DISCOVERING THE MAGIC FORMULA

YOU BUILD A WALL AROUND your heart the first time it breaks: the deeper the cut, the taller the wall. But even then, you know that one day someone will climb that wall. So you build it just for protection to give yourself time to heal and let only that special person in.

When your heart breaks for a second time, you might feel that building another wall won't keep the pain out. You learned from your mistake, and so you take the million little pieces left and discard them across the ocean. You know that it is going to be nearly impossible to put all the pieces together again. Love is now just a fairytale for you, yet you keep hoping that someone, someday, will begin a treasure hunt to collect all the pieces of your heart and, eventually, mend it in a most delicate way.

Love will always be a mystery for those who don't take the time to understand it fully. Unfortunately, few of us have ever given love enough time. It sometimes seems that modern society regards love as a nonnecessity and that it is often out of reach. From fairytales to rom-com movies, we've been brought up to believe that love either happens or it doesn't. We've been brought up to believe that love doesn't last forever or perhaps that it only lasts a short time, if we're lucky. So it's not surprising that so many people believe that love is magical but not entirely in our hands. In this book, we will explore a different kind of love, a different kind of magic. I will take you on a journey to see love and magic in a new light. Yes, love is magic; yes, love is a feeling; yes, love is a fairytale; and yes, love can be in your hands.

The Heartbreak

It took me almost six months and the help of my cousins to start healing and living again after I suffered a broken heart for the first time. Back then, I couldn't quite understand how my girlfriend could have emotionally connected with another man, which I considered the harshest form of cheating, or leave so suddenly after around eighteen months. However, just like Steve Jobs once said, *"You can only connect the dots looking backwards,"* and that is what I did when I was writing this book. While connecting the dots, I also noticed that a lot of relationships and marriages are platonic and more similar to a *settled-forever-after* "for the sake of the kids" rather than passionate love affairs (for which I constantly yearned).

After my second heartbreak, I decided that it was impossible to let my best friend go just like that. I succumbed to a feeling of "not again," and I just couldn't let the magical connection fall by the wayside. For the first time, I'd found someone I connected with on such a deep level, and I didn't want to lose that. It felt like a repetitive pattern, and the pain wasn't any easier to manage because of the familiarity. However, I understood that to ultimately win this woman's heart, I had to lose her friendship temporarily. That started with finding myself.

And so, after a week of complete and total mourning, I stopped playing the role of a victim and began to channel all of my energy and emotions into finding a solution. In my mind, this could never happen again, and I would do all I could to ensure that. After all, I had been in the personal development world for some time, reading many stories about patience, persistence, and hard work. Example after example ran through my mind. All of this inspired me not to give up, improve myself, and to gain a better understanding of the real problem between my ex-best friend and me. After numerous conversations, I finally knew why she wasn't attracted to me. It took some time for this particular light bulb to illuminate, but after it did, it led me on an entirely unexpected journey.

After weeks of intensive research and reading more than 1,200-plus articles, 200-plus books, and reviewing other resources, I finally found a solution to:

- Why we are attracted to bad boys/girls, and how to CREATE attraction with ANYONE

- Why we love nice guys/girls, and how to develop and MAINTAIN deep love and intimacy

- Why we are friend-zoned, and how to move from a FRIEND to a LOVER

- Why we are cheated on, and why we cheat and how to AVOID it

In Part I of this book, you will discover my answers to these situations. You will also understand the different solutions to love, or the "why" of each of the love problems outlined. I will also introduce you to the different "Relationship Character Types," and you'll discover which love character you are in addition to learning about the three stages of love and how you can trigger your biology and chemistry to be and stay in love. This inner journey will help you better understand yourself, discover your hidden magic, and become the hero of your own love journey.

Part II focuses on the "how" of the solution. There you will find a step-by-step plan to move you from being a lover and into a magical relationship; from being a friend and into a magical relationship; and from being in a passionless relationship to being in a magical one. The last chapter in Part II ties the knot of the Grey Dance of Love by sharing some of Mr. and Ms. Grey's most valuable nuggets of wisdom to make your romance sparkle and deepen your love. I divided this book in a logical, progressive, and easy-to-follow way. You will start with the love equation and then move to understanding the love problems through the equation. We all have an innate desire for love, and this book will help you evaluate, analyze, and progress in the direction of your ideal relationship.

This book is a bridge between four types of schools and brings you one simple formula to help you better understand love. You will discover love from different viewpoints, including biology, chemistry, psychology, anthropology, history, nature, nurture, mathematics, physics, spirituality, and philosophy. You will experience love as you never have before. The formulas outlined in this book have tremendous added value. Let me reassure you that whatever underdeveloped part is in your Love Formula, you can find the equilibrium and have the love you have been dreaming of.

I have gathered all the information in this book through a long research process. It is the accumulated contributions of countless authors, researchers, scientists, and the universe. Together with these timeless teachings, I have imparted my own formulas and experiences that will not only personalize the journey but give you the opportunity to learn from my own heartbreak.

It is time for you to take back the control. Taking control of your love life means adding **more** magic to your love life. The world is in dire need of love—some real, magical love. However, very few of us fully realize it and take action toward it. For all of you looking for love and who have encountered a brick wall because there was this "piece" that just wasn't right for you, this book carries the solution. You will discover the missing piece of love and how to develop it to become whole and at ONE with love. While you'll discover incredible concepts that you can apply immediately to your life, note that only with practice will you find what you're looking for.

There is a certain sexiness in never giving up. This never-giving-up attitude or drive is love at its highest level. Everyone can love when everything is rosy, but love—true love—is when you never give up and face the stormiest of the tornados. It is when you go to hell and back for the sake of your love to be together in a relationship. I am a firm believer that true love stands the test of time and space, and when you truly love, nothing and no one can stand in your way. It is true, pure, and divine. This is because love isn't ego-based, and it's not about needing someone. It is about wanting someone and doing whatever it takes.

The Three Love Problems

The problem likely feels similar to a common one, familiar in the sense that we have all experienced heartbreak in one form or another. However, with that pain also comes the endless desire to do all you can to ensure it never happens again. As delicate as the heart might seem, it is resilient and strong as well.

Think of this as a chemistry class where you hold the crucial ingredients to make your own love potion. All you need to do is find the right ingredients and mix them with the right dosages. Your result will be a magical elixir. In this chapter, I'll help you discover the three ingredients to transform you into a love alchemist, capable of taking control of and manifesting a truly magical and passionate love life. The Love Formula includes three magical ingredients:

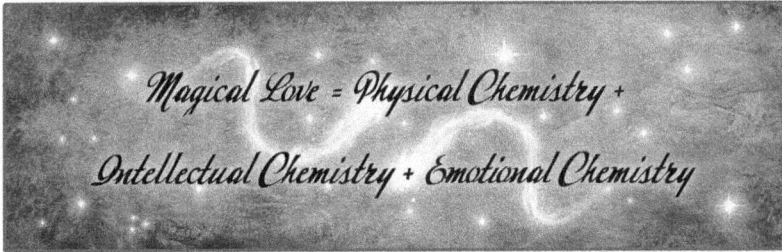

Magical Love = Physical Chemistry + Intellectual Chemistry + Emotional Chemistry

1. Physical Chemistry: Connection of the Body

2. Intellectual Chemistry: Connection of the Mind

3. Emotional Chemistry: Connection of the Heart

Magical love is the result of these powerful connections.

While I never truly embraced a heartfelt joy toward chemistry, it is now one of my greatest passions. Perhaps because the Law of Attraction states, "What you love and what you hate, you both attract."

To further illustrate this point, think about the answers to some of the following questions:

> *Have you ever wondered why we are often attracted to bad girls and bad boys?*

Why is it that sometimes you find the perfect person, but it just doesn't seem to click between the two of you?

Or you get married to the love of your life, only to find the fire quickly extinguishes?

Or why your love cheats on you, even though he or she loves you?

Why might you wander from your significant other and look elsewhere for fulfillment?

When it comes to love, we commonly see three forms or scenarios:

1) First Scenario: Love at First Sight

2) Second Scenario: Friend at First Sight

3) Third Scenario: Friend at Last Sight

Each of these carries unique and independent attributes and challenges.

I hope that by the end of this book, you will acquire a sense of awareness and knowledge to abandon dangerous love practices and move toward the following solutions:

1) From love at first sight to a passionate relationship

2) From friends at first sight to a passionate relationship

3) From friends at last sight to a passionate relationship

To that end, let us delve into the magic of love …

First Scenario: Love at First Sight

When you first meet someone, it is common to feel butterflies in your stomach, see sparks flying across the room, feel a sizzling sense of passion, and feel like you've found "The One." It's like a dream come true, isn't it? You've just found a person who connects with you on a physical and emotional level. That is when phenethylamine (PEA), also known as the "love molecule," shoots your emotions to your brain, triggering a message that you are in love.

While this is a wonderful feeling, don't shout "hooray" just yet. Why? Well, if you don't have any intellectual chemistry and common interests with your newfound partner, then once the PEA dissipates, you might find yourself wondering why you fell for that person in the first place. This is where all the questions of self-doubt start chiming in and negative thoughts begin to surface, such as *"My mom was right when she said she/he wasn't the right one for me."*

So let's revisit that initial encounter. Does it mean that those initial exhilarating emotions are just the PEA messing with your brain? Most of us learn about love from books and movies, and we've been disillusioned. From a young age, we believe that relationships are all about love at first sight or that sparks should always come first; that once you meet someone who makes you feel butterflies, then he/she sure is the real deal, the prince/princess of your dreams. It can work, but intellectual chemistry needs to be present for it to last.

Unfortunately, most of those movies start with strong, passionate love, but that's also where the story ends. Romeo and Juliet died young in the arms of one another; Jack in *Titanic* died while the love of his life, Rose, survived the capsizing of the ship. Cinderella married her prince, and then the movie ended; Belle met a Beast, who then transformed into a prince, who she then married. In those examples, the movies ended with these so-called "magical couples" never really living together or developing a long-lasting relationship. If they even did, it was likely a short one.

That is the world in which we grew up. Hollywood didn't mean to mislead us, but inevitably, it did. Our subconscious minds then take this "data" and shape our romantic futures based on those selective storylines. ***While those versions of love might seem amazing at first glance, they are just ONE part of the Love Formula.***

This is one of the many reasons why most of us go through life expecting our princes and princesses to magically appear out of thin air and then anticipate a happy forever after. However, upon arriving at the gates of the happy part, we don't know exactly what to do. We then end up with either a short, intense, passionate relationship that ends in heartbreak or else just the end of the relationship because the sparks are gone and we don't know how to rekindle them.

The problem: Most of us never really learned how to live the "after" part of the "happily ever after" mantra. We haven't been programmed or conditioned for this, so it is even more important that we become aware of it and focus our time and energy on it. Moreover, since our minds always require closure, the subconscious then fills in the rest of the story. In this case, we are conditioned to believe that *love* is always magical and happy and we always get what we want all of the time. However, when that first obstacle appears (and it's coming), we then start thinking that something is wrong and this couldn't possibly be love. We believe we have fallen out of love, but we don't understand that relationships require a daily dose of "home passion" to keep the fire alive. So it's important to learn the dance of love between passion and friendship.

Sometimes, you might fall in love at first sight and believe that you are compatible with your mate. While you're thinking *"This is it,"* I advise you to hold your horses. In the first scenario, we often find that there is a lack of common ground. This is why there are a lot of heartbreaks and a lot of misconceptions such as *I don't understand why I love him/her while he/she treats me so badly.* Let me reassure you that these feelings are quite normal. So the problem of the first scenario is that it lacks intellectual chemistry and (long-term) emotional chemistry.

The Solution to the First Scenario Using the Love Formula

You are the ultimate bad boy/girl and keep on having flings. But now you want a relationship with someone; however, you feel misunderstood when you date. You are the loner who doesn't need anyone. You are brilliant at igniting sparks, but you don't know what love is. You are waiting for this ONE person who will storm into your life, challenge you, and shift your life as romantic movie heroes or heroines do.

Your natural ingredients are: Physical Chemistry and (Short-term) Emotional Chemistry.

> Lover = (Normal to High) Physical Chemistry +
> (Normal to High) Short-term Emotional Chemistry
>
> Love at First Sight = (Normal to High) Physical Chemistry +
> (Normal to High) Emotional Chemistry + Spiritual Chemistry

With love at first sight, intellectual chemistry is not relevant. However, because of past-life connections, spiritual chemistry is.

As a lover, physical chemistry and (short-term) emotional chemistry are more important to you than intellectual chemistry, which is irrelevant. So, to find lasting love, you'll need to take the following steps:

Step 1: Start out as lovers with strong physical chemistry and (short-term) emotional chemistry.

Step 2: Build the intellectual chemistry (to understand each other better).

Step 3: Build the long-term emotional chemistry (to keep the sparks).

Step 4: Dance between the friendship and passion sides of love to create a long-term relationship.

Second Scenario: Friend at First Sight

Now imagine you've developed a close relationship with a friend, yet one or both of you don't feel any sparks. Wouldn't you want to ignite the relationship if you could? I mean, wouldn't it just be perfect?

You just found out that you are compatible on an intellectual and emotional level through sharing many common values, beliefs, hobbies, dreams, goals, and much more. While this creates a deep connection, to ensure the sparks are flying, physical and emotional chemistry must be present.

You keep wondering why you can't fall in love with this amazing person who is just like you, or you are on the other side not understanding how this amazing person doesn't feel like you. The truth is that the physical connection supports and maintains the emotional and mindful one. You simply cannot expect to have true and passionate love if one of these fundamental necessities isn't present.

So the problem we find in the second scenario is a lack of passion, or sparks, which results in being "friend-zoned." It is normal to worry about being caught in the friend zone, but you'll discover that this can actually be a blessing in disguise.

Keep the faith if you've been friend-zoned, as sometimes the best relationships start with a friendship. As friends, you already have a chemistry base, and it is a powerful one. Friends also have a lot of common values, goals, and tend to see life in a similar fashion.

Moreover, if you believe that you can't create the sparks, that they are either there or they are not (Chapter 2, "Physical Chemistry," will prove you wrong), or that it would be fake—not magical—to ignite things, then please visit www.greydanceoflove.com and read the omitted chapter "Rational Love, Emotional Love, or Magical Love?"

Sometimes, friends don't directly feel the sparks but passion can develop after a couple of dates, which is why dating experts say it's always good to give someone a chance when a basic level of compatibility exists. You'll discover, just as I did, that there is no perfect love, and that if you can *rearrange* the ingredients of the potion, you can indeed *create* some magic; sometimes, if you don't immediately feel those sparks, it doesn't mean they don't exist, but rather that they might just be asleep. This explains why people can stay friends for years and just a little shift in their relationship dynamic can ignite the most passionate sparks and turn a friendship made of legend into the hottest love affair ever.

The good news: Whether you know the person and are friends with that person or not, you can take the same approach to create the sparks. *The second scenario is where you will find the OTHER part of the Love Formula.*

Our conscious and subconscious minds play an important role in this development. In the first love scenario, the *subconscious mind* or *nature* rules. However, in the second love scenario, the *conscious mind* or *nurture* rules. So the problem of the second scenario is that it lacks physical chemistry and (short-term) emotional chemistry.

The Solution to the Second Scenario Using the Love Formula

You are the nice guy/nice girl, the one who is friends with everyone and keeps on being friend-zoned. You know how to build friendly trust and how to be helpful. You're always nice, doing everything possible, and because of that, people take you for granted. You keep trying to date, but you always get the "I love you, but I'm not in love with you" type of reply when you ask someone out.

Your nurtured ingredients are: Intellectual Chemistry and (Long-term) Emotional Chemistry.

Friend = (Normal to High) Intellectual Chemistry +
(Normal to High) Long-term Emotional Chemistry +
(Very Low) Physical Chemistry

Friend Zone (Best Friends) = (Normal to High)
Intellectual Chemistry + (High to Very High)
Long-term Emotional Chemistry +
(Very Low to Low) Physical Chemistry

As a friend, or best friend, with low physical chemistry, you'll, unfortunately, need to do some work to create the sparks. You can try to play on the emotional chemistry (short-term and long-term) as much as you like, but without physical chemistry, you won't be able to create the short-term sparks or ignite the long-term sparks. To create lasting love, you'll need to take the following steps:

Step 1: Start out as friends with strong intellectual chemistry and long-term emotional chemistry.

Step 2: Build the lover ingredient of the formula (physical chemistry).

Step 3: Build the short-term emotional chemistry to enhance the connection and to click.

Step 4: Dance between the friendship and passion sides of love to create a long-term relationship.

Third Scenario: Friend at Last Sight

You've been in a relationship for a couple of years, and you know your lover is also your "soulmate" or "The One." Over the years, you've developed a strong friendship and share many things in common. However, something has changed. You wake up one day and realize that something is missing—the sex, the passion, the sparks, the connection. You're left with just a friendly relationship with a person you really appreciate (or not so much anymore). The relationship dynamic has changed somehow over the years, but you haven't been paying attention to answer "why."

You feel confused, not understanding how the love of your life has turned into the person he or she is now. You start questioning if what you two shared was really love in the first place, as all you have now are the memories of better days.

At first, you think your feelings are normal. After all, you've been together for years. However, then you start getting irritated, perhaps because your partner didn't clean up his or her mess, forgot to take out the garbage, or can never seem to be on time. Those little irritations lead to one of the following scenarios:

1) You settle for the sake of the kids and/or to avoid what society will say; you accept things as they are, take separate rooms, and continue as if nothing happened.

2) You end up separating from each other to take time apart.

3) You get divorced.

In extreme cases, if you don't address those little irritations and issues, one partner might cheat on the other, causing irreparable harm. The irritations stem from a lack of emotional chemistry (more on that in Chapter 6), which then leads to a shift in the relationship dynamic (physical chemistry).

Moreover, if one or both of you can't find a resolution, then this may mark the end of the relationship.

So again, the problem we find in the third scenario is a lack of connection. While years have passed and you've consolidated friendship as part of the relationship, it was at the cost of the romance part. Yes, I know the kids, work, and life all got in the way. But when did you last have intimate contact (but not necessarily sex)? In the third scenario, one of the parties has been friend-zoned. You can be friend-zoned even when you are in a relationship. This is why love is a magical dance between passion and friendship. If you stop dancing on one side of the equation, the flow of energy will stop, and the relationship will die.

As Albert Einstein said, *"Everything is energy."* Relationships are included in this reference. When you stop the movement, you stop the flow. When you stop the flow, the relationship dies. So be sure never to take your relationship for granted. Therefore, the problem with the third scenario is a lack of emotional chemistry or connection.

The Solution to the Third Scenario Using the Love Formula
You had a wonderful honeymoon full of sparks and passion but became lazy or started to take your relationship for granted. Two scenarios emerged: you either fell into the "nice trap" and became a doormat, or you became very bossy and had an entitlement mentality.

Your nurtured ingredient is: Intellectual Chemistry.

Your dormant ingredients are: Emotional Chemistry and Physical Chemistry.

Even if you lost that spark, to restore your relationship, you need to build on intellectual chemistry, physical chemistry, and emotional chemistry by using the following steps:

Step 1: Recognize that you are now partners with strong intellectual chemistry.

Step 2: Rebuild the physical chemistry that you once had in order to recreate the sparks.

Step 3: Rebuild the emotional chemistry (short-term and long-term) to recreate the connection.

Step 4: Dance between the friendship and passion sides of love to create a long-term relationship.

The Intellectual Chemistry is what ignites the
relationship for the long-term, while it is the
Physical Chemistry that 'creates' the relationship and the
Emotional Chemistry that 'keeps' the relationship for the long-term.

Now, let's break down the Love Formula:

Magical Love = Intellectual Chemistry +
Physical Chemistry + Emotional Chemistry

Magical Love = Happily Married Forever After

Intellectual Chemistry = Similarities = Certainty =
Friendship = Nurture = Understanding = Upbringing

Physical Chemistry = Differences = Uncertainty =
Attraction = Nature = Tension = Sparks = Biology

Emotional Chemistry = Connection = Seduction +
Playfulness = (Short-term or Masculine)
Emotional Chemistry + (Long-term or Feminine)
Emotional Chemistry

So:

Magical Love = Intellectual Chemistry + Physical Chemistry + Emotional Chemistry				
=	Similarities	+ Differences	+	Connection
=	Certainty	+ Uncertainty	+	Seduction
=	Friendship	+ Attraction	+	Playfulness
=	Nurture	+ Nature	+	Presence
=	Understanding	+ Tension	+	Grounding
=	Friendship	+ Sparks	+	Vulnerability
Magical Love = Fireworks				

Friendship Is the Light Side of Love.

Attraction and Sparks Are the Dark Side of Love.

> = > The Grey Dance of Love is the marriage between friendship, attraction, and emotional connection, and this dance never ends, because if it does, so does love.

Understanding the Love Cake

The Love Formula is easy to apply. If all you want is a short-term relationship or a fling, just focus on physical chemistry and (short-term) emotional chemistry. If you only want friendship, then you need to work on intellectual chemistry and (long-term) emotional chemistry. And, if you want a long-term relationship, a love story for the ages, you will need to work on all three ingredients. So think of it like baking a cake—a love cake.

The Love Cake					
=	Intellectual Chemistry	+	Physical Chemistry	+	Emotional Chemistry
=	Processed Ingredient	+	Raw Ingredient	+	The balanced mix and Connection of Raw and Processed Ingredients

When we understand the Love Formula, we can see that relationships often fail to materialize or can't be maintained because:

Attraction was all there was, and they couldn't get past intellectual chemistry.

Friendships couldn't get past physical chemistry and (short-term) emotional chemistry.

"Happily forever after" fails because they couldn't get past the emotional chemistry.

This formula shows us that most relationships can strive to achieve a higher rate of success. However, creating a relationship and keeping a relationship are very different and, therefore, require the Grey Dance of Love.

Creating a relationship is achieved with physical chemistry and emotional chemistry.

Keeping a relationship is achieved with intellectual chemistry and emotional chemistry.

Creating and keeping a relationship is achieved with intellectual chemistry, emotional chemistry, and physical chemistry.

That is why both sayings "like attracts like" and "opposites attract" are true.

> "Like Attracts Like" = Intellectual Chemistry
>
> "Opposites Attract" = Physical Chemistry

That is also why research has proven that the ideal combination is "matched opposites."

"Matched Opposites" = "Like attracts like" + "Opposites attract"

$$= \text{Similar Wants} \quad + \quad \text{Complementary Needs}$$
$$= \text{Same Thinking} \quad + \quad \text{Opposite Biology}$$

In his book *How to Make Someone Fall in Love with You in 90 Minutes or Less*, relationship counselor Nicholas Boothman labels "matched opposites" as similar in values and motivators and opposite in behavior and personality.

Now that we have finally ended the never-ending debate of which is true ("like attracts like" or "opposites attract"), let me reassure you, this alone won't guarantee you love. Yes, I know, it was too good to be true, or was it? we can turn to the missing piece of the puzzle: emotional chemistry. This is how you make the other person feel, and what ignites the fire. In fact, I'd go as far as to say that:

Emotional chemistry is the secret of all successful long-term relationships.

You see, physical chemistry and (short-term) emotional chemistry create the sparks; the combination of intellectual chemistry and (long-term) emotional chemistry creates the home feeling; and (short-term) emotional chemistry and (long-term) emotional chemistry are the keys that link the sparks with a friendship to set love on fire. The value of the different ingredients of the Love Formula can be summarized as follows:

Intellectual chemistry and emotional chemistry determine whether you are going to be in a casual relationship or develop into a more serious relationship.

Physical chemistry and emotional chemistry determine whether you are going to be just friends or develop into something more—and this can change anytime. You can go from friend to lover even after years of friendship, and vice versa.

Physical chemistry and emotional chemistry determine if you are going to fall out of love, or rather, out of sparks, which explains why you can be in love for a long time and then suddenly become too friendly and the sex disappears.

Yet again, physical chemistry and emotional chemistry determine if you are going to be cheated on.

Love cannot be left to fate or taken for granted. It can start out strong, but even the strongest castles are susceptible to attack if not carefully maintained and as a result weakens with time. Or our journey in love starts out as castles made of sand, ready to be washed away at the threat of one big wave and then fortifies with time. Both, of course, this is to no fault of our own.

However, as we obtain a more insightful understanding of how love is lost, and even how to build love, we find ourselves better positioned to build strong castles able to withstand all the elements of life and maintain them. In the next chapter, after demystifying our love problems and discovering the Love Formula, we will focus on the first ingredient of the Love Formula to start unlocking our own underdeveloped ingredient for our happy forever after.

CHAPTER 2
PHYSICAL CHEMISTRY

IN THE FIRST CHAPTER, WE discovered that love could be in our hands but that we can be limited in our visions of it. While numerous origins and reasons for each love problem exist, they all manifest into one of the three scenarios, each with its own set of limitations and reasons a relationship might fail or not take form. Often, this results from ingredients related to nature and nurture and how they mix or blend. In the end, by working on your underdeveloped ingredients for love, you will create the relationships you want based on the Love Formula.

Unlike People
ATTRACT

Like People
REPEL

As part of that journey, let us shift our attention to the first ingredient of the Love Formula: *physical chemistry*, which is when masculine meets feminine and they "complete" or "chemistrify" each other.

I first learned about polarity in chemistry class. Our teacher showed us an experiment with two opposite sides of different magnets. The magnets would attract each other when we moved the positive side of a magnet to the negative side of the other magnet. However, the two magnets would repel each other when we moved the same polar side of the different magnets. As a young man, I hadn't yet realized that this was a tremendous metaphor for love and relationships. In fact, physical attraction looks and feels very similar to magnets. Little did I know that the law of polarity, evidenced by the magnets, would offer a valuable lesson in my future love relationships.

The Law of Polarity states that everything has an equal opposite; the positive has an equal and opposite force in the negative, the yin has the yang, and, similarly, for relationships, masculinity and femininity are two sides of the same coin. Just like the North and South Poles of the Earth create a force of magnetism, the masculine and feminine poles create a flow of sexual polarity between two people.

Now, it is not as easy as characterizing physical energy in form as either masculine or feminine. In reality, men and women have characteristics of masculine and feminine energies inside of them. Just like a magnet, they are two sides of the same person. The *masculine energy* can't be without the *feminine energy*, just as the head side of the coin can't be without the tail side of the coin, and vice versa.

When balance results between the masculine and feminine energies, a man or a woman will find polarization. A polarized man is assertive, while a polarized woman is radiant. When an **Assertive Man**, acting from his nature, meets a **Radiant Woman**, acting from her nature, you can be sure that the sparks will fly. This is how a relationship is polarized.

Throughout this book, you'll discover that it is important to work on polarizing yourself and your relationship. When you polarize yourself, you are working at a **microlevel**, focusing on what you can do to find love from within. When you polarize your relationship, you are working at a **macrolevel** because you are working to better the pair. Contrary to magnets, men and women can interchange their masculine and feminine energies at any time. External circumstances, life changes, and other people will all affect the **micropolarities** and **macropolarities** of men and women.

At the foundation of our conversation is the recognition that masculine and feminine energies carry a very specific archetype. They should be studied for their differences as much as celebrated for their uniqueness. The better your understanding of the specific qualities associated with each "energy," the more adept you will be at understanding why you and your companion act a certain way. To that end, let's now unpack the differences and qualities of masculine and feminine energy and explore how they manifest in us and our relationships.

Masculine Energy Archetype

The Masculine Energy Character

With a dominant masculine energy, your character reflects boldness, confidence, and a conquering attitude. You are determined, driven, and decisive in pursuing your goals. You work to achieve your goals relentlessly because closure is important. You love to be in control, and you focus on providing safety, strength, and protection. You prefer a simple, predictable, quiet, and free life. You find peace of mind in solitude and disconnection. When you have a more masculine essence, you will always be driven by a sense of mission or purpose.

The Masculine Energy Focus

You are focused on a purpose and make it your life's mission. You will relentlessly pursue what you want with strength, drive, determination, and perseverance until you get it.

The Masculine Energy Activities Lifestyle

When you have a dominant masculine energy, you are likely to be attracted to extreme sports and activities; you are a thrill seeker. Your quiet moments energize you. The masculine energy lifestyle is imposing. You're likely to prefer an imposing style of dress with sharp lines.

The Masculine Energy Communication Style

You show strength and stability with your monotone voice, which is grounding. You have a direct style of communication and always say what you mean. Your words have a purpose; you only talk to reach an objective. You find gossip a waste of time and prefer to talk about something useful that will bring something to you or someone else. The goal of your words is to communicate information. You think before you speak, only speak if you have something to say, and stop when you've made your point.

The Masculine Energy Body Language

Masculine energy body language is imposing. You take up space. From an evolutionary viewpoint, or biologically speaking, space is status. As such, the more space you occupy, the more imposing and higher the status you reflect.

You walk in as if you own the place. You walk with a purpose, have an air of confidence and cockiness, and walk tall with your head up, chest out, and are smiling and/or laughing. This shows confidence, that you're interesting, have something to offer, are having fun, and are fun to be around.

When a person sits, you may prefer to stand and place a hand over their shoulder; you might even give the person a pat on the back—these are subtle cues of dominance. The feminine energy is naturally attracted to you.

Masculine energy takes up a lot of space and knows how to mark its territory.

Feminine Energy Archetype

The Feminine Energy Character

With a dominant feminine energy, your character reflects care, sensuality, and a nurturing attitude. You are emotional, vulnerable, and soft when pursuing your relationships. You flow with a relationship until you surrender with love to your partner because you trust him or her. You love to receive, and you focus on nurturing acceptance, love, and intimacy. You love a complicated, unpredictable, talkative, and committed life. You find peace of mind in togetherness and connection. You magnify things, know how to multitask, motivate, and pursue creativity and self-expression. When you have a more feminine essence, you will always be energized by love and relationships.

The Feminine Energy Focus
You are focused on relationships and make this your life's mission. You open up and surrender with vulnerability and openness when you trust that you can abandon yourself completely to your partner.

The Feminine Energy Activities and Lifestyle
When you have a dominant feminine energy, you are likely to be attracted to dancing and singing; simply put, you love life. You are energized by talking and may vent when you're feeling upset. The feminine energy lifestyle is changeable, depending on the mood of the day. You are likely to dress in soft fabrics with flowing lines.

The Feminine Energy Communication Style
You show flow and playfulness with your voice; it is attractive. Your communication style is indirect; you always hint at what you mean. You talk to feel connected and can talk freely for hours nonstop for no reason. The goal of your words is to share and feel connected. You keep talking to build rapport and find common ground.

The Feminine Energy Body Language
Feminine energy body language is sensual and flirtatious. You flow and walk in a room with grace. When you sit, you may prefer to cross your legs, but otherwise, you display an open body language that invites communication. You sit with your legs crossed, with exposed wrists and neck (it is intimate for women), and play with your hair (to show youthfulness). Feminine energy is all about flirting.

Understanding the Masculine and Feminine Energy Dynamic

While there are many distinct and defining qualities that differentiate masculine from feminine energies, in fact, they complement each other. Masculine energy provides feminine energy with strength, presence, and strong bounderies as well as solutions. In return, feminine energy provides nurturing, appreciation, and receptivity. The strength of the masculine energy balances the softness of the feminine energy. Their differences complement each other and make them stronger. With that in mind, you can communicate better when you are aware of your partner's energy at any given moment, while noticing whether his or her masculine or feminine energy is dominant.

For example, a man or woman with a dominant masculine energy who is full of ambition will want a dominant feminine energy partner who will praise and nurture them. On the other hand, a dominant feminine energy man or woman who likes to play will want to have deep conversations with his or her partner.

Continuing with our example, since masculine energy and feminine energy have different communication styles, it wouldn't be wise for a woman with feminine energy to talk to her masculine energy partner in the same way she would talk to her girlfriends. He will likely feel exhausted if she makes him guess, asks him indirect questions, or just gossips. He would feel disconnected, annoyed, or want to run away. Similarly, if the man talks to his woman the same way he would talk to his guy friends (i.e., masculine energy language), such as being direct and only talking when he has a point, she would feel disconnected, become annoyed (start thinking she did something wrong), or try to talk more and more (because that is how she connects).

It is important to understand the different characteristics between masculine and feminine energy. As you gain a more insightful and direct grasp of their fundamental qualities, you will also be able to use this information to better relate and connect first and foremost with yourself and ultimately with your partner.

The Difference Between Masculine and Feminine Energy

Masculine energy has a direct, factual, and clear communication style. Its vision is simply black or white, wrong or right. When masculine energy receives energy from the outside world, it reacts through intellect and senses by rationalizing the energy/communication and pushing it out by translating it into action fast so that it isn't affected by it. On the other hand, feminine energy has an indirect, emotional, and unclear communication style because it is safer and allows the possibility of change (changing the decision). Its vision is grey, wrong or right. When feminine energy receives energy from the outside world, it processes the energy/communication through emotions and intuition by emotionalizing and absorbing it and by experiencing it and then repressing it, which leads feminine energy to be affected by it, and as such, it processes slowly and deeply. Feminine energy requires time to consider how to respond.

It is a positive thing that masculine energy blocks and rejects the outside energies and isn't affected by them by emanating and pushing them directly. It is similar to the point that it can also be a positive when feminine energy absorbs and pulls in the outside energies and is affected by them by accepting and welcoming them in.

Feminine energy isn't to be considered weak or negative; it is powerful, and female leadership excels and achieves much better results than male leadership in certain situations and vice versa. Masculine leadership tends to be task- or goal-oriented, assertive, and persuasive, while female leadership tends to be more people- or process-oriented, collaborative, and empathetic. Both types of leadership are strong in their own way, and we need both energies in balance.

Now, take a moment to compare the healthy and unhealthy feminine and masculine energies.

Feminine		Masculine	
Healthy Traits	Unhealthy Traits	Healthy Traits	Unhealthy Traits
Wise (Learns and Shares Lessons)	Plays the Victim and Complains	Leadership and Support	Closed and Repressed
Open, Trusts, Surrenders, Vulnerable	Critical and Judgmental	Focused, Authentic, and Grounded	Self-centered, Incongruent, and Motivated by Power
Sensitive, Sensual, Soft, Playful	No Bounderies, No Self-Control, Chases Love	Boldness, Confidence, Present, Holds Space	Macho without Substance, Move Away from Love
Creativity, Expressiveness, and the Arts	Inauthentic	Awareness, Mentorship	Overbearing, Always Wants to Be Right
Heart over Mind	Refuses All Rational Thought, Very Emotional	Mind over Heart	Refuses All Emotional Thought via Addictions (Work, Alcohol, Drug)
Intuitive, Tunes into People and Situations	Secretive, Manipulative	Service to Others	Puts Own Priorities Above Others
Transformation and Growth, Manifests	Stays Stuck in Old Patterns and Beliefs	Purpose and Mission, Doer	Doesn't Follow through with Ambition, Lacks Drive
Caring, Nurturing, Connects	Fearful of Being Hurt So Stays Closed	Integrity, Safety, Strength, Validates	Bullies, Rigid, Controls

A Deeper Understanding of the Polarities

It is important to differentiate between masculine and feminine energy of men and women. Masculine energy is not necessarily a male characteristic, just as feminine energy is not necessarily a female one. To be whole and complete, men and women need BOTH forms of energy.

In the three stages of the relationship section, we'll delve deeper to explore why men are born with a dominant masculine energy and women are born with a dominant feminine energy, how nurture might have affected the dynamic of relationships, and how to reconcile nature with nurture. Discussing this will help you better understand and become more aware of your current state of being as well as your (potential) partner's current state of being, with the goals being to first find a greater balance of the energy inside of you and then understanding your (potential) partner's energy before finally reconciling your differences.

Once you find a balance between your masculine and feminine energy, you can, and should, adjust your polarity to match your partner's current needs if you have one and then revert back to your dominant energy. Energy can change because of the stressors of life situations such as work and personal challenges. As you develop a better ability to change your energy to adapt to your partner, you will find a healthier and more meaningful connection between the two of you. However, it is inadvisable to change your energy to match a person you're interested in, as this won't be sustainable in the long term. In such a case, work first on living in your core energy and developing your nurture energy before approaching your love interest. And let's remember that physical chemistry is based on biology and nature.

Now that we have unraveled the first ingredient of the Love Formula and dissected it to its core, we can move with a greater sense of awareness of the underlying chemistry that leads to certain behavioral traits of men and women and identify the type of love partner you are. You will learn more as we enjoy this journey together.

Chapter 3
Which Love Partner Type Are You?

Masculine and feminine energies shape not only the qualities and behaviors of each participant in a loving relationship but also the interaction of the two, which can predetermine the success and compatibility of two lovers. To that end, in this chapter, I will share with you the great importance of knowing not just yourself, but also your partner. The old saying goes "You reap what you sow"—meaning, you'll eventually have to face the type of person you attract simply because they are mirroring an aspect of yourself that you want to heal (more on that later in this chapter). With that in mind, let's first ponder the men or women you've been attracting or the partner you are in a relationship with and start by considering whether they carry a predominately masculine or feminine energy. This might give you some very important insight into why you are looking for one type of partner but seem to be finding the opposite. This can also help you know which side of the energy you are on.

To better help you do this, I have created eight unique characters, the "Relationship Character Types', that embody the types of chemistry we often see in relationships. While some characters fit each other better, you will discover that since relationships are dynamic, we can always adapt our new skills to fit a different character. Having a basic understanding of all eight will help you identify the energy you fall into and what you need to become to shift your energy, while also understanding where your friend or partner stands at in their own space. Remember, these are simply buckets to help you better analyze the type of man or woman you are and the type of man or woman you are searching for. When you are playing in the love field, note that a man can show his feminine side once he has shown his masculine side, and a woman can show her masculine side once she has shown her feminine side.

I have made the characteristics of the eight characters extreme, and you may not see yourself in them all the time. That is not important. What is important is that you ask yourself which of these characteristics shows up within you and under which circumstances. Let's now look at each of the eight characters.

Mr. Bad Sparks (Highly Masculine)

Meet Mr. Bad, the unhealthy masculine man who attracts all women for the short term. Mr. Bad is an extreme masculine archetype that makes women melt like ice under the sun. Note that Mr. Bad doesn't build friendships; he wins hearts but never keeps them.

Personality in a Relationship

Mr. Bad is egotistical, and his relationships focus on his need for physical pleasure with no emotional attachment. He is domineering, judgmental, and trusts only his own opinion. He overly emphasizes the importance of money and material things.

Mr. Bad expresses an excess of masculine energy and a lack of feminine energy. He hides his fear of emotional connection with his dominating attitude and becomes aggressive around emotions. He feels the need to control his emotions because he is lost and doesn't know how to love and connect. He creates strong and rigid rules to hide his hopelessness, and he shows a fake sense of being in control of his emotions. He projects his immature masculine energy on women, which means that he dominates, can be aggressive, and controls and creates strong rules for them.

Mr. Bad finds romantic partners easily but rarely has long-term relationships; if he does, he will probably end up cheating anyway. He connects sexually but is unable to connect emotionally.

What Do Women Find Attractive in Mr. Bad Sparks?

Mr. Bad projects his desire to women who accept it; they love it when men find them sexually attractive and want them, and in return, they may want men too. He is pretty good with living on the edge, which is also the edge of sexual desire. Women love the mystery of Mr. Bad, the fact that he lives on the edge (a calculated edge), tests his limits from time to time, knows people and situations, is seductive, solid and grounded, has self-control (especially emotionally), and is independent, present, goal-oriented, humorous, and sexually desired.

Women believe that Mr. Bad can PROTECT them and make them FEEL like a little girl again. He has a great PRESENCE about him and stands nice and tall. He APPEARS to have a lot of confidence and is good at what he does for a living. He is really good at sports. As Jennifer Nielsen, blogger of *Hot Alpha Female*, says, *"A man with presence is more than likely going to make a woman feel more calm, feminine, and relaxed. All these naturally help her process her emotions. When a woman can process her emotions, she is more able to react in more predictable ways."*

The Eleven Traits That Mr. Bad Sparks Subconsciously Creates

1) Powerful Eye Contact (he has the look)

2) Strong Masculine Body Language

3) Self-confidence

4) Leadership (he is perceived as strong and powerful, which makes it appear that he can solve all the world's problems, take risks, and accept responsibility)

5) Presents a Challenge (knows how to create intrigue)

6) Experienced

7) Emotionally Intelligent (although this is just an appearance) and Passionate

8) Skilled in Making Others Feel Safe and Secure with His Presence and Grounding

9) Independent and Never Seeks Approval

10) High Standards

11) Integrity (gives him credibility and trustworthiness)

The Problem with Mr. Bad Sparks

Mr. Bad is not long-term relationship material. His number-one priority is himself, so you'll never fix him. Mr. Bad has a big ego and is always seeking power. He wants to win at all costs and believes the end justifies the means. As long as he gets what he wants, it doesn't matter if someone gets hurt along the way. Mr. Bad is focused when solving problems; he doesn't get distracted for whatever reason until a task is done. Flexibility is not in his dictionary.

Mr. Bad is an attraction junkie. While he seeks to satisfy his lust with women at any cost, he does so at the expense of his future. Mr. Bad is a great example of living in the now to the extent that he leaves his past behind and doesn't even consider his future. So, ladies, is he the right one for you? Is he the one you want to build your future with?

Mr. Bad is challenged by how he sees himself versus what society expects from him. The more extreme or unhealthy his masculine side is and the more macho he is, the more difficult it will be for him to love himself while adapting to those around him.

Mr. Bad lives in nature and doesn't want to adapt to nurture or what society expects of him. Society expects men today to be nice. Because of this discrepancy, Mr. Bad doesn't love himself. He feels like an outcast, that he is misunderstood and unloved. The extreme side of Mr. Bad is actually a form of protection or a plea for help. The more extreme he is, the more he is seeking love through attention; and being extreme is the only way he knows how to be. Since Mr. Bad doesn't love himself, how can he give love to another?

Mr. Bad seeks external love through praise from the women he loves. He needs to hear that he is good and doing good; he is a praise junkie. Mr. Bad seeks acceptance and emotional support from people, most notably his woman. But he also has an excess of hate energy that he wants to release to be filled with love. However, Mr. Bad's unbalanced masculine energy means he finds it difficult to create a healthy relationship. The masculine energy in Mr. Bad is releasing the hate, and the feminine energy in Mr. Bad is pulling in the love.

Since Mr. Bad is not respecting his internal feminine energy, it appears to be reflected outside of him in the form of disrespecting women. Mr. Bad controls with power and may abuse women because he needs to release his emotional poison or burden. It is the INTENSITY or EDGE of the hate in him that attracts women.

Mr. Bad ALWAYS needs to be right. His need to be right is stronger than his need for the relationship. Don Miguel Ruiz, the author of *The Four Agreements and The Mastery of Love*, says, *"The need to be right is the result of trying to protect the image we want to project to the outside. We have to impose our way of thinking, not just onto other humans, but even upon ourselves."*

Mr. Bad, being very masculine, wants to go out with a very feminine woman. She would be an extension of his own internal feminine energy. Mr. Bad recognizes the femininity inside himself in the feminine woman.

Our relationships are mirrors of ourselves; they show us what we need to work on by triggering and pushing our buttons. Mr. Bad not honoring or treating women right is only a reflection of not honoring the feminine side inside of him. It is a reflection of his inner struggle.

Ms. Bad Sparks (Highly Feminine)

Meet Ms. Bad, the unhealthy feminine woman who attracts all men for the short term. Ms. Bad is the extreme feminine archetype who makes men excited like the first time they undressed a woman. Note that Ms. Bad doesn't build friendships; she wins hearts but never keeps them.

Personality in a Relationship

Ms. Bad is egotistical, and her relationship focuses on her need for physical pleasure and no emotional attachment. She is manipulative and seductive, dependent and high maintenance, unpredictable and moody, and a relationship strategist. She uses humor as a shield and weapon and is skilled at making remarks that reveal others' insecurities. She places high values on the men she dates but will often use sex to achieve personal fulfillment.

She hides her fear of emotional connection possibly due to her abandonment issues with her needy attitude. She feels the need to control her emotions because she is fearful of being hurt and doesn't know how to love and connect. She manipulates and seduces to hide her fears and insecurities, and she plays the role of the victim and drama queen to get some attention. She always reacts to her emotions, which are on autopilot. She projects her immature feminine energy onto men, which means that she manipulates, seduces, and controls them by being sexually vulnerable, nurturing, radiant, and appealing to their egos.

Ms. Bad finds romantic partners easily but rarely has long-term relationships; if she does, she will probably end up cheating. This is because she connects sexually but cannot connect emotionally due to an excess of feminine energy and a lack of masculine energy.

What Do Men Find Attractive in Ms. Bad Sparks?

One of the biggest turn-ons for a man is when a woman acts as if he is her hero, waiting to be rescued. Ms. Bad praises men and validates their egos. Men want to be seen as warriors and saviors; they want to feel they are heroes who are on a mission to save their princesses from the mighty dragons. A woman can tame a man by praising his actions (big and small). In turn, he will do anything for her. So, ladies, you see how powerful being feminine is? Do you see where your power lies? Do you see that feminine energy can be stronger than masculine energy? Praise makes a man feel truly masculine; a man wants to feel how much you need him. The more you praise him, the more he will be at your disposal.

Men crave the fact that Ms. Bad is mysterious, is always flowing and in movement, lets things be, is vulnerable enough to give up control, is soft and light, seductive, dependent (the savior complex), present, relationship-oriented, humorous, physically fit, immaculately groomed, and flirtatious with a strong sexual desire. Men believe that Ms. Bad can PRAISE them and make them FEEL like a hero. She has a great PRESENCE about her and is nurturing and soothing.

The Twelve Traits That Ms. Bad Sparks Subconsciously Creates

1) Powerful Eye Contact (she has the look)

2) Strong Feminine Body Language

3) Self-confidence and Low Self-esteem (she needs the man)

4) Enjoys Being Led and Taken Care Of

5) Presents a Challenge (knows how to create intrigue)

6) Experienced

7) Emotionally Intelligent (to get what she wants from others but not for herself) and Passionate

8) Nurtures and Cherishes Others with Her Presence

9) Dependent and Always Seeks Approval

10) High Standards

11) Charming Personality

12) Craves Physical Connection Over Emotional Connection

The Problem with Ms. Bad Sparks

Ms. Bad is not long-term relationship material because her priority is not you but herself, so trying to fix her won't happen. Like Mr. Bad, Ms. Bad will not stay faithful; she is an attraction junkie and will leave you at the first sign of greener pastures. She craves drama and excitement, so if she finds it elsewhere, she will not be asked twice.

Ms. Bad has a big ego and is always seeking love. She wants to win at all costs. Her motto is "The end justifies the means." As long as she gets what she wants, it doesn't matter if someone gets hurt along the way. Ms. Bad is overwhelmed when emotional, easily distracted, and is not driven by goals.

While she seeks to satisfy her lust with men at any cost, she does so at the expense of her future. Ms. Bad is very much present-oriented and is the perfect example of living in the now, to the extent that she leaves her past behind and doesn't even consider her future.

You want challenges (which happens with polarity), and you believe there is something about her, but she won't fight for you or your passions. She projects her immature feminine energy on men as a way to manipulate them so that she can get what she wants. She is like a child who always wants to get what they want. She just doesn't know what she is doing; she needs to be told. So, gentlemen, is she the right one for you? Is she the one you want to build your future with?

Ms. Bad is challenged by how she sees herself versus what society expects from her. The more extreme or unhealthy the feminine side is, the bitchier she is and the more difficult it will be for her to adapt to society and the less she will love herself.

Ms. Bad lives in nature and doesn't want to adapt to nurture or what society expects of her. Society expects women today to be equal to men (i.e., independent). She doesn't quite agree.

Because of this discrepancy, Ms. Bad doesn't love herself. She feels like an outcast and misunderstood, and as such, she feels unloved. The extreme side of Ms. Bad is actually a form of protection or a call for help. The more extreme she is, the more she seeks love through attention, and being extreme is the only way she knows.

Since Ms. Bad doesn't love herself, how can she give love to another?

Ms. Bad seeks external power through protection from the men she loves. She needs to feel safe and secure. She needs strong bounderies. Ms. Bad seeks validation and support from people, most notably her man.

Ms. Bad has excess power energy that she is trying to grasp in order to be filled with power.

The feminine energy in Ms. Bad is grasping the power, and the masculine energy in Ms. Bad is pulling in the power. Since Ms. Bad is not respecting her internal masculine energy, this is being reflected outside as her not respecting men.

Ms. Bad uses her love to control and abuse men because she needs to release her emotional poison or burden. It is the INTENSITY of the desire of power in her that attracts men.

Ms. Bad ALWAYS needs to be right. Her need to be right is stronger than her need of the relationship.

Ms. Bad, being very feminine, wants to go out with a very masculine man; he would be an extension of her own internal masculine energy. Ms. Bad recognizes the masculine energy inside her in the masculine man. Our relationships are mirrors of ourselves; they show us what we want to work on by triggering and pushing our buttons. Ms. Bad not honoring or treating men right is only a reflection of not honoring her own internal masculine energy. It is a reflection of her inner struggle.

She is emotionally immature, mainly because of the nurture part. This is because of one of three scenarios: she grew up without a strong, balanced woman in her life; she got everything she wanted all of the time; or she entered into relationships with guys early (she became dependent and unstable). As such, she didn't learn how to process her emotions. She expects others to fulfill her needs because that's what she has been taught or grew up with. This led to her not being self-sufficient, not loving herself, and needing constant approval from the external world (men in particular).

Seducing Women

In the seduction phase, the man must be present, grounded, hold space and be confident. The more the woman feels your strength, the more attracted she will be. The more masculine, authentic, nonjudgmental (when listening), and unashamed of your desire for her, the more she will want you. Deep down, she is insecure and seeks reassurance, and when she finds it in you, you can get anything from her. Women feel with their hearts first, and then they open up sexually. By reassuring her, you are filling her heart with love; once you do, she will open up to you completely. A woman wants to be led by the strongest. When you are nice, you are her equal. When you are her equal, the polarity and flow of the relationship dies, the sparks die, and the attraction dies. She wants you to lead her with strength and presence, bounderies, your ability to listen, and guard her emotions. She will test you, both your integrity and your masculinity.

She wants her children to be the strongest, so testing you is just her way of seeing if you can have her children. The two most powerful and recurrent tests she will put you through are to test your bounderies and how you handle her emotions. If you act with integrity (you act the same way you would act when calm and when she tests you), then you will pass. She will test you until the attraction diminishes, and once it does, you will have proven to her that you are not man enough. The best way to pass her tests is to act with integrity, remain consistent, and respond with calmness (not emotionally) and perhaps even tease her about it.

Mr. Nice Mirror (The Wounded Masculine Man)

Meet Mr. Nice, the wounded masculine man who started out as Mr. Bad but has been tamed by Ms. Nice. He tends to have long, passionless relationships, but that's because Mr. Nice doesn't build relationships; instead, he builds friendships.

Personality in a Relationship

Mr. Nice is emotionally dependent and sexually frustrated. He is submissive to Ms. Nice, and this has led him to lose his true identity and repress his nature side. Since the relationship dynamic has changed, Mr. Nice has become more sensible, stagnant, and amorphous, and he has let himself go to an extreme (when it comes to the dating world). This has led him to live in the past. He lost his once-epic interpersonal skills and never really learned how to express his true feelings. Mr. Nice has a bad habit of discussing his relationship problems at work and his work problems in his relationship. He has low personal values, as he acts in accordance with what society expects of him. He feels like a victim. Mr. Nice is in denial and has low self-esteem.

Although Mr. Nice is a strategist when it comes to finding personal peace of mind with Ms. Nice, he doesn't know how to communicate with her.

Mr. Nice expresses a wounded masculine energy and an excess of feminine energy. He projects his wounded masculine energy on Ms. Nice, which means that he is submissive to her most of the time (without necessarily agreeing).

He is in a relationship with Ms. Nice, but it's more of a friendship because it lacks passion. He will cheat if they have issues. He is now sexually disconnected and still unaware of how to connect emotionally.

The Problems between Mr. Nice Mirror and Ms. Nice Mirror

Mr. Nice has two problems: physical chemistry and emotional chemistry. Because you sexually rejected him or because you didn't know how to speak with him, he felt criticized instead of praised. You killed the sexual connection (his source of connection). This wounded his masculine energy, and he then felt rejected. So he withdrew from the couple, and the relationship died. He is now withdrawn from the relationship and focuses on his children, his work, and his friends; basically, everything except you because you 'betrayed' him.

He may or may not stay faithful, but he will be loyal to you. Now, now… be patient and listen until the end. Mr. Nice will receive his part of the blame as well. You want your man back, don't you? I mean, you've spent so many years with him, and he was so great at the beginning. What happened? How can you help him? You will find the solutions in Part II, but meanwhile, learn how masculine energy communicates and start speaking it with him; remember, he is not your girlfriend.

The Real Problem with Mr. Nice Mirror

Mr. Nice is challenged by how he sees himself versus what society expects from him. The more wounded his masculine side might be, the more withdrawn he is from the relationship, the more difficult it will be for him to heal his nature, and the less he will love himself.

Mr. Nice lives in nurture and repressed his nature in order to adapt to what society expects of him. Society expects men today to be nice. Because of the discrepancy, Mr. Nice doesn't love himself. He feels he is misunderstood, and as such, he feels unloved. The wounded side of Mr. Nice is actually a call for help. The more wounded he is, the more he is seeking love through attention. He is often withdrawn and initiates a cold war in response.

Mr. Nice seeks external love through praise from Ms. Nice. He is a praise junkie, appreciating acceptance and sexual support from Ms. Nice. Since Mr. Nice is not respecting his wounded masculine energy, this is reflected outside as Ms. Nice not respecting her wounded feminine energy.

Once rejected a few times (it can be as little as three times), Mr. Nice stopped expressing his sexual desire with Ms. Nice and needs a lot to repair his broken ego. He will direct his desire toward his secretary, the sexy neighbor, or even your best friend, and Ms. Nice, you will only have yourself to blame. Rejecting a man sexually is like rejecting a woman emotionally; it is literally a relationship killer. The relationship died the moment you rejected him sexually because when you reject him sexually, you reject his nature, the very essence of who he is.

Ms. Nice Mirror (The Wounded Feminine Woman)

Meet Ms. Nice, the wounded feminine woman who started out as Ms. Bad but became dominant over Mr. Nice. She tends to have long, passionless relationships, but that's because Ms. Nice doesn't build relationships; she builds friendships.

Personality in a Relationship

Ms. Nice is emotionally dependent and sexually frustrated. She dominates, controls, and manipulates Mr. Nice to get what she wants. This has led her to lose her true identity and repress her nature side. Since the relationship dynamic has changed, Ms. Nice has started nagging and complaining, became a control freak, and was moodier and more rigid. Ms. Nice can be high-maintenance. She wears her masculine mask to perfection and doesn't let herself be vulnerable and let go (in the relationship). This has led her to live in the past. The masculine mask hides her extremely fragile interior and instead shows a tough exterior. She lost her once epic vulnerability and nurturing side. Instead of sharing her feelings, she gives orders and expects to be obeyed on the spot. Ms. Nice has low personal values, as she acts in accordance with what society expects of her. She feels like a victim. Ms. Nice is in denial and has low self-esteem.

She is a narcissist and an emotional manipulator. After she tames her partner, she focuses her control on her children, wears a mask outside the house ("My life is perfect; I smile all the time"), and places high value on her children (if they fail, she has failed; if they succeed, it is thanks to her). Ms. Nice loves gossip, and while she surrounds herself with friends, she often feels lonely. She gives love and devotion until it hurts, offers too much just to get approval/attention or affection, and doesn't set bounderies (this leads her to anger and resentment).

Ms. Nice expresses an excess of masculine energy and a wounded feminine energy. She projects her wounded feminine energy onto Mr. Nice, which means that she dominates him most of the time. Ms. Nice is in a relationship with Mr. Nice, but it's more of a friendship because there is no passion. In case they are having issues, she would be likely to have a long affair, and lately, she is the one asking for a divorce because her emotional needs are not being met. To that end, she doesn't know how to communicate her needs to Mr. Nice. She is now sexually disconnected and still unaware of how to connect emotionally with Mr. Nice.

The Problems between Ms. Nice Mirror and Mr. Nice Mirror

Ms. Nice has two problems: physical chemistry and emotional chemistry. You rejected her emotionally by refusing to listen to her, so she felt unloved. You've wounded her feminine energy, so she started pushing more and more to receive validation from the couple, and eventually, the relationship died. So you killed the emotional connection (her source of connection). She is now fighting constantly to be heard, and while she shifted her search for validation to her children, her work, and her friends, what she craves the most is a connection with you. She may or may not stay faithful, but she will be loyal to you. So, you see, both Mr. and Ms. Nice carry equal blame.

You want her back, don't you? I mean, you've spent so many years together, and things were so great in the beginning. What happened? How can you help her? You will find the solutions in Part II, but meanwhile, learn how the feminine energy communicates and start speaking it with her; remember, she is not your guy friend.

The Real Problem with Ms. Nice Mirror

Ms. Nice is challenged by how she sees herself versus what society expects from her. The more wounded her feminine side is, the pushier she is in the relationship and the more difficult it will be for her to heal her nature and the less she will love herself. Ms. Nice lives in nurture and repressed her nature to adapt to what society expects of her. Society expects women today to be wonder women (in other words, a leader at work and a boss/bitch at home, excuse my language).

Because of this discrepancy, Ms. Nice doesn't love herself. She feels that she is misunderstood, and as such, she feels unloved. The wounded side of Ms. Nice is actually a form of protection or a call for help. The more wounded she is, the more she seeks love through attention, and being pushy/bossy and ordering you around is the only way she knows.

Ms. Nice seeks external love through being cherished by Mr. Nice. She needs to be heard venting when she asks for it (and it should be immediate), she wants to dump her emotions at the speed of a dial, and she is impatient. Ms. Nice seeks validation and emotional support from Mr. Nice. Since Ms. Nice is not respecting her wounded feminine energy, this is being reflected outside as Mr. Nice not respecting his wounded masculine energy.

Because Ms. Nice has been emotionally rejected, she will increase her nagging, bitching, and complaining with Mr. Nice until he starts listening to her and her problems. It will take a lot of time for him to repair her broken ego and trust.

She will direct her control toward her children, and when, after some time, she sees no reaction, she will have a long-term affair. The affair will be slow to start, but once it does, you can be sure that she is never coming back, and you, Mr. Nice, will only have yourself to blame. Rejecting a woman emotionally is similar to rejecting a man sexually; it is literally a relationship killer, because that means you are not accepting her for who she is.

Mr. Friend Amore (The Feminine Man)

Meet Mr. Friend, the unhealthy feminine man who will be attracted to Ms. Friend for the short term. A feminine father and a masculine mother raised Mr. Friend; as such, he models after his father by living through nurture while not being aware of his nature (later in the book we will see how we subconsciously shape our relationships by modeling or reproducing the relationship of our parents or caretakers). Note that Mr. Friend doesn't build relationships; he builds friendships.

Personality in a Relationship

Mr. Friend is not masculine enough. He has no backbone, is not assertive or authentic, lacks integrity, and his relationship focuses on his need for emotional attachment at the detriment of physical pleasure. He is a people pleaser, friendly, has low self-esteem, and fulfills everyone's needs except his own. He maintains a calculated niceness by always expecting something in return for his nice deeds. Because Mr. Friend is unaware of his nature side (having modeled a feminine energy figure), he experiences a loss of identity.

Mr. Friend expresses a lack of masculine energy and an excess of feminine energy. He hides his fear of sexual connection with his self-deprecating and shy attitude and becomes filled with self-doubt around emotions. He feels the need to control his sexual urges and creating sparks because he fears rejection and believes he is not good enough. He uses sarcasm and humor to hide his hopelessness. He projects his excess feminine energy on women, which means that he is caring, attentive, sentimental, needy, and puts women on a pedestal. He connects emotionally but cannot connect sexually.

The Problems of Mr. Friend Amore for Women

Mr. Friend has two problems: physical chemistry and emotional chemistry. Because a feminine father and masculine mother raised him, this became his model for how a relationship is. His feminine energy makes women see him weak and inauthentic with his feelings toward them. While he is a good listener and can create a good emotional connection, he cannot create a sexual connection, meaning there is an issue with physical chemistry and short-term emotional chemistry. Mr. Friend doesn't know how to create the sparks. Mr. Friend is good with the *brain in love* but terrible with the *brain in lust*.

He is your best friend, and you can't seem to feel anything sexual or some sparks. Just help him out, and you won't regret it. You will find solutions in the Chapter 7 with regards to biology as well as in Part II, but in the meantime, help him be more masculine and you will see how your whole life can change. Drop your masculine mask, put your ego aside, and be vulnerable because that is true love—that is divine and beautiful and shows that you can love unconditionally. I promise he will repay you a thousand times over.

Mr. Friend is challenged by how he sees himself versus what society expects from him. The more developed his feminine side is, the less assertive he is, and the more difficult it will be for him to discover his nature and the less he will love himself. Mr. Friend lives in nurture and is unaware of his nature. Society expects men today to be nice, but Mr. Friend is too nice; he lacks a backbone.

Because of this discrepancy, Mr. Friend doesn't love himself. He feels he is misunderstood and, as such, he feels unloved. The search of Mr. Friend for

The One or for love by making someone his friend first is actually a form of protection or a call for help. The more feminine he is, the more he seeks love through attention and waiting for The One. Making a woman his friend is the only way he knows.

Mr. Friend seeks external validation and appreciation from his partner. He needs to hear that he is good and doing good, as he is a praise junkie. Mr. Friend seeks acceptance and emotional support from women. Mr. Friend doesn't respect his masculine energy that is being reflected on the outside by attracting masculine-energy type of women. Mr. Friend's needy vibe is a huge turnoff, and it automatically gives the control of the relationship to the woman.

One of Mr. Friend's main issues is that he is not familiar with his "cave" (his alone time); as such, he doesn't know he needs to pull away to recharge his testosterone. Mr. Friend unconsciously creates arguments in his relationships to justify pulling away because he used to witness his mother's disapproval of his father's emotional distancing. Because he doesn't enter his cave to recharge, Mr. Friend becomes sensitive and irritable. The more he delays his cave time, the harder he tries to please, the more feminine he becomes, and the more he loses part of his masculinity. While Mr. Friend might feel guilty when he's entering his cave, he loses his desire and passion and becomes passive and overly dependent when he isn't there. Mr. Friend might hate to be alone because he fears losing love. According to psychology, this is due to childhood memories of a mother rejecting the father or directly rejecting the child.

Mr. Friend Amore's Interaction with Women

When interacting with women, Mr. Friend often hears things like:

"You are amazing, but I can't be with you right now (I have to focus on my career, I have other problems, etc.) ..."

"It's not you, it's me."

"You are really perfect, but ..."

Does this sound familiar to you? This is what women try to tell you, but what they really mean is:

"I don't feel any sparks or sexual tension with you."

"You are not challenging me. You are not being masculine enough, and you are not authentic with yourself."

Let's be honest—you have been a people pleaser all your life, especially with women you like. You have tried to fulfill all their needs, and while they loved you for that, it is exactly what killed the sparks or sexual tension. You are an overthinker. You do everything while having something in mind. You do something nice for someone because you expect to receive something nice back. Women feel it when you are trying to buy their affection or seek their approval (through flowers, dinners, etc.), which is why they reject you. While trying to be attentive, loving, and to show that he's a reliable provider, Mr. Friend lacks integrity and sex appeal.

The Nice Guy versus the Bad Guy

The nice guy and the bad guy are two sides of the same coin. Mr. Bad is the unhealthy masculine man, and Mr. Friend is the unhealthy feminine man; they just manipulate differently.

Mr. Bad is afraid of commitment (fearful of both boredom and losing the intensity of the sparks), while Mr. Friend is afraid of his emotions (fearful of owning his emotions and being vulnerable and authentic). Because of societal taboos that make sex and sexuality "shameful," Mr. Friend is ashamed of expressing his true feelings and raw desire, as he doesn't want others to perceive him as a creep.

Power, integrity, and self-worth are all important if you want to build attraction. By power, I mean controlling the relationship dynamic; by integrity, I mean being your true self; and by self-worth, I mean not putting her on a pedestal and being a puppeteer. If you are hard on yourself, you will be hard on women. They don't like that.

Because of the huge discrepancy between Mr. Friend's inner image and that of society's ideal image, he has repressed his inner bad boy and pushed the nice boy image to be accepted by society. Perfectionism was created in the first place because of Mr. Friend's expectations of his image versus what society wants him to be. By accepting himself and his raw emotions and desires for who he is Mr. Friend will have regained his authenticity.

So, you see, we all have a bad boy and a nice guy inside of us. Who you let out depends on your self-image and the preferred image of society. Mr. Bad wants to please himself, Mr. Friend wants to please society, but Mr. Grey wants to please himself *and* society by being authentic and doing the Grey Dance of Love.

Mr. Bad and Mr. Friend are two sides of the same coin: just like Mr. Bad has an *extreme* masculinity and a *weak* femininity on the outside and Mr. Friend has a *weak* masculinity and an *extreme* femininity on the outside, the *weak* femininity in Mr. Bad is screaming on the inside and the *weak* masculinity in Mr. Friend is screaming on the inside. This is why it is important to be balanced.

Why Women Should Choose Mr. Friend Amore over Mr. Bad Sparks

1) He defends you and the relationship.

2) He values your views.

3) He praises you with a pure heart.

4) He really loves spending time with you (not only for sex).

5) He likes the things you like.

6) He likes planning the future.

7) He likes to give you gifts for no reason.

8) He remembers the important dates.

9) He likes asking you for help.

10) He is always there to help.

11) He gives you the best side of the bed.

12) He respects your opinion.

13) He wants to know about your day and listens attentively.

14) His face glows with happiness when he sees you.

15) He can really do anything to solve your problems.

16) He always checks in on you.

17) He always texts you "Good morning."

18) He is thoughtful (sends you flowers or small notes to let you know he is thinking about you) and will put your well-being before his.

19) He will do everything he can to cheer you up when you are stressed, troubled, or afraid.

20) He cares about how you feel and will gladly open his heart to you.

21) He wants to be your home and safe place.

22) He wants to know everything about you; he wants to discover you just like he would discover a new planet.

Of course, these points are just to get you started, as there is much, much more. And yes, it is true that these points are more about intellectual chemistry (as you will discover in the subsequent chapters), but this is the most powerful base for a long-term relationship. All you need is to help Mr. Friend become more masculine and work on his physical chemistry (which is a piece of cake, to be honest) and you'll be in for a love story that goes beyond a fairytale.

Tip 1
Studies have shown that attractive people feel more connected to a stranger who acts indifferent to them at first but gradually warms up to them over time. Why? Because you show that you are not impressed by their looks as such. When you slowly warm up to them, they will feel as if they've won you over through their personality. This makes them feel really good; you didn't win them over by something that was given to them naturally but rather by something they worked for.

Ms. Friend Amore (The Masculine Woman)

Meet Ms. Friend, the unhealthy masculine woman who will like Mr. Friend for the short term. A feminine father and a masculine mother raised Ms. Friend; as such, she modeled her mother by living through nurture while not being aware of her nature. Note that Ms. Friend doesn't build relationships; she builds friendships.

Personality in a Relationship

Ms. Friend is seen as "one of the guys" (definitely not erotic nor feminine) and as sexually frustrated. In a relationship, she dominates, controls, and manipulates to get what she wants. Because Ms. Friend is unaware of her nature side (having modeled a masculine energy figure), she experiences a loss of identity. Ms. Friend learned how to nag and complain from Ms. Nice, is a control freak, rigid, and always places her needs above others'. She wears her masculine mask to perfection and doesn't let herself be vulnerable and doesn't know how to show her true feelings and let go (in the relationship). She is the frightened little girl who is afraid of being hurt and abandoned and is scared to let her guard down and allow another person in. This has led her to live in the past. Her masculine mask hides her extremely fragile interior and shows, instead, a tough exterior. Ms. Friend has low-personal values as she acts by following society's expectations and feels like a victim. Ms. Friend is in denial and has low self-esteem.

She is passive aggressive, overcompensates, and spends a lot of time at work (as a form of controlling her life and showing that she doesn't have time for love). Ms. Friend loves gossip, and while she surrounds herself with friends, she often feels lonely. She gives love and devotion until it hurts; offers too much just to get approval/attention or affection; and doesn't set bounderies, which leads her to anger and resentment.

Ms. Friend projects her excess of masculine energy on men. She hides her fear of intimacy with her bossy attitude. She feels the need to control her sexual urges and creating sparks because she fears rejection. She uses sarcasm and humor as a shield and weapon to hide her fears and insecurities. To that end, she doesn't know how to communicate her needs to men. She connects emotionally but cannot connect sexually.

The Problems of Ms. Friend Amore for Men

Ms. Friend has two problems: physical chemistry and emotional chemistry. A feminine father and a masculine mother raised her, which defines her understanding of a healthy relationship. Being masculine, men view her as strong or sometimes a bitch, as she is not authentic with her feelings toward men. While she can be a good listener and can create good emotional chemistry, she cannot establish a sexual connection, meaning there is an issue with the physical chemistry and short-term emotional chemistry. Ms. Friend doesn't know how to create the sparks. She is good with the brain in love but terrible with the brain in lust.

She is your best friend, and you can't seem to feel anything sexual or any sparks. Just help her out, and you won't regret it. You will find the solutions in Chapter 7 with regards to biology as well as in Part II, but meanwhile, help her be more feminine, and you will see how your whole life can change. Put your ego aside and be vulnerable, because that is true love, that is divine and beautiful, and that shows that you can love unconditionally. I promise she will repay you a thousand times over. So, you see, Mr. and Ms. Friend are to be blamed equally.

Ms. Friend is challenged by how she sees herself versus what society expects from her. The more developed her masculine side is, the bossier she is, and the more difficult it will be for her to discover her nature, and the less she will love herself. Ms. Friend lives in nurture and is unaware of her nature, so she lives by what society expects of her. Society expects women today to be wonder women, but Ms. Friend is too bossy and a control freak.

Because of this discrepancy, Ms. Friend doesn't love herself. She feels she is misunderstood; as such, she feels unloved. Ms. Friend's search for The One, the fairytale, or for the sparks, is a search for self-protection or a call for help. The more masculine she is, the more she seeks love through attention. Waiting for The One who will make her feel the butterflies in her stomach is the only way she knows; and by the way, this is NOT love, it is attraction, which you can have with anyone (more on that later).

Ms. Friend seeks external love, validation, and emotional support from men. Since she does not respect her feminine energy, this is reflected outside as her attracting feminine-energy men. Ms. Friend's independent vibe is a huge turnoff and automatically gives men the impression that she doesn't need them.

One of Ms. Friend's main issues: She's not familiar with what Dr. John Gray describes as her "well." She doesn't know she needs to connect even more to recharge. A woman needs her partner the most when she is going down in her well. However, since Ms. Friend is masculine, she disconnects even more, which makes her more sensitive and irritable. The more issues she has, the more she will disconnect, and the harder and more masculine she will become.

The Nice Girl versus the Bad Girl

The nice girl and the bad girl are two sides of the same coin. Ms. Bad is the unhealthy feminine woman, and Ms. Friend is the unhealthy masculine woman; they just manipulate differently.

Ms. Bad is afraid of commitment (afraid of losing the intensity of the sparks and afraid of boredom), while Ms. Friend is afraid of her emotions (afraid of owning her emotions, of being vulnerable and authentic). Because of the societal taboos against sex and sexuality, Ms. Friend is ashamed of expressing her true feelings and raw desire, as she fears she'll be perceived as a bitch. She often forgets that if you are too independent and don't act as if you need men, it's likely that they won't like you and will run away from you.

Mr. Friend, because of the huge discrepancy between your inner image and the ideal societal image, you repressed your inner bad girl and pushed the nice girl image to be accepted by society. You created perfectionism in the first place because of your expectations of your image versus what society wants you to be. By accepting yourself and your raw emotions and desires for who you are, you will have regained your authenticity. In *The Mastery of Love*, Don Miguel Ruiz says, *"That image of perfection tells us how we should be in order to acknowledge that we are good, in order to accept ourselves."*

So, you see, all women have an inner bad girl and inner nice girl. Who you let out depends on your self-image and the preferred image of society. Ms. Bad wants to please herself; Ms. Friend wants to please the standards of society; Ms. Grey wants to please herself *and* society by being authentic and doing the Grey Dance of Love.

Ms. Bad and Ms. Friend are two sides of the same coin, because just like Ms. Bad has an *extreme* feminine energy and a *weak* masculine energy on the outside and Ms. Friend has a *weak feminine* energy and an *extreme masculine* energy on the outside, the *weak masculine* in Ms. Bad is screaming on the inside and the *weak feminine* in Ms. Friend is screaming on the inside. This is why you must be balanced.

Mr. Grey Dance (The Healthy Masculine) and Ms. Grey Dance (The Healthy Feminine)

Meet Mr. and Ms. Grey, a.k.a. "The Magical Couple." This is where the healthy masculine man who will attract and love Ms. Grey forever meets the healthy feminine woman who will attract and love Mr. Grey forever. Mr. and Ms. Grey won each other's hearts and keep each other's hearts.

Mr. and Ms. Grey have balanced their masculine and feminine energies, understand each other's favorite communication styles, and keep on growing together (contrary to Mr. and Ms. Nice, who are growing apart). They have mastered the Grey Dance of Love.

Relationship Type: Long—they dance between intense and friendly.

Friendship Type: They are best friends and have developed a deep understanding of each other.

Close Relationship: They trust each other blindly and grow together hand in hand.

Hobbies: They do masculine energy type of hobbies and feminine energy type of hobbies together. They can go shopping Sunday morning and watch a boxing match in the afternoon.

They Are Relationship Experts

Mr. and Ms. Grey are always present and clear. They have a purpose and show their feelings. They hold space and are grounded. Mr. and Ms. Grey are strong, intelligent, and humorous. They create preventive strategies in case of emergencies; they ask about each other all the time (they never take each other for granted); they communicate fluently the Eleven Love Connections; they say what they mean without playing mind games; they keep on courting each other even after years of marriage; they don't let the sparks die (instead of playing petty games *on* each other, they play games *with* each other: playing hot and cold versus going on an adventure together); they make agreements when they can't convince each other. They are sexually and emotionally balanced; they dance between sexual intimacy and emotional intimacy. They trust each other. Mr. and Ms. Grey express balanced masculine energy and balanced feminine energy.

What Do Mr. and Ms. Grey Dance Find Attractive in Each Other?

Mr. and Ms. Grey openly project their desire to each other without any sexual taboos. They assume their sexuality and intimacy with maturity. They have an intense sexual and emotional intimacy that they take beyond the bedroom. They are truly authentic, honest, and mature. Similarly, their relationship changed from challenging each other immaturely to challenging each other more maturely. They dance between sexual intimacy and emotional intimacy. They trust each other with all their secrets, and they assume their sexuality and emotionality.

How They Transformed Their Relationship

They did this through shifting the mystery from; between each other to discovering new things together (from inside to outside, from me versus you to us versus the world). Instead of keeping mysteries from each other, they discover mysteries together (such as learning a new language or traveling to a new country). They, of course, still court and flirt with each other, groom regularly, and are faithful and loyal. They learned to be present for each other and talk to each other with their own love connections.

Their relationship is now a priority for Mr. and Ms. Grey (even before their children and/or work). They have learned to put their egos aside from time to time for the sake of the relationship, and they seek love over power. They dance between the positive nostalgia of the past, living in the present, and properly planning the future. Mr. and Ms. Grey know that they didn't find The One—they are building it together.

How Mr. and Ms. Grey Dance Found Balance
Mr. and Ms. Grey have closed the gap between their inner image and the image society expects them to live up to. They have healthy masculine and feminine energies, and they both love themselves.

Mr. and Ms. Grey dance between nature and nurture. They love themselves internally and express this externally toward each other from a place of unconditional love. They have what we call "a balanced sexual pole"—they are both complete and feel complete by themselves.

Mr. and Ms. Grey don't need each other. They are codependent of each other, help each other out, and take each other's advice, thoughts, and feelings into consideration. It is not an "I versus you" relationship, but rather a "we" relationship. Mr. and Ms. Grey each have healthy masculine energy and healthy feminine energy. Mr. Grey follows through on his promise (when he says something, he will do it), brings the best out of Ms. Grey (challenges, inspires, encourages, etc.), is thoughtful (he remembers the details), patiently works through any issue, and is always there for Ms. Grey.

Ms. Grey is emotionally mature. She has a sense of self-control, accepts and controls her urges, learns from her mistakes, reflects, is personally responsible, is accountable for her actions (sets her own bounderies, autonomous, aware, etc.), is independent, and makes her own decisions.

Ms. Grey is optimistic because she knows she can turn around and control life at any time. She speaks up for what she wants. Instead of acting upset, Ms. Grey states what she wants.

Which Love Partner Are You?

So the question remains: Which type of love partner are you? Forging a successful and happy relationship starts with an in-depth analysis of your qualities, characteristics, and energy so that you can find the right type of partner for you. Not all partners are good fits for each other.

Real love is a choice. It is an unconditional commitment to an imperfect person. It is about knowing that after all the butterflies have gone and after the honeymoon is a distant memory, your partner has stayed with you to fight with you and for you. Despite all your insecurities and imperfections, he or she wants to be with you for the journey to experience your growth and your awesomeness because they know that butterflies have their seasons, but they also know that they can rekindle those butterflies anytime.

Ultimately, we all should strive to build a relationship that mirrors Mr. and Ms. Grey's. They not only provide balance to the other but they also perfectly fit together simply because they have worked on their relationship at a microlevel (internal) and macrolevel (external). They are the yin to the yang, possessing different yet complementary characteristics. They have healthy masculine and feminine energies and recognize there are times they must shift, adjust, and rebalance to maintain the synergy of the relationship. However, before they were Mr. and Ms. Grey, they were each on a journey to find themselves and their own path to love.

This same journey starts for you. Step after step, endure the path and open your eyes to the type of lover you might be. Are you satisfied in that box? Would you like to change your practices? Are there areas that you can improve? The importance of this cannot be overstated. The real work begins when two become one. That is the topic of the next chapter.

CHAPTER 4
THE THREE STAGES
OF A RELATIONSHIP

EACH AND EVERY ROMANTIC RELATIONSHIP goes through three stages. None of these stages is better than the other. In *stage one*, we experience physical chemistry; in *stage two*, we experience intellectual chemistry; and in *stage three*, we experience emotional chemistry. Each relationship passes through and dances between all three stages, but if the relationship gets stuck in one of the stages, then it is likely to be in jeopardy. Sometimes, relationships start in stage one (love at first sight), and other times relationships start in stage two (friends at first sight). There is no set-in-stone rule the three stages of relationships follow. It all depends on your journey and what you want to experience. However, understanding the three stages means that you will be able to choose the love environment you want to be in. You can enter and leave any of the three stages of the relationship at any time depending on your relationship dynamic. To that end, let's unpack each of the three stages and determine where you fall.

Stage One: The Immature Stage (I Need/I Feel—First Love—Ideal Love—Nature—Falling In Love)

Stage Two: The Reverse Stage (I Need/I Think—Growth Love—Nurture—Falling Out of love)

Stage Three: The Balance Stage (I Want/I Think and I Feel—Forever After—Nature and Nurture—Being in Love)

Referencing our eight characters, Mr. and Ms. Bad are stuck in stage one. Mr. and Ms. Nice are stuck in stage two, along with Mr. and Ms. Friend. Mr. and Ms. Grey are enjoying stage three and are dancing in all three stages. The following diagram should help you better understand the differences of each stage.

The Three Stages of Relationships		
Stage One: **The Immature Stage**	**Stage Two:** **The Reverse Stage**	**Stage Three:** **The Balance Stage**
The man wants his woman to satisfy his emotional needs	The man wants his woman to satisfy his Basic Needs	The man wants his woman to satisfy his self-actualization needs
The woman wants her man to satisfy her basic needs	The woman wants her man to satisfy her emotional needs	The woman wants her man to satisfy her self-actualization needs
Conditional love	Conditional love	Unconditional love
First Love/Ideal Love	Painful/Growth Love	Compassionate Love
Falling in Love	Falling out of Love	Being in Love
Nature	Nurture	Embracing Nature and Nurture
Feel Incomplete Alone	Feel Incomplete Alone	Feel Complete Alone
They fight over text	They fight over the phone	They fight face to face
They judge you on your past	They judge you on your past and present	They help you carry your past and present
The Need to Be Right	The Need to Be Right	The Need to Solve
Fear of Being Alone	Fear of Being Taken Over	Love of Being Alone and Taken Over
Intimacy Through Gaining Sense of Self	Intimacy Through Loss of Self	Ability to Let Intimacy In
Maintains Power through Attachment	Maintains Power through Dominance	Maintains Power through Unity
Dependence Stage	Independence Stage	Codependence Stage
Sees the Relationship as a Destination	Sees the Relationship as a Destination	Sees the Relationship as a Journey

Stage 1: The Immature Stage (The Ego)

In this stage, the man has immature feminine energy and the woman has immature masculine energy. This is why they both feel incomplete. They attract each other because their opposite energies complement each other. This leads us to the notion that opposites attract. Opposites attract each other because they complement each other. Mr. Bad, the highly masculine man, searches for his feminine side outside himself through the woman. Ms. Bad, the highly feminine woman, searches for her masculine side outside herself through the man. They both look for their underdeveloped part outside themselves and in the other; they believe they NEED the other.

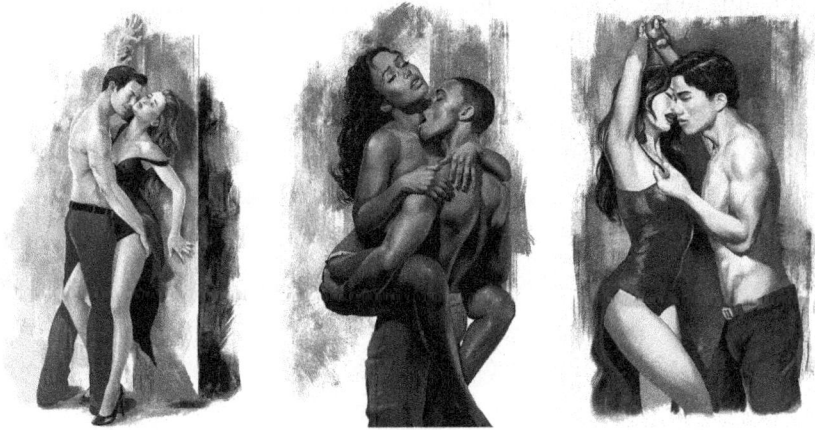

Mr. Bad's lack of feminine energy inside of him pushes him to be overly masculine, so he tries to compensate by controlling, dominating, and ruling the woman. Similarly, Ms. Bad's lack of masculine energy inside of her pushes her to be overly feminine, so she tries to compensate by seeking external validation through needy love, feeling secure, and feeling safe with her man.

This is the nature and biology stage where physical chemistry is most relevant. It is the most intense and polarized relationship stage. Mr. Bad is always *externally* controlling the woman and making her dependent on him for her basic needs, while Ms. Bad is always *internally* controlling the man and making him dependent on her for his emotional needs.

This is where the honeymoon period takes place, and it is also the karmic stage where much is to be learned about our opposite polarities. However, in this stage, love comes from a scarcity mindset; it is conditional love, and it is based on punishment and reward. "I love you if . . ."

Building only the masculine or only the feminine breeds a sense of separation, whereas the masculine/feminine polarity is two sides of the same person. One can't be without the other. There can be a great deal of conflict between who we are on the inside and whom we project to the world around us. When there is great conflict between the two, we generally feel at a loss, and this is from where the lack of self-love stems. This is why it is important to see and feel positive reinforcement and acceptance via other people—it helps to reduce the conflict.

You'll need to work on your self-image or develop your opposite polarity inside yourself if you're stuck in this phase of relationships and want to move to the third stage. In this stage, the man believes that the woman is less important while the woman believes that the man is more important. Your partner should love you just the way you are; no one is more or less important than the other. The woman wants to be rescued physically (wants her basic needs to be met), and the man wants to be rescued emotionally (since he has his basic needs met). It's all about what YOU need, what YOU feel. It's about your first love; it's the stage where you fall in love because you only want to experience the extreme feelings, the adrenaline rush. You want to feel alive and needed.

Stage one is love based on fear. We don't have love inside, so we seek it outside ourselves, and when our outside source (our partner) is tired and exhausted, we move on. Filling our emptiness from the outside will always make us feel empty. You can only feel full by feeling love from the inside. With that said, here are the positive and negative attributes of this stage:

This is the ego stage and the attraction stage (attraction is based on polarity, which is physical and based on ego and conditional love). Since stages one and two are based on the ego, they play not to lose, while in stage three, Mr. and Ms. Grey play to win.

The Positives of This Stage (The Attraction Stage)

Mr. Bad and Ms. Bad live in their core natural energies; they are at ease.

Mr. Bad is very powerful, physically strong, and provides protection and support to Ms. Bad.

Ms. Bad is very loving, nurturing, radiant, sexy, and affectionate toward Mr. Bad.

This is the most powerful stage with regards to attraction; this is where the sparks happen (between two extreme polar opposites). The more opposite Mr. and Ms. Bad are to each other, the more attraction and sparks build between them.

The Negative of This Stage (The Ego Stage)

Mr. Bad and Ms. Bad did not learn to adapt to the other and have not developed their opposite energy. This leads to them living in the extreme.

Mr. Bad can be violent and abusive and use physical or financial force to get his way.

Ms. Bad can be jealous and lie or manipulate to get her way.

This is the most powerful stage with regards to ego; this is where the needy vibe happens ("I need you to complete me," "I feel like you are my destiny," "You make me feel whole," etc.).

Mr. Bad needs Ms. Bad's love just as much as Ms. Bad needs Mr. Bad's power.

The Purpose of This Stage

Mr. Bad, lacking feminine energy inside of him, seeks that energy outside of him from Ms. Bad. Ms. Bad, lacking masculine energy inside of her, seeks that energy outside of her from Mr. Bad.

Mr. Bad completes Ms. Bad's basic needs externally.

Ms. Bad completes Mr. Bad's emotional needs externally.

This type of relationship is based on need and only works for a while until the need is met or the energy is not met.

Stage Two: The Reverse of Power Stage (The Ego)

In this stage, the relationship is between a feminine man and a masculine woman, and we find two scenarios at play.

The First Scenario

Here, the man has a wounded masculine energy, and the woman has a wounded feminine energy, leading them both to a feeling of incompleteness. They fight with each other because they are not living in their core natural energies. Because of that, they feel tired most of the time.

Mr. Nice, the wounded masculine man, searches for healing his broken ego and masculine side outside himself through Ms. Nice. Ms. Nice, the wounded feminine woman, searches for healing her feminine side outside herself through Mr. Nice. They try to heal their wounds outside themselves and in the other; they believe they NEED the other.

Mr. Nice's wounded masculine energy pushes him to retreat and seek outside of himself what he is unaware of having inside. Masculine energy is about control, power, and rules. Mr. Nice feels powerless and not in control of his relationship because Ms. Nice is now masculine. So, he tries to compensate by seeing other women who will make him feel powerful and in control, or, if his masculine energy is too wounded, he will become a couch potato.

Similarly, Ms. Nice's wounded feminine energy pushes her to talk, nag, and complain more and seek outside of herself what she is unaware of having inside. Feminine energy is about love, connection, and caring. Ms. Nice feels unloved, not cared for, and lonely because Mr. Nice is now in his feminine energy. Ms. Nice then tries to compensate by drowning herself in work until a man comes and makes her feel loved, cared for, and connected, or she just continues to play out the victim role by nagging and complaining more.

When you are stuck in this stage, you no longer believe in true love. You feel hopeless and shameful. Being in love is less important than being in a relationship, and each of you is stuck in your own pattern and do not want to listen to your partner.

The Second Scenario

The man has repressed his masculine energy, and the woman has repressed her feminine energy, leading to a feeling of incompleteness. They both feel imbalanced because they have not discovered their natural energies. Mr. Friend, the feminine man, searches for his masculine side outside himself through the woman. Ms. Friend, the masculine woman, searches for her feminine side outside herself through the man. They look for their undeveloped part outside themselves and in the other; they believe they NEED the other.

Mr. Friend's lack of masculine energy pushes him to be overly feminine, so he tries to compensate by seeking external validation through needy love, feeling secure, and feeling safe with a woman. Similarly, Ms. Friend's lack of feminine energy makes her overly masculine, so she tries to compensate by controlling, dominating, and ruling men.

When you are stuck in this stage, you don't believe in true love; you feel ashamed of sexuality and feel guilty about sex. In this stage, Ms. Nice and Ms. Friend want to prove they don't need men, which leads men to feel emasculated; this goes against biology, which is why women are in a contradiction as well as men.

This is the nurture and society stage where intellectual chemistry is the most relevant. It is also the friend-zone stage. It is the unpolarized stage where the polarity is dead or reversed. There is an imbalance in the relationship, the man has excess feminine energy, and the woman has excess masculine energy.

Mr. Nice is always internally controlling Ms. Nice and making her dependent on him for her emotional needs, while Ms. Nice is always externally controlling Mr. Nice and making him dependent on her for his basic needs. This is the stage after the honeymoon when the PEA disappears and they both start feeling that something inside them is missing. It is also the soulmate stage, where there is much to be learned about being self-dependent. However, in this stage, love comes from a scarcity mindset. It is conditional love too. "I love you if ..."

People can give so much, but when life starts to happen after the honeymoon, the man and woman start feeling that something is missing, not only inside them but also in their partner. They can no longer rely on their partner to fulfill their needs. While the man sought the feminine energy in his woman, she stopped fulfilling that part, so he now seeks it inside himself or starts looking for it in another woman. Moreover, while the woman sought the masculine energy in her man, he stopped fulfilling that part, so she now seeks it inside herself or starts looking for it in another man.

Therefore, the relationship dynamic transforms from *dependency* on the partner to *independence* of the partner, while each person looks for another way to fill their needs. The woman assuming the masculine role wrongly believes that she doesn't need her man. She believes that if she can work, bring money home, do the cooking, raise their children, and so on, then why does she need a man? In this relationship stage, this is what a woman wants because she had to assume the masculine role because the man didn't "man up." If you are the man and you have spent too much time in your feminine energy, or if you have spent too much time in your masculine energy if you are the woman, you might have pushed your friend (Mr. and Ms. Friend) or your partner (Mr. and Ms. Nice) to go into stage one, seeking the masculine man or the feminine woman.

If you are stuck in this relationship phase and want to move to the third stage, I suggest you start working on healing your wounded energy (Mr. and Ms. Nice) or discovering your repressed energy (Mr. and Ms. Friend) and work on developing your opposite polarity inside yourself. In this stage, the woman believes that the man is less important, and the man believes that the woman is more important. Your partner should love you just the way you are; no one is more or less important than the other. The woman wants to be rescued emotionally (she already has her basic needs met), and the man wants to be rescued financially (since he has many more expenses). It's all about what YOU need, what YOU feel. It's about learning to grow love; it's the stage where you fall out of love because the polarity has died, the hormones no longer blind you, and they no longer give you the rush of attraction. You no longer feel alive and needed; you feel love is hard and only about hard work. You disconnect from your feelings and your partner's feelings.

In stage two, because of society's attempt to make men and women equal, men have been emasculated and women have been defeminized, and so society has killed the polarity. Yes, men and women should be similar, but certainly not identical. With that said, here are the positive and negative attributes of this stage:

Mr. Nice and Mr. Friend are feminine; Ms. Nice and Ms. Friend are masculine.

The Positives of This Stage (The Search for Balance Stage)
Mr. Nice and Mr. Friend and Ms. Nice and Ms. Friend live in their core nurture energies.

Mr. Nice was once Mr. Bad and is now adopting his feminine energy to become more balanced.

Ms. Nice was once Ms. Bad and is now adopting her masculine energy to become more balanced.

Mr. Nice has learned how to be more nurturing and affectionate.

Ms. Nice has learned how to be more independent.

The Negatives of This Stage (The Independence Stage)

Mr. Nice and Mr. Friend and Ms. Nice and Ms. Friend are not living in their core natural energies, which has caused a decrease in polarity and attraction.

Mr. Nice lost himself and forgot all about his masculine energy. Ms. Nice lost herself and forgot all about her feminine energy.

Mr. Friend never knew about his natural masculine energy because he saw his father (Mr. Nice) acting more feminine, which society applauded.

Ms. Friend never knew about her natural feminine energy because she saw her mother (Ms. Nice) acting more masculine, which society applauded.

Mr. Nice and Ms. Nice didn't balance their masculine and feminine energies. Mr. Friend and Ms. Friend didn't know they had repressed their natural energies.

The Purpose of This Stage

Mr. Bad, unable to get feminine energy from Ms. Bad (outside of him), seeks it inside of himself and disconnects from Ms. Bad, becoming Mr. Nice.

Ms. Bad, unable to get the masculine energy from Mr. Bad (outside of her), seeks it inside of herself and disconnects from Mr. Bad, becoming Ms. Nice.

Mr. Bad disconnects from Ms. Bad's basic needs externally for her to complete her basic needs internally.

Ms. Bad disconnects from Mr. Bad's emotional needs externally for him to complete his emotional needs internally.

Mr. Friend discovers he has been repressing his masculine energy and now starts to express it.

Ms. Friend discovers she has been repressing her feminine energy and now starts to express it.

This stage of the relationship is based on independence and self-sufficiency, and this only works until there is too much independence, which defeats the whole purpose of a relationship.

Stage Three: The Balance Stage (The Repolarized Stage)

Neale Donald Walsch, the author of the book series Conversations with God, said, *"The purpose of a relationship is not to have another who might complete you, but to have another with whom you might share your completeness."* This is what stage three feels like.

In this stage, the man has healthy masculine energy and the woman has healthy feminine energy, leading both of them to feel complete. After attracting their polar opposite in stage one and then attracting their similar pole in stage two, they learned to dance as opposites *and* similars. They are now complete from the inside and dance between their complementarities on the outside. Both man and woman have embraced the healthy sides of their masculinity and femininity and begin to perform the Grey Dance of Love.

Mr. Grey, the healthy masculine man, IS masculine & feminine and wants to PLAY with the woman.

Ms. Grey, the healthy feminine woman, IS feminine & masculine and wants to PLAY with the man.

They are now both complete. They stopped looking and are now BEING. They have developed their underdeveloped part, and they believe they want to dance with the other. Mr. Bad's healthy masculine energy allows him to be masculine and feminine inside and to reflect his masculine energy outside. He no longer dominates or controls, but rather he sets strong boundaries and holds space to allow his woman just to be.

Similarly, Ms. Bad's healthy feminine energy allows her to be feminine and masculine inside and to reflect her feminine energy outside. She no longer seeks validation, but rather she flows freely between the strong bounderies and radiates with her beauty to allow her man just to be.

This is the stage of embracing nature *and* nurture; this is where emotional chemistry is the most relevant. It is the stage where the man and the woman feel the most connected. Mr. Grey is allowing the woman to just BE by holding space for her and allowing her to experience growth through strong bounderies, while Ms. Grey is allowing the man just to BE by appreciating him for who he is.

While you might shout hooray too soon, remember that relationships are dynamic. External circumstances can create a shift in the polarity in you or your partner; but now you are complete, so you can interchange in order to accommodate the changes in your partner until your partner goes back to his or her natural state.

In this stage of relationships, basic and emotional needs are met by the man and the woman. So the dynamic shifts from NEED to WANT and from ME to US. It's about forever after; it's the stage where you grow IN love because you only want to experience the connection.

This is also the stage when the PEA (the love hormone) is recreated, and you can both start dancing. It is also the *twin flame* stage where most is learned about the self as well as learning about the other. In this stage, love comes from an abundant mindset, and it comes from unconditional love.

Mr. and Ms. Grey value growth over the outcome of their relationship; they trust that they will work out their differences. They certainly don't have an "entitled" mentality, and they don't expect their partner to act in a certain way. They also don't repress themselves to please their partner. They set their partner free and allow him or her to be.

Mr. and Ms. Grey own their baggage, their wounds, and their hurts, and they know that even if they are the ones who trigger them, it is not the partner's responsibility to deal with them, only to help and be there. Mr. and Ms. Grey also understand that telling the truth and being authentic with their own feelings, even if it hurts, is the only way to truly connect and to feel known, seen, and understood. With that said, here are the positive and negative attributes of this stage:

Mr. Grey and Ms. Grey are both masculine, feminine, and balanced.

The Positives of This Stage (The Balance Stage)

Mr. Grey dances between living in his core natural masculine energy and his developed nurture feminine energy.

Ms. Grey dances between living in her core natural feminine energy and her developed nurture masculine energy.

Mr. Grey is powerful and loving, strong and nurturing, and protects and gives affection.

Ms. Grey is loving and powerful, nurturing and strong, and affectionate and protective.

The Negatives of This Stage (The Timing Stage)

There are no negatives, just a word of caution: Don't get too comfortable.

Mr. and Ms. Grey have to know when they should recreate the sparks and when they should dance toward friendship.

The Purpose of This Stage

To dance and grow together.

Mr. and Ms. Grey dance between certainty and uncertainty, friendship and fights, at will.

Mr. and Ms. Grey dance between being best friends and being lovers.

Mr. Bad, Mr. Nice, and Mr. Friend become Mr. Grey.

Ms. Bad, Ms. Nice, and Ms. Friend become Ms. Grey.

Mr. and Ms. Grey are complete internally and want to have fun with their partner.

This type of relationship is based on playfulness and discovering each other, and this works forever (as long as the dance continues).

> For a relationship to thrive, your partner has
> to be your soulmate, your life partner, and your best friend.
> The soulmate challenges you, the life partner connects
> with you, and the best friend supports you.

The Development of Relationships through Each Stage

Let's now focus on how relationships develop through each of these three stages. Physical chemistry kicks off most relationships. The man is masculine, the woman is feminine, and everything is rosy. After a couple of months or years, life gets in the way, and the physical chemistry gives space to the intellectual chemistry. Therefore, we move from *biology* or *nature* to *friendship* or *nurture*.

This begins a reverse in polarity. The woman becomes more masculine; the man becomes more feminine. Biology is not helping. After the honeymoon period, biology needs to recharge as we have exhausted our physical chemistry; as such, we're moving to the polar opposite of our core energy. Because of an excess release of testosterone (masculine energy) that the partner takes in (feminine energy), a man's testosterone level decreases when he is in love, while a woman's testosterone level increases. We got used to each other at the same time, and the habits settled in.

The third stage is about being aware of the shifts that happened because of stages one and two, and start the Grey Dance of Love. Because the man is masculine in the long term and the woman is feminine in the long term, a dance between masculine and feminine in the short term can help a lot.

In the second stage, the man is depleted of his masculine energy and the woman is depleted of her feminine energy. As such, they start behaving with the opposite of their core energy.

To recover, the man goes into caving mode, reconnects with his male friends, goes to the gym more often, stays late at work, and so on. Meanwhile, the woman wants to connect more, reconnects with her female friends, wants to meet people, dance, and so on. The man needs to pull away to recharge his testosterone and feel like a man again. When the man feels like a man, he feels safe. A woman will make her man feel safe by making him feel like a man. The third stage involves balancing the releasing and pulling in of testosterone between the man and the woman.

The Evolution of Relationship Needs over Time

To better understand why we shift and move through the three stages of relationships, look back thousands of years to how relationships have evolved and how they relate to Maslow's hierarchy of needs. If we compare our love needs with the societal needs described by Maslow, we see that our values and expectations have changed over time. As such, the rules and strategies of relationships that used to apply to our ancestors no longer apply to us.

So we must upgrade our relationship skills, just like we regularly update the software of a computer. The hardware remains the same (our *biology* or *nature—physical chemistry*), but the software changes (in this case our nurture or upbringing—intellectual chemistry). The pyramid on the next page, which is based on Maslow's hierarchy of needs, can illustrate your relationship's hierarchy of needs.

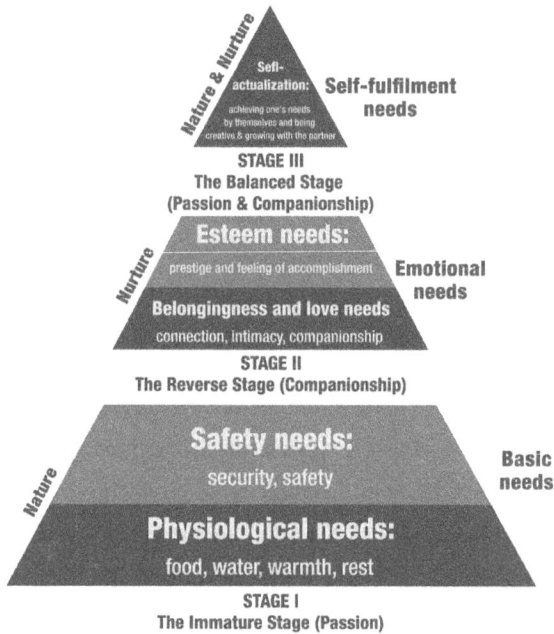

Notice the correlation between the three stages of relationships with the three stages of needs.

- Stage 1: Basic Needs
- Stage 2: Psychological or Emotional Needs
- Stage 3: Self-fulfillment Needs

While each is important, our ancestors were content and satisfied by fulfilling their basic needs of physiology and safety. They lived when safety was of paramount importance and was their primary need. They didn't have the luxury of tending to their emotional needs.

Today, on the other hand, we meet most of our safety needs and, as such, our primary needs shifted from the basic to the emotional needs. We moved up the ladder of needs from safety first and romance second to romance first (since we've met our basic safety needs). Dr. John Gray, the author of *Men Are from Mars, Women Are from Venus*, said, *"Today's wives do not leave husbands because they're not being provided for. They leave because they are emotionally and romantically unfulfilled."*

While moving up the ladder is great, it is crucial to adapt to change, and many of us have failed miserably at doing that. Our ancestors' strategies were great for fulfilling their basic needs, but then we started moving to the romance needs with the same strategies, which is now leading to a skyrocketing divorce rate. The same strategies simply cannot and will not work.

If we are to continue working on the same strategies with our relationships, we will always have two options: divorce or stay and be cheated on. Neither of these two is an adequate option. So we can go back to the basic needs of our ancestors and be content with them, or we can learn new skills and move up the hierarchy of needs.

Our ancestors' strategies worked for them because they were not aware of any other needs; they were busy taking care of their basic needs. Our parents started to feel the internal conflict, especially with the rise of the feminist movement, and although they became aware of the problem, they didn't find the solution. Being aware of the problem helps us find a solution that we can implement, which requires a lot of work. The problem is that our children will then pick up on our new relationship patterns too.

The Real Reason We Want to Be in a Relationship

We are living in the third plane of existence, on planet Earth, to grow and experience our full potential. Relationships are our best way to experience it. Relationships are our mirrors and trigger what we need to change the most inside of us. We are always attracted to our opposites, because our opposites challenge us to move forward and transform us, and yet too much opposite destabilizes us, which is why a balance between opposite and similarity is important. In other words, we want to change safely or experience change in a safe environment. Since relationships trigger old wounds, both partners can work on healing in order to then grow together.

People's reasons for being in a relationship change over time, and such a change often depends on which stage you are in during your relationship.

If you are in stage one, you are in a relationship to have your basic needs taken care of. If you are in stage two, you are in a relationship to have your emotional needs taken care of (since your basic needs are already taken care of). Moreover, if you are in stage three, you are in a relationship to grow together and form deeper connections from a place of unconditional love and an ego-free space.

The chart following should help you better understand the relationships between our characters, their desires, and their energies:

The Relationship Dynamics

Mr. Bad Sparks and Ms. Bad Sparks	Control vs. Submission	Masculine vs. Feminine
Mr. Bad Sparks and Ms. Nice Mirror	Control vs. Submission	Masculine vs. Feminine
Mr. Bad Sparks and Ms. Friend Amore	Control vs. Submission	Masculine vs. Feminine
Mr. Nice Mirror and Ms. Nice Mirror	Indifference vs. Indifference	Masculine vs. Masculine
Mr. Nice Mirror and Ms. Bad Sparks	Control vs. Submission	Masculine vs. Feminine
Mr. Nice Mirror and Ms. Friend Amore	Submission vs. Control	Feminine vs. Masculine
Mr. Friend Amore and Ms. Friend Amore	Submission vs. Submission	Feminine vs. Feminine
Mr. Friend Amore and Ms. Bad Sparks	Submission vs. Rebellion	Feminine vs. Feminine
Mr. Friend Amore and Ms. Nice Mirror	Submission vs. Control	Feminine vs. Masculine

Creating the Sparks

We all want the sparks of a healthy and loving relationship. We create them by the friction or collision of two opposites. In a relationship, we find those sparks through the friction of the masculine energy with the feminine energy. When the man and the woman act from the same polarity (masculine or feminine), the flow of energy between them becomes blocked and static. Remember when we talked about two similar sides of the magnet would repel each other?

Since energy always flows between two opposite poles, this means that in a relationship when both are on the same side of the pole, there is no energy and there are no sparks. There is no flow. The energy is blocked, which keeps the sparks from flying. The higher the difference in poles, the stronger the intensity of the flow, and the more magical the sparks. A man and a woman can have NOTHING in common, but if they have a strong polarity, they can't resist each other.

When you have dominant masculine energy and your partner has dominant feminine energy, you make your partner feel more feminine with your masculine energy and your partner makes you feel more masculine with their feminine energy. If you want to create polarity in your relationship, one person has to be the leader and the other the follower (you can exchange roles anytime). If you want to create even more polarity, in addition to both having balanced masculine and feminine energies inside them, the man has to be the ravisher and the woman the ravished. In other words, the man has to be more masculine and the woman more feminine because nature (biology) is still stronger than nurture (society or cultural upbringing).

The two sides of polarity are never static. Sometimes the roles of masculinity and femininity shift per the current situation. If one of the partners shifts their energy because of work or for some issue at home, the other partner's energy will follow suit and shift to the opposite pole to keep the spark going. You can be masculine at work and feminine in your relationship, and vice versa; and you can be masculine with someone and feminine with someone else. Relationship coach Janie Terrazas says that: *"A woman who exudes mostly masculine vibes and a man who exudes mostly feminine vibes, will initially have a strong attraction to each other. However, if they enter into a relationship, they'll eventually have problems because she'll discover times when she wished he was more masculine (take charge and make decisions), and he'll wish she was less controlling and more nurturing ... especially in the bedroom."*

While it is true that opposite poles attract, our nature, having centuries of precedence, is stronger than our nurture, which is why a woman will always want to go back to her core feminine energy and a man will always want to go back to his core masculine energy. So the masculine woman will, unconsciously, expect her man to "man up."

The more masculine the woman is at work, or the more masculine her job is, the more she will want to be feminine outside her work. My ex-best friend, for example, is an architect, which is a masculine type of job; she craves to be feminine outside of her work. Understanding the polarities is key to relationship success.

The Grey Dance of Love

The Grey Dance of Love is all about dancing back and forth, as shown on the map below.

A relationship is a dance between similarities and differences. It is never static and always moves along the line or map.

If you want more sparks, move toward the fight zone. If you want more compassion (because you feel there are too many fights), move toward the friend zone.

The Fight Zone (Where Lovers Thrive): This is the zone of opposites. This is where Mr. Bad and Ms. Bad live. Mr. Bad is purely masculine, and Ms. Bad is purely feminine. Lovers thrive in uncertainty.

The Friend Zone (Where Friends Thrive): This is the zone of similarities. This is where Mr. and Ms. Nice and Mr. and Ms. Friend live. Mr. Nice and Mr. Friend are dominantly feminine, and Ms. Nice and Ms. Friend are dominantly masculine. The friend zone happens with Mr. Nice and Mr. Friend because both partners are feminine, and this leads to having no one leading the relationship. Similarly, Ms. Nice and Ms. Friend find themselves in the friend zone because both partners are masculine. This leads to having two leaders and no follower in the relationship. Friends thrive in certainty.

The Love Zone (Where the Greys Thrive): This is the zone of complementarity. This is where Mr. and Ms. Grey live. Mr. Grey is dominantly masculine with Ms. Grey, who is dominantly feminine with him. Love happens between them because they are both balanced in masculinity and femininity from the inside, and they project their core (nature) energy on the outside with their partner. The Greys dance between certainty and uncertainty.

The Grey Dance of Quantum Physics: In quantum physics, when two subatomic particles bond and then are separated, they demonstrate an awareness of each other after they've been disconnected; this is called entanglement. This is why we need to separate. We need to separate not lose awareness of our individuality.

The Grey Dance of Love: Finding Your Balance

Any meaningful relationship begins with loving yourself. A relationship is a reflection of your soul, your inner image. The happier you are within, the happier your relationship is. The more love you have for yourself, the more loving your relationship. If you're in an unhealthy relationship, it's probably because there are parts of you that need to grow and need more self-love. The starting point in then forging a healthy relationship with another is fundamentally evaluating how relationships begin and how they transform and shift through each of the three stages.

Learning how to dance between masculine and feminine activities can help your relationship grow in love. You can have crazy, funny dates, do random stuff, eat weirdly, be spontaneous, and so on to spice things up and keep things light and fun. At the same time, you can be traditional by bringing flowers and gifts and going out for dinner or to the movies.

The most important aspect of all this: Embrace both sides of love—the light and the dark—so that you both feel complete. If you focus on having fun only, there is no substance. If you are too traditional, there is no fun. So remember to embrace nature *and* nurture.

Remember: It's about finding a balance between nature and nurture. Nature wants fun and spontaneity. Nurture or society wants tradition and culture. That balance is often based on loving communication, mutual trust, and honesty. Can you trust that your partner will handle your raw emotions with care and protect them no matter what? To deeply connect with your partner, establishing and building trust is paramount, so ask yourself this: *Do I tell my partner how I truly feel? Do I tell him/her the truth?* Being honest with each other will help you work together to find solutions and avoid resentment, which is important for the success of the long-term relationship. However, trusting your partner is also the sexiest thing you can do, as it opens you up like nothing else. Friends sugarcoat, lovers embellish, but partners tell the truth because they know that both can handle it. When you tell your partner you will do something, do it. He or she knows they can count on you at all times. Last, learn the art of being present. Being present involves listening without judgment and shows that you care about your partner. It makes them feel important and valued. It makes them feel that they matter.

Nicholas Boothman, the author of *How to Make Someone Fall in Love with You in 90 Minutes or Less*, reminds us that, *"It's not about length of time, it's about emotional progression, with each stage unfolding in precisely the right order. If you understand the architecture of falling in love, the stages involved, and how to build and choreograph them properly, it's absolutely possible for two people to fall in love in 90 minutes or less."* The journey through my book, *The Grey Dance of Love*, is very much a voyage through love, where we drop in and out of the various challenges and tremendous victories love can offer. In this chapter, we found a better recognition of the different love stages and how you can dance amongst each one. With a sense of awareness and great balance toward the masculine and feminine energies, you can position yourself to find your dream relationship.

CHAPTER 5
INTELLECTUAL CHEMISTRY

NOW THAT WE'VE EXPLORED THE differences between men and women (*physical chemistry*), let's look at the similarities (*intellectual chemistry*) because while it is true that opposites often attract, it is also true that like attracts like. Moreover, while nature has made us different, nurture brings us closer to each other, and the more we share goals and values, the stronger the bond of our friendship becomes.

While physical chemistry is about fulfilling our basic needs, intellectual chemistry is about our emotional needs. This covers things like friendship, shared similarities, upbringing, how we match, and so on. In other words, it is your mindset, attachment style, behavioral type, and communication style. Remember, though, that friendship has one dynamic; it is only a third of the success for a long-term relationship. Mr. and Ms. Friend are champions when it comes to intellectual chemistry. They are born with this talent and have developed it to an extreme.

The Different Ingredients of Intellectual Chemistry

Intellectual chemistry has everything to do with how much you have in common with someone. However, it's not what you think. To have strong intellectual chemistry, you need to share three types of identical or complementary ingredients:

1) Fixed Mindset Versus Growth Mindset

2) Avoidant, Anxious, and Secure Attachments

3) Extroverted and Introverted Types

If you have one or more of those ingredients in conflict with your partner, you may be in for some trouble long term unless you or your partner adapts. While many combinations of beliefs, values, interests, desires, and motivations exist—and the more you have in common the better—there are some deal-breakers.

The First Ingredient of Intellectual Chemistry:
Fixed Versus Growth Mindsets [1]

The Fixed Mindset

People with a fixed mindset live in fear. They ALWAYS want to prove themselves (ego), are sensitive about being wrong or making mistakes, and believe nothing can be changed (i.e., we love each other, or we don't; we are attracted to each other, or we're not; I have to find The One, or else it's not going to work, etc.).

---

1 Based on Carol S. Dweck

That's why the Bads and the Nices play the victim. They live in paralysis, and that results in failed relationships. The Bads don't believe in making an effort. They take their partner and their relationship for granted. The Nices complain about their relationship, thinking *poor me, oh poor me*. They don't understand that just like Rome wasn't built in a day, a relationship takes time.

For the fixed mindset, it is all about finding and staying with The One. However, when things get complicated, this depresses them because they don't understand. "My mom promised me I would live happy forever after if I found my prince," they tell you. They often get stuck in relationships because it would be a shame to be wrong; I mean "You're smart, right?", "You're talented at finding The One, right?", "You can never be wrong.", "You made the right choice; you just have to wait for destiny or fate to change your partner." Irony aside, this doesn't often work.

They want a relationship that feeds their egos. They put their partners on a pedestal, and no one is allowed to touch or go near them; they worship them. They seek perfection and instant gratification. They believe that if you have to work at a relationship, it is not good enough. It has to be The One. Unfortunately, this means they are living in the past. In movies, characters meet The One, get married, and live happy forever after, so that MUST be true in real life as well, right? They are terrified that they might not find The One because that is what they have been taught. If you don't meet The One right from the start (instead of building The One), it robs you of your excuses. They believe a relationship is a finished product. You get what you have, and that's it. How depressing is that?

The fixed mindset links their actions to their identity, so if they fail at something, they believe they are a failure, their self-esteem gets affected, and they just play the role of the victim and take no action to resolve the situation. My ex-best friend wanted to give us a chance because she was looking for a nice guy for a change. I was a real gentleman, and I recall her saying that she enjoyed every minute we shared. However, I think she freaked out when things became serious. She really liked me, but I experienced her pushing me away and not wanting to take the risk of potentially not having our relationship work. As Carol S. Dweck, author of *Mindset*, puts it, *"If people believe their qualities are fixed, and they have shown themselves to be smart or talented, why do they have to keep proving it? After all, when the prince proved his bravery, he and the princess lived happily ever after. He didn't have to go out and slay a dragon every day."*

On a similar note, when you find someone, you have slain one dragon; but when you enter a relationship, you have a whole different set of dragons that you don't know about, lying in wait for you. Therefore, you MUST learn new skills and techniques if you want to kill different dragons. **Biology and psychology** agree *that attracting someone and being in a relationship with someone requires different skills and stems from different processes.*

The Problems of Fixed Mindsets in Relationships

Problem 1: If You Have to Work for a Relationship, It Is Not Meant to Be

They expect everything good to automatically happen—that this will magically occur through their love, sort of the way it happened for Sleeping Beauty. They believe that if it were the right relationship, they would just know and understand each other's needs. They have an entitlement mentality: If we are compatible, then everything should just come naturally. Dr. John Gottman, of The Gottman Institute, reminds us that, *"Every marriage demands effort to keep it on the right track; there is constant tension … between the forces that hold you together and those that can tear you apart."*

Ms. Nice is culpable of wanting—*no* expecting, *no wait*, demanding—of Mr. Nice to read her mind. "I mean, we have been together for so long … you should know me better." No, please stop this behavior. Throughout the years, you change and your partner changes, and that means your relationship dynamic changes as well. Instead of expecting your partner (entitlement mentality) to grow like you, ask for what you want.

Mr. Nice, on the other hand, is culpable of agreeing on everything to buy his piece of mind from all the endless nagging. So he has become Ms. Nice's doormat. Next time, Mr. Nice, remember that a relationship is between two individuals first and a couple second. Of course, you may think that we shouldn't have to work on relationships, as they should just be natural. And, in the past, when relationships counted solely on nature and biology, you'd have been right; but nurture means we need to adapt.

The benefits of working on the relationship:
1) Helps your brain work better.
2) Increases your energy.
3) Increases your creativity.
4) Puts you in a positive frame of mind.
5) Helps you look at opportunities.
6) Helps you live longer.

So choose to have a growth mindset. According to Bob Proctor, the author of *You Were Born Rich*, *"When you make a decision, you flip your brain onto a different frequency. You begin to attract whatever is on that frequency."*

Problem 2: Character Flaws

The second issue with the fixed mindset: It leads to character flaws. When it comes to relationships, blame is the fixed mindset's favorite pastime. People blame themselves, their partners, the cat, you name it. Since fixed-mindset individuals link action with identity, whenever their partner does something they don't like, they blame him or her for it and associate the action with failure.

Therefore, their partner is a failure, and there is nothing that can be done about it. So they become dissatisfied with their relationship. This is the moment they realize they were duped and that their partner is not The One, which is when they realize there must be someone else out there. Someone with a fixed mindset sees a relationship as a finite product that is perfect. "I mean, you are my partner … you should be perfect. You should know everything all the time."

The Growth Mindset

Dr. Robert Sternberg, psychologist, psychometrician, and professor of human development at Cornell University, says, *"The major factor in whether people achieve expertise is not some fixed prior ability but rather purposeful engagement."* Growth-mindset people believe that you can develop any quality with some effort (i.e., we can grow in love; we can create and recreate attraction by following the process; etc.).

> **Tip 2**
> Do you know that most successful people have a growth mindset? Albert Einstein and Thomas Edison were thought of as stupid in school. Michael Jordan was kicked off a basketball team. Walt Disney was fired from his job because he lacked imagination. I could go on and on, but I believe you get my point. If they could do it, so can you.

Mr. and Ms. Grey have a passion for learning: learning about themselves, learning about each other, and learning about their relationship. Carol S. Dweck celebrates this by stating, *"The passion for stretching yourself and sticking to it, even (or especially) when it's not going well, is the hallmark of the growth mindset. This is the mindset that allows people to thrive during some of the most challenging times in their lives."*

Mr. and Ms. Grey developed an ability to have fun with their setbacks by transforming them and playing with them through perseverance and practice. They love to learn new ways of growing together and new ways of loving each other. They know that when they enter a relationship, all the "home passion" will start. This is when the real fun begins.

They want a relationship that challenges them to grow. They want their partner to point out their weaknesses and help them overcome them; they want their partner to grow with them and learn from them. They know that we are here on earth to learn from experience, and that also applies to relationships. They seek progress and delayed gratification. They know that a relationship is a work in progress.

While failure still affects a growth mindset, they don't let it define them. They learn how to face and deal with the problem, and sometimes they get energized and even more determined to solve it. They take every new problem the same way a child learns to walk; they stumble on and on until they stand tall and proud. They know that similar to how people are dynamic and change with time, so do relationships. So they learn, grow, and adapt. They believe that they have to work to have their happy forever after. Moreover, while those with a fixed mindset praise the ego (smart and talent), those with a growth mindset praise the progress (action and improvement).

For a relationship to work, the two partners must either have a fixed mindset or a growth mindset. It will not work if one partner has a fixed mindset while the other has a growth mindset. Remember, relationships are not static; they are dynamic. Most people enter a relationship with the idea that they will never change. However, in the end, that is one of the reasons relationships fail. Now, let's discuss in greater detail some of the other reasons.

The Second Ingredient of Intellectual Chemistry: Avoidant, Anxious, and Secure Attachment

Patterns of Attachment, an interesting study presented in a book by Mary D. Salter Ainsworth, Mary C. Blehar, Everett Waters, and Sally N. Wall, found that we tend to fall into one of three categories when it comes to attachments. Which one you are in depends on the quality of your childhood.

Secure attachment (*relatively good childhood*): Finds it easy to get close to others, is generally comfortable relying on people and having people rely on them. They don't have a problem being on their own. A secure person is balanced and does not manipulate things to get your attention.

Anxious attachment (*unfulfilled childhood*): This is a stark contrast to secure attachment. Can never get enough love from others and tends to have lower self-esteem and self-confidence. They often go overboard on affection and intimacy. People who fall into this attachment style may not be in love with you, but they do become increasingly obsessed.

Avoidant attachment (*poor childhood experience*): Finds it hard to trust others and prefers to be on their own. They likely experienced trauma or abuse in childhood, which makes them afraid to form deep attachments. They don't want a relationship, so when an attachment begins to form, their natural tendency is to pull away. Love may be in the air, but they may not welcome it; they close themselves off and shut their feelings down. They often question the motives of others and shy away from intimacy. Sometimes, avoidants idealize an ex not because the ex was perfect but because it helps deactivate feelings for a new partner.

When referring to the different attachment types, Dr. Leslie Becker-Phelps and Megan Kaye, authors of *Love: The Psychology of Attraction*, say, "*We simply transfer out attachment from our primary caretaker to a new 'base.'*" You develop your attachment type in your childhood by learning what to expect from your parents. According to Dr. Becker-Phelps and Kaye, if your parents are warm and attentive, you develop a secure attachment (you know your needs will be met). If your parents are inconsistent with their attention and are not always responsive, you will develop an anxious attachment, and it is based on conditional love (if you act the right way, you might earn love). If your parents are distant and cold or harsh and critical, you will develop an avoidant attachment; you learn not to trust anyone.

The authors further state, "*So we unconsciously choose partners who remind us of past experiences and who therefore—we hope offer us a chance to heal old wounds. The problem comes if we try to resolve unfinished business by changing our partner rather than by understanding the issues they trigger and asking for their support. Addressing old securities has to be mutual, so we need a partner who is willing to work with us. If you find someone who'll collaborate on mutual healing, you may find that old mistakes turn into new confidence.*"

Here is a diagram to better help you understand the different aspects of each attachment style: [2]

---

2 Dr. Leslie Becker-Phelps and Megan Kaye, *Love: The Psychology of Attraction* (DK, 2016).

Attachment Style	Parenting Style	Child's Baseline Emotional State	Child's Expectations of Life
Secure	Warm, Attentive, Relatively Consistent, and Quick to Respond	Happy, Confident, and Curious	"My needs will be met."
Anxious	Inconsistent: Sometimes Responsive and Sometimes Not	Insecure, Anxious, and Intensely Emotional	"If I act in the right ways, I might earn love, and my needs might be met."
Avoidant	Distant and Cold, or Harsh and Critical	Emotionally Shut Down	"I can't trust anyone to meet my needs. I must meet my own needs."

A Relationship between a Secure and an Anxious/Avoidant Person: Of the three types of attachment, people who are secure tend to fare better in relationships, which are, therefore, more secure. Secure people can find love with anxious or avoidant people. The secure person tends to have more intimacy with an anxious person. In a relationship, only one person needs to be secure and make the compromises. This person provides stability and reassurance to their partner and is available when their partner needs him or her, which allows the anxious person to be more at ease and demonstrate some of their best qualities. Those qualities include being loyal and having a loving presence. The secure person, who tends not to take things personally, can provide comfort to an avoidant person, who has a tendency to worry about being tied down. They give the avoidant person time alone and a sense of freedom.

The problem, however, comes with a relationship between two insecure types, as Dr. Becker-Phelps and Kaye claim.

A Relationship between Two Anxious People: *"The relationship may be close, even passionate, but there will be a lot of conflicts instead of communicating their feelings directly. If the relationship lasts, it will be volatile."*

A Relationship between Two Avoidant People: This combination has a tendency to not last the test of time. Theirs is a detached and convenience-based marriage. Their lack of ability to grow close may result in infidelity, lack of intimacy, and no connection with their partner.

A Relationship between an Anxious and an Avoidant: Dr. Becker-Phelps and Kaye state that among the three combinations, this is the worst type, though also the most commonly occurring. They further characterize that an avoidant person sees an anxious person as "clingy," "needy," "melodramatic," "demanding," and "obsessed" by commitment, while a secure person sees an anxious person as "affectionate," "worried," "upset," "companionable," and "loyal."

They also characterize an anxious person as seeing an avoidant person as "distant," "confusing," "selfish," "mean," and having "commitment issues." A secure person, however, sees an avoidant person as "private," "cautious," "self-sufficient," "conflicted," and "independent."

A secure person, on the other hand, can find love with an anxious or an avoidant person, but intimacy is better with an anxious person.

Dr. Becker-Phelps and Kaye remind us that, *"With work and patience, we can adjust our models for a kinder view of life. Self-affirmations and self-compassion can help you tackle those fears, as can Cognitive Behavioral Therapy."*

The Third Ingredient of Intellectual Chemistry: Extroverted and Introverted Types
Now that we have discussed the two mindsets and the three attachment types let us move on to the two behavioral types: *extrovert* and *introvert*.

For a relationship to work long-term, both partners must be either extroverted or introverted. If one partner is extroverted and wants to go out all the time and the other partner is introverted and wants to stay at home, it will not work. An extroverted type tends to be energized by people, while an introverted type is energized by time alone. As time goes by, they will forge different habits and activities that do not necessarily complement each other.

Developing a Deeper Intellectual Chemistry

With a powerful base and a solid match of the three ingredients of intellectual chemistry, you can start forging a stronger bond with your partner. One of the best ways to develop a deeper friendship and intellectual affinity or connection is to spend more time together. Learning a new language together, starting a project, joining a group, and going on a weekly walk by the beach are some activities that you can regularly do.

Over the course of a relationship, sexual chemistry will naturally fluctuate. It can grow as you become closer; it can diminish as you build emotional walls between you; and it can even be lost and reignited. This is why falling in love with your best friend can be the most fulfilling emotional experience. Studies report that couples who were friends before they became romantically involved have more successful and satisfying marriages. Dr. John Gottman reaffirms that by saying, *"Happy marriages are based on a deep friendship. By this I mean a mutual respect for and enjoyment of each other's company."* However, if you have issues with needing to be in control or being afraid of being controlled by others, you may choose partners toward whom you feel little or no sexual attraction to keep yourself safe. Moreover, if you are uncomfortable with emotional or sexual intimacy, you will attract a partner that will be unavailable.

Intellectual chemistry is crucial to connection and building a meaningful and loving relationship. It is absolutely a deal-breaker, and without it, even if you enjoy strong physical chemistry with your partner, that physical chemistry will eventually subside. However, should you put in the home passion and dedicate yourself to developing intellectual chemistry, you will find the rare love we are all trying to obtain. In the next chapter, we will discuss the role emotional chemistry plays in forging a beautiful romance.

CHAPTER 6
EMOTIONAL CHEMISTRY

NOW THAT WE HAVE A basic understanding that physical chemistry is related to your nature and intellectual chemistry is connected to your nurture, what is *emotional chemistry*? And maybe more importantly to answer—what role does emotional chemistry play in your journey to find meaningful and lasting love? We answer those questions in this chapter.

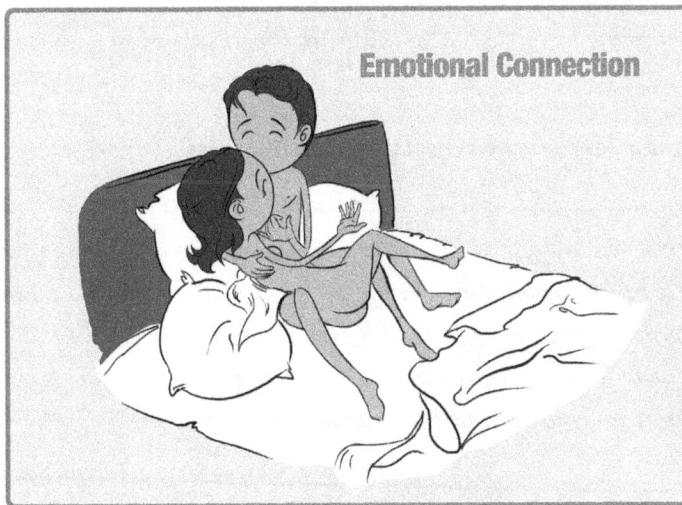

Emotional Connection

When we have the right physical chemistry (i.e., living in your core energy), we create the sparks; when we have the right intellectual chemistry (similar mindsets, attachment types, and extroverted and introverted types, i.e., living in your nurture energy, in addition to having similar goals and values), we create friendship. Similarly, the more extreme your masculine and feminine energies are, the more sparks you experience between your partner and you. The more goals and values you have in common, the stronger the friendship. However, even then, is that enough to sustain a meaningful relationship?

Many relationship experts claim that the polarity (a.k.a. physical chemistry) creates sparks, while others say that sometimes polarity doesn't work by itself. I agree with both. Sparks alone do not work, friendship alone does not work, and sparks and friendship can work for the short term. However, there is still a piece missing for the magic to happen in a long-term relationship: emotional chemistry.

Emotional chemistry is about accepting the differences and celebrating the similarities. It's about learning to be playful and light in the face of challenges while flirting and teasing along the way. Emotional chemistry is about connecting our differences with our similarities and becoming one; about connecting nature with nurture, being present for our partners, developing trust, and establishing an unshakeable bond. This is where we connect the lover side of us with the friend side of us to become best friends.

Flirting is a dance that connects similarities with differences.

"When you begin flirting with us, we're imagining what kind of lover you'll be in a relationship. A fun and playful man will always have surprises waiting for us and will keep the romance alive both in the bedroom and out. (When a man is direct we imagine an executive boardroom with no sense of humor and no time for us)."

—Tiffany Taylor, author of *Tiffany Tells All: The Attraction and Seduction Audio for Men*

The collision that happens between masculine and feminine energies creates intense friction that leads to tension, which in turn creates the sparks.

The more extreme the polarities, the more the tension rises, and the more the sparks start to fly.

A **friendship** has one dynamic.
A **loveship** has one dynamic.
A **relationship** has two dynamics.
A **magical relationship** has three dynamics.

The Different Types of Emotional Chemistry

In stage one, Mr. and Ms. Bad use the first type: short-term seduction (sexual connection).

In stage two, Mr. and Ms. Nice and Mr. and Ms. Friend use the second type: long-term seduction (emotional connection).

In stage three, Mr. and Ms. Grey use the short-term *and* long-term seductions (sexual and emotional connection).

Sexual connection alone does not work, as it is a type of "get-love-quick" scheme (mainly used by pickup artists). Moreover, emotional connection alone does not work because it is like trying to get a car to move forward without any fuel.

Sexual Connection: The First Ingredient of Emotional Chemistry (Stage One)

Attraction has less to do with how much you have in common and more to do with how playful you can be with your differences, the silences between your words, and your physical chemistry. Attraction happens in the pauses, in the mystery, in the tension, in the opposites. So if you want more attraction and more sparks, increase the mystery, the tension, and the differences between your polarities. This is what makes someone magnetic and sexy; **it has nothing to do with similarities.** Let's give it a try. Say their name and smile the next time you want to increase the tension while in a conversation with your partner. Then take a few seconds before answering their question. They will go ballistic.

The three things needed to create a **sexual connection** are:

1. Biology (Nature)

Nature created man with a penis and woman with a vagina. Nature has made men more masculine and women more feminine. This is biology. So to have the sexual tension and the sparks, the man has to be a man and the woman has to be a woman. Again, this is biology talking. Attraction has almost nothing to do with looks. When the man is masculine and the woman is feminine, the tension will rise because of their differences and attraction will happen. Remember when you wondered how this stunning babe was dating this ugly man? Or when this handsome man was dating this ugly woman? It has nothing to do with what society put in our heads. Money and fame are not attractive to women—masculine energy is. Physical beauty is not attractive to men—feminine energy is.

2. Being Comfortable with Your Sexuality (Nurture)

Society trains us to think that sex is wrong or shameful, which can often block your sexual energy. However, when you fall for that, you are simply repressing your natural energy. So, Mr. Friend, learn to express your masculinity rather than to repress it, and Ms. Friend, learn to express your femininity rather than to repress it. (This doesn't apply to Mr. and Ms. Bad since they decided to stay in their natural energies.)

3. Playfulness (Connecting Nature and Nurture)

Playfulness is a dance between similarity and differences. Two things can help you become a master of playfulness:

> **Mystery.** Mystery creates anticipation in your partner's mind, and it is anticipation that creates excitement and makes it more pleasurable. So keep a zest for unpredictability, as attraction grows in mystery. Dating is a game that never ends. Sexual attraction is about wanting something you don't have. If you delay information, it builds emotional experience and creates mystery and wonder.

Tension. The more opposite the polarity of energies, the more the sexual tension increases. When you play with your differences, you are not afraid of showing who you truly are and accepting each other despite the differences. Men can play with women's emotions, and women can play with men's egos.

This is where you tease each other. When you are cocky and funny, you are showing that you have a good sense of humor, which means that when life gets tough, you will know how to handle the problems. When you start to feel the tension, don't ease up on it. Enjoy it. Enjoy being uncomfortable. It is the art of being present. Men, be problem-creators; women love drama and emotional roller coasters, but they will deny it because it is not what they want (i.e., nurture) but it is what they need (i.e., it is in their nature).

The Two Things That Kill Sexual Connection

Finding true love and a long-lasting relationship isn't just based on considering those positive things you can do; it is also heavily reliant on avoiding the threats to your sexual connection. The greatest threats we often see in our current environment are:

1. Porn. If you watch porn, you will be less willing to have your needs met in real life. This means that the tension won't be high and that you (men) are more in your feminine energy (yes, it means you are more passive).

2. Friendship. When you get too comfortable and too friendly, you kill the tension, the mystery, and the attraction.

Sexual Connection = Physical Chemisty + Playfulness

Emotional Connection: The Second Ingredient of Emotional Chemistry (Stage Two)

Emotional connection is the second ingredient of emotional chemistry. A number of common misconceptions exist around emotional connection. We will start off by discussing those at length.

The First Misconception: The Different Perception of Romance—What Men Think Versus What Women Feel

The first misconception is the difference between what men think versus what women feel. I came across a powerful and enlightening article by Liz Rave, dating coach and sexual attraction expert. In "Romance vs. Logic," Rave differentiates what men and women perceive as "romance."

For instance, I always thought that when a woman wanted romance, it was all about the flowers, romantic dinners, and the like; however, after reading this article, I learned I was completely off. Rave says, "When a woman says she wants (more) romance, what she is really saying is that she wants more sexual energy. When women want to be seduced, they will often ask for 'romance,' not sex."

Tip 3

When a woman nags and complains all the time, she is just lacking some romance time or, more specifically, sexual energy from you.

So if you're always friend-zoned, it's because a woman wants you to feel her—feel her like the artist would feel his painting. You make or create the feeling, and she follows it. Masculine leads; feminine follows. You act, and she is open to receive. So it is not her feeling, but rather it is you creating the feeling for her and her accepting it. When you look at her, it is not the look but rather the feeling behind it. It is how you feel about her and you trying to send her such a feeling. It is not the rose itself but the feeling you give her when you offer the delicate rose.

The following examples illustrate this point:

Scenario 1: You give her a red rose.

Scenario 2: You are walking along a bay, and a merchant of red roses approaches you. You tell him to give you his most beautiful rose. While giving it to your partner, you tell her, "Do you see this rose? It pales in comparison to the beauty I see in you." You can add more, such as, "If you have a lighter, now you can see this red rose in flames. Imagine a plane of more than a million red roses in flames. That is how I feel about you."

Do you see the difference between the two?

Romance is about feeling desire and acting on it while getting lost in the object of your desire. If you are expressing your desire or feelings to some-one and they are not responding, it is because they are not accepting their feminine energy, and they are not letting or allowing the energy to just flow. Instead, they are in a controlling and nonsurrendering state. (Tip: Increase your masculine energy.)

Tip 4
Passion delivered nonverbally is irresistible to women.

What Women Are Not Doing Right

If you love your friend, the nice guy, don't shun him. You will lose a gem. All you need to do is teach him how to have the bad guy's characteristics that you crave. Teach him how to win your heart. Teach him once, and he will cherish you for the rest of his life. He will treat you better than both the nice guy and the bad guy combined. You would have made Mr. Friend version 2.0 (an updated version of Mr. Friend) even happier, and for that, he will make you the happiest woman. He only needs your guidance, because in all honesty, he doesn't know any better; nobody taught him.

I know and I understand that it is a turnoff to have to explain romance to a man and that explaining it kills the romance. However, look at it this way: Teach him once, and while you might kill the romance for the day, you win the romance for the next 18,000 days you will be spending with him. I promise you he will romance you as you have never seen. Or if you choose not to teach him and hope that the next guy will know, or maybe the next, or the next …

What is one day of turnoff versus your whole life?

The Second Misconception: The Two Emotional Chemistry Connections

To better understand the two emotional chemistry connections, let us look at the different perception of connection and the flow of sexual energy, or why men connect sexually versus why women connect emotionally.

Christina Antonyan, sexual educator, wrote an interesting article on the flow of sexual energy. In the piece, she illustrated that a man's positive energy flows from his penis while a woman's positive energy flows from her heart. This explains why a woman becomes more aroused if you foreplay with her breasts. More than 800 nerve endings exist in the nipples, and stimulation of the area increases oxytocin production—a hormone that boosts relaxation and happy feelings. While Antonyan focuses on sexual energy, we are going to take that and explore another layer: emotional energy.

Antonyan also describes how kissing can increase the passion between you and your partner: *"Women can get heavily aroused just from passionate kissing. If you want to amplify this intimate feeling, then caress her bottom lip gently with your thumb."* This is why foreplay is so important for women because they are receptors. They enjoy being nurtured, teased, and touched prior to the sexual act. Penetration is the masculine part, so until she relaxes in her femininity, it is difficult for a woman to feel aroused. She can let go once she is nurtured and then the flow of energy starts to be exchanged.

Women are biologically programmed to feel with their hearts first, because the heart is their active, energetic pole, before they can feel with their vaginas, while men are biologically programmed to feel with their penises first since the penis is their active, energetic pole. After a man feels with his penis, he can then feel with his heart. *Since a woman's vagina is passive and receptive, she needs time to warm up for sex; she wants her man to romance her out of her heart. Since a man's heart is passive and receptive, he needs time to warm up for communication; he wants his woman to inspire him out of his head.* This explains why men always want sex first and why women always want to talk (especially about their emotions) first. It also explains that the process of men wanting sex and women wanting to talk about their emotions is a biological loop. It further enhances that our differences complement each other.

From a woman's heart (active), her emotions go out (she lets go and trusts) to a man's heart (receptive). From a man's penis (active), his thoughts go out (he lets go and trusts) to a woman's vagina (receptive). The woman trusts her emotions to her man while her man trusts his thoughts to his woman.

Since women live in their hearts and men live in their heads, trust is important.

Women "release" their emotions while men "release" their thoughts.

Men "pull in" their emotions while women "pull in" their thoughts.

The primary form of connection for men is through sex. It is not purely physical but biological because it is how men feel connected (just as women feel connected through emotions).

As we previously discussed, the positives for a man is his penis, and for a woman, it's her breasts. A man connects (plugs in) with his penis; a woman connects (plugs in) with her heart. Men and women are inversely matched. For men, connecting first with sex doesn't mean that they don't like emotions; for women, connecting first with emotions doesn't mean that they don't like sex. It just means that this is how we should begin with connection.

Do you want more proof that men and women are the same but express themselves differently?

Do you know that both men and women have a penis?

Men express their penis outward, while women express their penis inward.

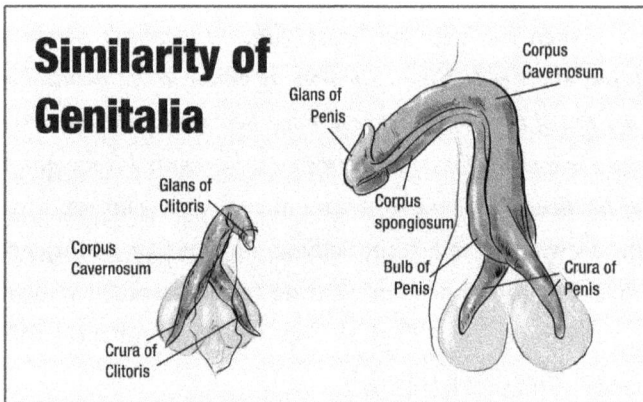

Still not convinced? Here's another illustration:

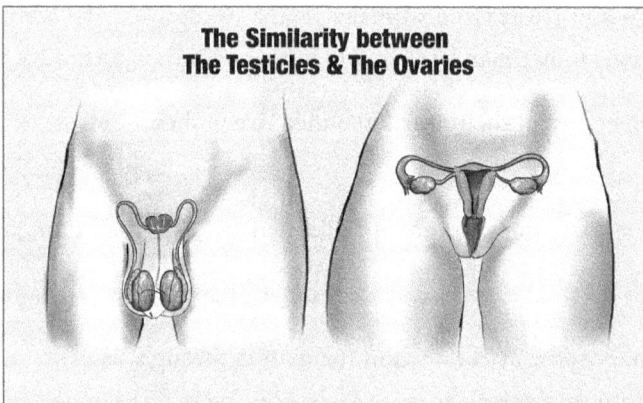

If the man or the woman breaks that loop (a woman withholding sex or a man not listening to his woman venting), then their emotional connection is lost.

Ms. Nice, keep in mind the following thought: Intimacy is the difference between friendship and relationship, and sex is one part of intimacy. In fact, sex is man's way of feeling loved. It is how men connect, so if you deprive Mr. Nice of sex, he will feel unloved and will start looking somewhere else.

However, here's a dilemma: Men feel love through sex, yet women feel vulnerable with sex. The solution? It is important for a man to make a woman feel safe, to be grounded, to be present, and to set strong bounderies for the woman to be open and vulnerable for sex. Ladies, also remember that just as you feel love through emotional connection, men feel vulnerable (yes, the opposite of sex). So you must make him feel safe, grounded, present, and protected in order for him to be open and vulnerable with his emotions.

Dr. John Gray, the author of *Men Are from Mars, Women Are from Venus*, says, *"We now have biological evidence that when you talk about feelings and how you feel inside without trying to solve problems, just talking and sharing, it stimulates high amounts of hormones called oxytocin, and that hormone lowers stress in women, but it doesn't lower stress in men. Which is why men do not understand why women always want to talk about the problem."* Men and women want different kinds of sex (romantic sex, love sex, quick sex, hot and exciting sex, nurturing sex, etc.). To that end, Dr. Gray offers some valuable sex tips for us to consider:

1) Quickies are important if time is an issue or if the woman is hesitant.

2) Men feel rejected when there is not enough sex. It starts when the man is in the mood and his partner rejects him.

3) If a man is not in the mood, self-pleasure will get him turned on.

4) The following is a good strategy to reject your partner without hurting their feelings: "Oh I'm so tired, but let's do it in the morning. I so look forward to that."

Each is a subtle and important reminder about the role sex might play in the development of a relationship. Each one helps build emotional chemistry and promotes positive love practices.

A Deeper Understanding of the Two Emotional Chemistry Connections

While men often complain about not understanding women's emotions, women also complain about not understanding men's love of oral sex. However, as we explored earlier in the chapter, a woman's positive flow of energy starts in the breasts (or heart) while the negative polarity ends in her vagina. Similarly, a man's positive flow of energy starts in his penis while the negative polarity ends in his breasts (or heart).

So while women first have to feel before sex, men first have to have sex before feeling. A woman must first feel, while a man must first be sexually satisfied because men and women are inversely programmed to feel and be satisfied in opposite (and yet complementary) ways.

Men love oral sex because, according to Renee Wade, dating and relationship expert, *"Oral sex is one of the ultimate feminine acts of love."* Oral sex shows a man that his woman is willing to perform an act of submission to him; she is showing her vulnerability, her admiration, a perceived love, and a sense of connection. Wade goes further by saying, *"It's not all about sex for men, but rather, it is how men perceive love, acceptance, and admiration."* It makes men feel accepted and received.

Ladies, just as you feel safe and trust your man with your emotions and your heart, your man feels safe and trusts you with his penis. By submitting to your man, you make him feel more like a man. When you as a woman allow yourself to be vulnerable with him, this shows your man that you trust him. Whether it is about trust, presence, or any of the ideas that are related to relationships or connection, men and women work inversely.

Men, if you want your woman to love you, protect her emotions. Women, if you want your man to love you, protect his penis. This is pure biology. Just like women are hardwired to feel first, men are hardwired for sex first. Men and women experience the same emotions but inversely; men connect sexually first and emotionally second, while women connect emotionally first and sexually second.

Moreover, a woman's breasts/emotions are as close to the heart of her womanhood as you can get. Women subconsciously or consciously see it as part of what makes them a woman. If a man rejects this part of her, she thinks that he isn't attracted to her or that he doesn't love her. Similarly, a men's penis is as close to a man as you can get. Men subconsciously or consciously see it as part of what makes them a man. If a woman rejects this part of her, he thinks that she isn't attracted to him or that she doesn't love him.

Men must speak to women with their *emotional connection of emotions*, just like women must speak to men with their *emotional connection of sex*.

Why Masculine Energy Disconnects and Why Feminine Energy Connects

Masculine energy seeks freedom, while feminine energy seeks love.

Masculine energy seeks detachment, while feminine energy seeks attachment.

Men's core energy is masculine, and women's core energy is feminine. With that in mind, when men or women get tired and drained, they act opposite of their natural energy. That is because they give so much of their energy that they become depleted of it, so the only energy left is the opposite one.

Gerald Rogers, a transformational leader, speaker and coach, claims the act of men disconnecting starts in infancy. This is contrary to the girl who becomes conscious of her gender by connecting with her mother (because her mother is the same sex as she is). On the other hand, the boy, when he becomes conscious of his gender, distances himself from his mother, realizing he is different from her. As time passes, while the girl expands her pattern of connecting with her mother to all sorts of people (friends, husbands, employees, and more), the boy expands his pattern of distancing himself from his mother to all areas of his life. This is why men disconnect with the opposite sex, while women want to connect.

Rogers goes further by stating that men fear commitment or intimacy because they unconsciously believe that their identities (formed through distancing) might be engulfed and annihilated by relationships.

I loved Rogers's explanation for why men are less affected by their emotions. He uses meditation to explain that it enables a man to distance himself from his thoughts and emotions by viewing them from afar. This allows him to become more aware and to decide what to do with the thoughts rather than becoming identified by them. He says that, *"In other words, the initial detachment and distancing stance leads to greater connection and loving attachment."*

Similarly, feminine energy craves connection. Bonding and connection are the main focus and priority of feminine energy. Relationships allow it to reach out and talk (this is how feminine energy connects), especially about its problems since this is its way of solving them (by talking about them). When in a relationship, feminine energy tends to nag a lot when dissatisfied because this is its way of chasing masculine energy—remember that they communicate indirectly.

Emotional Chemistry (Stage Three) = Sexual Connection (Stage One) + Emotional Connection (Stage Two)
Magical love only happens in stage three of relationships. After the sexual connection of the masculine and feminine energy and the playfulness that

happened in stage one (physical chemistry), you polarized yourself (masculine and feminine energy), and you polarized your relationship (by adding playfulness). Once you made sure that you have similar or compatible mindsets, attachment types, and energy types, and you started spending more time together with activities you both enjoy, you have developed a deeper bond out of stage two (intellectual chemistry). Now comes stage three, where you can merge sexual connection and emotional connection to form emotional chemistry. Once you have mixed your physical chemistry, intellectual chemistry, and emotional chemistry, you will have created a magical love. Moreover, while you can certainly have an emotional connection if you are in stage two, you can only have emotional chemistry in stage three.

You connect the ingredients of stage one and stage two in this stage, and add one more ingredient to ensure that you create a love that lasts. You add the emotional connection of emotions and the emotional connection of sex, which I call: *men sexual connection* and *women emotional connection*.

Magical Love = Physical Chemistry +
Intellectual Chemistry + Emotional Chemistry

Magical Love = (Masculine Energy + Feminine Energy) +
(Mindset + Attachment Types + Energy Types +
Time Spent Together) + (Playfulness + (Men Sexual Connection +
Women Emotional Connection))

Sexual Connection = Physical Chemistry + Playfulness

Emotional Connection =
Men Sexual Connection + Women Emotional Connection

Emotional Chemistry = Sexual Connection
+ Emotional Connection

How Masculine and Feminine Energies Connect Differently

With a basic understanding of why masculine energy disconnects and why feminine energy connects, we can now shift to a conversation surrounding how, when they do connect, they go about it in different ways. Men and women love their partners similarly, but they express it differently. For example:

The type of presence men seek in a woman is through sex.
The type of presence women seek in a man is through communication.

The type of trust men seek in a woman is through sex.
The type of trust women seek in a man is through communication.

The type of vulnerability men seek in a woman is through sex.
The type of vulnerability women seek in a man is through communication.

The type of bounderies men seek in a woman is through communication.
The type of bounderies women seek in a man is through sex.

The type of grounding men seek in a woman is through sex.
The type of grounding women seek in a man is through communication.

The type of holding space men seek in a woman is through sex.
The type of holding space women seek in a man is through communication.

The type of intimacy men seek in a woman is through sex.
The type of intimacy women seek in a man is through communication.

The type of foreplay women seek in a man is through sex.
The type of foreplay men seek in a woman is through communication.

The type of validation men seek in a woman is through sex.
The type of validation women seek in a man is through communication.

The type of love men seek in a woman is through sex.
The type of love women seek in a man is through emotions.

I am sure you see the stark contrast between the two styles. Men emotionally connect through sex, women through communication. Recognizing that will help you begin the process of forging a stronger level of emotional chemistry.

> Men and women attract differently (physical chemistry); attach similarly (intellectual chemistry); and connect inversely (emotional chemistry).

Isn't the Grey Dance of Love beautiful?

The Best Ways Men and Women Feel Emotional Chemistry

Remember, emotional chemistry is the link between sexual connection and emotional connection. It is a dance between physical chemistry, playfulness, sexual connection, and emotional connection through foreplay, presence, and special rituals. Emotional chemistry is the link that glues marriages together; it is the link that bonds couples closer. It is the magical ingredient that will keep you at an orgasmic state of passion, fulfillment, appreciation, understanding, acceptance, and love and love and looovveee. Yes, emotional chemistry is that powerful.

Foreplay

Remember, **while a woman needs foreplay before sex, a man needs foreplay before communication.** Authors Dr. Leslie Becker-Phelps and Megan Kaye, in their book *Love: The Psychology of Attraction*, say, *"Sexual desire is generally categorized as four stages (desire, arousal, orgasm, and resolution)— but Rosemary Basson argues that arousal and desire are often reversed, and that for women in particular, sexual desire is often responsive rather than spontaneous: being approached by a partner or starting to do sexual things creates arousal, which in turn creates the desire for sex."*

Tip 5

Sex isn't just about pleasure; during orgasm, the body releases oxytocin hormones associated with bonding.

This further solidifies the validity of my theory of the inverse connection between men and women. Men feel desire first and then get aroused, while women get aroused first and then feel desire. Similarly, with communication, women feel the need to vent to feel understood and accepted, while men want to feel accepted before wanting to communicate.

Presence

Just as women want their men to be present and grounded when they are talking about their emotions, men want their women to be present and grounded when they are having sex. Why? Simple: This is their way of feeling love from their partners.

The man is emotionally present for the woman during communication (masculine presence), while the woman is sexually present for the man during sex (feminine presence). By being "in the now," by being grounded, by holding space, both partners will feel safe and trust their respective partner.

Being present is about you giving your undivided attention to your partner at the right moment; it is creating a safe space for him or her to express concerns and share love in the rawest manner possible. By validating your partner's feelings, acknowledging him or her, and showing love with no judgment, you are giving unconditional love. Being present for your partner is one of the most powerful connection rituals you can ever practice, as it will open the door to their soul and magnify the attraction between you.

Masculine emotional presence and feminine sexual presence are about being in the moment, focusing on your partner, being vulnerable, grounded, holding space, setting bounderies, having intimacy (eye contact, hugging, touching, laughing, etc.), and Tantra (spiritual union) ...

For your partner to trust you and be totally honest with you.

For your partner to feel safe with you and confide their deepest secrets.

For your partner to feel validated and loved.

(Note that validation, in this case, is a stage one feeling; you need external validation because you are not validating yourself internally.)

The Five Qualities Women Find Irresistible in a Man [1]

1) Presence (the here and now), connected with her, with your purpose, with yourself (Practice meditation to build presence)

2) Purpose (It's hot to have a purpose, and working on it gives you a sense of direction)

3) Direction (Purpose is knowing what you are here to do, and direction is doing it); Plan and Act on It (makes feminine energy feel safe)

4) Trust and Honesty

5) Integrity

Setting Bounderies

Men and women can develop emotional chemistry by creating bounderies. Bounderies set expectations. It is important to have them because they make you feel safe in a relationship. Men can set safe bounderies during sex, while women can set safe bounderies during communication. That is how both partners will feel safe and trust the other.

1) Clearly identify your bounderies.

2) Understand why you need those bounderies; the why is important in order to stick with your decision when your bounderies are tested.

3) Be straightforward.

4) Always start with tight bounderies.

5) Address boundary violations.

6) Use a support system to stick with your bounderies.

Five Nonsexual Ways to Build and Deepen Intimacy, Trust, and Connection

1) Eye Contact

2) Nonsexual Touch (such as hugging or cuddling)

3) Laughing Together

---

1   Influenced by Shelly Bullard

4)   Doing a Form of Art Together (such as dancing or painting)

5)   Mindful Eating

The Grey Dance of Eye Contact [2]

As mentioned previously, the three ways to build emotional chemistry with your lover are through *foreplay*, *presence*, and *special rituals*. Moreover, as part of *presence*, one of the easiest things you can do to enhance your emotional chemistry is to utilize eye contact to promote and build a connection. Eye contact is one of the most powerful ways to build attraction, and this is backed by science and research. In fact, Harvard psychologist Zick Rubin conducted an experiment on eye contact. He found that couples that are truly in love look into each other's eyes for much longer than couples who aren't in love. In fact, when talking, these in-love couples tend to look at each other 75 percent of the time while talking.[3] Rubin goes on, saying that eye contact can go as far as releasing PEA. Furthermore, when you increase eye contact, this leads to a deeper level of intimacy and connection. [4]

So if you want to know how emotionally connected you are with your partner, look no further than your eye contact. When you gaze into your partner's eyes, listen without judgment, just be present, and your connection will deepen. That is how you will increase the intimacy. From a biological standpoint, the left eye is connected to the right hemisphere of the brain while the right eye is connected to the left hemisphere. By looking at the left eye, you are looking at the emotional side of your partner; by looking at the right eye, you are looking at the thinking side of your partner, that is if you are right-handed (it is the opposite with left-handed people). This is where the Grey Dance of Eye Contact must happen. Knowing that the left eye is the emotional side and the right eye is the thinking side, it is important to dance between the left and right eye while looking 80 percent of the time in the left eye. Keep in mind that the only way to be present while maintaining eye contact is by gazing from left to right and right to left.

---

2   Based on *Evolution: Male*

3   Andrew G. Marshall, *I Love You, but I'm Not in Love with You* (Bloomsbury Paperbacks, 2016).

4   Brendan T., *Evolution: Male*, https://evolutionmale.wordpress.com/.

Tantra

While most people associate Tantra with sex, it is much deeper than that. It has tremendous healing powers. Tantra is one of the most ancient and powerful methods to express love. It is the best and most profound way to connect with your partner at a soul-to-soul level. According to Psalm Isadora, sex expert and relationship guru, *"It is about getting out of your head and into your body, letting go of shame, and owning your desire. It's about learning to let go of control."*

Tantric sex has many other benefits, including healing past traumas, achieving multiple orgasms, and sexual and emotional merging.

Special Rituals

This is the third way to build your emotional chemistry and take it to the next level. Engaging in special bonding rituals with your partner will create a deeper bond, sense of belonging, and connection. Special rituals help you magnify the good things you do for each other as well as make the difficult days easier. They become a source of "home feeling" and in turn help you feel safe, grounded, and loved, and the bond between the two of you will grow stronger and stronger.

I've dedicated an entire section to discovering and applying special rituals that Mr. and Ms. Grey apply. You can find it on www.greydanceoflove.com.

It's amazing that something as simple as eye contact can enhance connection, develop love, and take you to a higher level of emotional chemistry. That is just one way to increase it. Perhaps it is a forgotten art, but something so simple can be so powerful. If you want to build a lasting and passionate relationship, you have no choice but to maintain a high level of awareness and focus on emotional chemistry. This chapter should have helped guide you to accomplish that. It might take some time and energy, but the lasting results will show inside the bedroom and out.

CHAPTER 7
THE BIOLOGY AND CHEMISTRY OF LOVE

AS YOU CHECK OFF AN ever-developing intellectual, physical, and emotional chemistry, you'll begin to recognize and enjoy a supercharged relationship with your partner. Focusing on each of these integral areas will help forge the bond we all can only dream of. However, love is as much biological as anything else. Understanding the chemistry of love will help you explain why you might feel or act in a certain way. To fully light your life on fire, you have to focus on your biology so that you can recognize why you feel the way you do and how you can change the way you feel.

Love Potion ingredients:
1/3 Physical Chemistry (Attraction/Passion)
1/3 Intellectual Chemistry (Attachement/Friendship)
1/3 Emotional Chemistry (Connection)

In their theory of the two factors of love, psychologists Elaine Hatfield and Ellen Berscheid claim that we associate love with excitement and excitement with love. This explains why we tend to be very attracted to someone if we feel an adrenaline rush. This is a beautiful realization. Why? Because chemically speaking, while it is very difficult to recognize and separate one feeling from another, it is interesting for us to play with our hormones to help our brains move into attraction. In *Love: The Psychology of Attraction*, Dr. Leslie Becker-Phelps and Megan Kaye explain this by stating, *"We may think we know our feelings, but the physical sensations of fear, excitement, and desire are almost identical."* Dr. Becker-Phelps and Kaye further remind us that attraction can be triggered by fear (horror movies, roller coasters, parachuting and extreme sports, etc.), anger (a common outrage at some injustice in society), urgency (deadlines and bounderies), drama, and sexual arousal. In fact, they go so far as recommend to *"look through a few naughty pictures or read a bit of erotic fiction before the date; some mild sexual frustration might make your date look all the hotter."*

Tip 6

If you are struggling to create attraction, do something thrilling on your dates. Since fear, excitement, and desire have the same physical sensations (and they are located in the same region of the brain), watching a horror movie, going on a rollercoaster, doing an extreme sport, or even doing something new will get your friend or partner excited, and his or her desire for you will automatically increase by sharing these experiences.

This can really make things interesting for each of us. We feel something, anything, but we aren't always sure what it means. What causes this overwhelming and emotional feeling? The answer: Many different hormones are at work behind the scenes that cause you to feel the way you do. As we unpack each at length, you should begin to sense how these chemical reactions can impact your ability to love and be loved.

The Different Hormones That Will Help You in the Different Stages of Relationships

The human brain experiences three chemical reactions that it processes in each of the three stages of relationships. While in the different stages of relationships, our bodies simultaneously release those different hormones during each stage. The brain and the body act in sync as these hormones are released.

Stage One: Attraction (Physical Chemistry)

Stage Two: Attachment (Intellectual Chemistry)

Stage Three: Connection (Emotional Chemistry)

For the purpose of simplification, we are going to discuss two brains: the *brain in lust* and the *brain in love*.

The *brain in lust* is stage one whereas ...

The *brain in love* is stages two and three, and...

The *brain in lust and love* is stages one, two, and three.

Mastering the process of the brain in lust will help you attract anyone you want; this is the key to creating the sparks.

Mastering the process of the brain in love will help you get attached and connected; this is the key to being in love.

Mastering the process of the brain in lust and love will help you attract, be, and stay in love for a lifetime; this is the key to growing in love.

Let's look at each one in greater detail.

The Brain in Lust

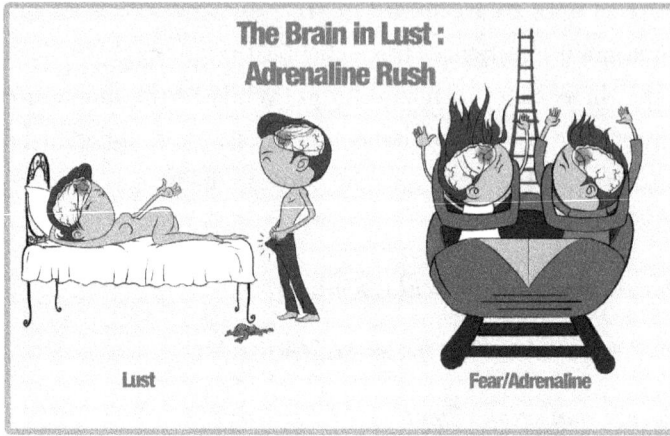

In the process of attraction, our brains release three types of hormones:

1. The sex hormones, also known as the lust hormones (testosterone and estrogen)

2. The smell hormones (pheromones)

3. The attraction hormones (serotonin, noradrenalin, and dopamine)

The human body reacts as if it is hungry or thirsty when the brain releases the attraction chemicals. This is because, as mentioned earlier, excitement, fear, and desire are located in the same place and are all linked to the same chemicals. Allan and Barbara Pease, authors of *The Mating Game* and *The Body Language of Love*, say, *"During lust, two key parts of the brain become active—the hypothalamus, which controls our primordial drives, such as thirst and hunger, and the amygdala, which is a center for arousal. Dopamine is heavily secreted during lust, and it triggers the production of testosterone, causing sexual attraction to occur."*

The Sex Hormones

The brain is heavily affected by sex hormones like testosterone and estrogen when in lust. The sex hormones, testosterone for masculine energy and estrogen for feminine energy, are produced in the sex organs and are based on instant attraction. When the sex hormones are released (during sex or intimacy), the effects last between a couple of weeks and even up to a year. This is the stage Mr. and Ms. Bad excel at and, unfortunately, this is also the stage at which they fizzle out. This is why they cannot form long-term relationships.

Testosterone

Testosterone is the masculine energy sexual hormone. It is responsible for the development of facial and body hair, acne, a deeper voice, broader shoulders, narrow hips, and helps shrink bellies. From testosterone comes power and strength. **Men are wired with testosterone, which in high levels keeps a man from wanting to settle down with one woman. Studies show that lower levels of testosterone increase a man's demeanor toward commitment.** A 2006 study at the University of Chicago found that testosterone levels in married men and dads are much lower than single men who are still chasing after their counterparts. This is because fathers are now playing the role of parental figure and nurturer, which leads them to have higher oxytocin levels. [1]

Even our hormones show us that we need to dance between desire and love, between attraction and friendship. The higher testosterone is important for the attraction phase, whereas lower testosterone is important for the attachment phase. Jed Diamond, the author of *Male Menopause* and *The Irritable Male Syndrome*, helps explain this phenomenon: *"Many of us are drawn to high testosterone people for excitement and sex, but lower testosterone people make the best spouses."*

Dr. Theresa Crenshaw states that testosterone is twenty to forty times more present in men than women and that it is testosterone, not estrogen, that causes the heightened erotic sensitivity of the clitoris, breasts, and nipples. It maintains the fullness, thickness, and health of a woman's genital tissue as well. A deep voice reflects testosterone levels, which is attractive to women. In fact, increased body fat reduces testosterone. [2]

---

1   Allan and Barbara Pease

2   Jed Diamond

How to Increase Your Testosterone and Last Longer in Bed

According to Psalm Isadora, intimacy expert, you can work to increase your testosterone and last longer in bed by:

1) Working out in the gym and increasing lower body strength (hip- thrusting, dead lifts, and squats workouts)

2) Cardiovascular high-intensity interval training (sprints at intervals)

3) Mental games (change where you are getting your pleasure)

4) Play your own edge (masturbate until you almost get an orgasm)

A recent study on testosterone from the University of Aberdeen identified that men with higher levels of testosterone exhibited a stronger preference for more feminine faces, whereas women with higher levels of testosterone were attracted toward more masculine faces. Dr. Kluger states that just in case women's testosterone could use a boost, men pass it along in their saliva during passionate kissing. That helps explain why men and women spend time kissing as foreplay to sexual intercourse. However, it doesn't stop there. Testosterone can change by the minute. Jed Diamond states: *"Testosterone fluctuates daily, seasonally, and drops when we hit menopause (in women) and andropause (in men). Now we know that men are as 'hormonal' as women and our hormonal cycles have a significant impact on our love lives."*

Testosterone plays an important role in creating a meaningful love relationship, but you can have too much of a good thing. There will always be natural physiology at play, regulating your behavior and sexual desire. However, knowing how testosterone impacts what you do and how you feel can be a real game-changer as you move through the three stages of relationships.

Estrogen

Estrogen is the counterpart to testosterone. It is the feminine energy sexual hormone. Estrogen is responsible for the development of female secondary sexual characteristics during puberty, including breast development, widening of the hips, and female fat distribution. Women with a high level of estrogen are more attractive to men because estrogen is also an indicator of fertility. In males, estrogen regulates certain functions of the reproductive system important to the maturation of sperm and may be necessary for a healthy libido.

While estrogen levels are significantly lower in males compared to females, estrogen, nevertheless, also plays an important physiological role in males. Men who have too little estrogen may have excess belly fat and a lower libido. Men with too much estrogen may grow breasts and have poor erections.

Women who have low-estrogen levels may have a lessening of menstruation, may also experience symptoms of menopause such as hot flashes, insomnia, and a lower libido; mood swings and dry skin are also a problem. High-estrogen levels can cause weight gvain (binge eating) and menstrual changes. Estrogen is also involved in the sex drive of women and men. Sex drive is dependent on testosterone levels only in the presence of estrogen, but without estrogen, testosterone levels decrease sexual desire.

How to Increase Your Estrogen Level

1) Moderate sports (jogging, yoga, etc. Note that excessive sports will decrease estrogen, so moderation is key.)

2) Good amount of sleep (7 to 8 hours)

3) Decrease stress

4) Eat a healthy, balanced diet

The Smell Hormones

Pheromones

Most all of us have heard of testosterone and estrogen, but pheromones are likely just as important to sexual attraction and lust. Pheromones are airborne scent chemicals that send signals about our moods and genetic makeup to alert a potential mate. These chemicals are excreted and trigger a social response. They are capable of acting outside of the body to trigger an impact on the behavior of the individual who receives them. They impact the other person by their response physiologically and also behaviorally to the person releasing them. Some people will be attracted to your natural scent, while others will be repelled by it.

Pheromones are primarily perceived through olfactory sensors, and studies suggest several areas of the body, including the skin, sweat glands, saliva, and urine, excrete them. In fact, several studies have shown that **people who produce higher than average amounts of pheromones have greater success with members of the opposite sex.** Several studies also show that pheromones can read the moods of individuals. In one study, researchers collected tears of women and placed them under men's noses (without telling them what the substance was). The results showed reduced sexual arousal and testosterone levels. In another study, researchers asked women to rate the odors of T-shirts worn by different men. The results showed that women preferred men whose DNA was different from their own (note: physical chemistry, masculine/feminine), and they could even tell whether the person was anxious.

Androstenone is a male's primary pheromone secretion. In a woman, androstenone is also secreted but as a secondary pheromone. Her primary pheromone, copulin, causes an increase in testosterone levels in men.

Pheromones can act as powerful catalysts of sexual attraction. As humans secrete these chemicals through perspiration, they are subconsciously detected by the nose, brain, and nervous system.

Men primarily release androstenone through their skin and hair. While men and women excrete trace amounts of it through their urine, men excrete up to four times as much as women do. This particular pheromone, which is produced by the adrenal glands of both sexes, is also present in sweat under the armpits of both sexes. In addition, it is present in smegma, which is the substance secreted by the sebaceous glands of the penis and vagina.

Back to copulin, the pheromone I previously mentioned. Studies of the vaginal secretions of sexually alluring women have demonstrated the presence of copulin. The appearance of these chemicals appears to correlate with hormonal variations corresponding with changes in the female menstrual cycle.

How to Increase Your Pheromone Level

1) Exercise regularly. It boosts your testosterone level, which naturally increases pheromones. The sweat you excrete through your pores will help spread your body's natural pheromones over your skin.

2) Take a bath in soapless, hot water and use a mild exfoliating soap. Natural pheromones are released from the skin; soap washes away your natural pheromones. Instead, try sandalwood essential oils to destroy bacteria that can result in offensive body odor.

3) Eat zinc-rich foods. Doing so increases testosterone and male fertility.

4) Get enough sleep. When you don't get enough, your testosterone production slows down.

> **Tip 7**
> Consider your antiperspirants and deodorants, as they can cause clogged pores in the armpits, one of the strongest sources of pheromones, and this limits or blocks their emission.

The Attraction Hormones

Estrogen, testosterone, pheromones, oh my! It is a lot to consider. Attraction hormones are the third category of hormones that impact the lust within your brain. In the early stages of a relationship, attraction and/or sparks are caused by the combination of three neurochemicals: phenethylamine, noradrenalin, and dopamine. In the later stages of a relationship, three other neurochemicals replace them: *oxytocin, serotonin,* and *endorphins. Phenethylamine,* or PEA, is an amine that naturally occurs in the brain and some foods, such as chocolate. It is a stimulant that causes the release of *noradrenalin* and *dopamine.* PEA controls the transition from lust to love.

When we fall in love or when we feel attraction, our palms sweat, we can stutter and become breathless, we can't think clearly, and it feels like we have butterflies in our stomachs. This is all due to the surging brain chemicals dopamine, noradrenalin, and serotonin (called *monoamines*). Noradrenalin and serotonin excite us, while dopamine makes us feel happy. Biologically speaking, with the combination of dopamine, noradrenalin, and PEA in your body, you're experiencing something similar to a cocaine high. Moreover, it doesn't matter whether you just met this special person, or you've known them for ages; these love signals can be released at any time.

The attraction hormones noradrenalin and dopamine are triggered when we start becoming attached due to certain activities we are doing together. When the attraction hormones are released, the effects last between eighteen months to three years.

Studies show that looking at the picture of our beloveds lights up the dopamine receptors in the brain. Men, being more visual than women, are more prone to this, which suggests that men falling in and out of love faster than women may have a biological basis.

Psychologists Donald G. Dutton and Arthur P. Aron conducted three experiments and found direct correlations between attraction and anxiety. Two equally attractive females were placed on separate bridges. One stood on a suspension bridge, and the other stood on a regular bridge. The females stopped passing men and asked them to fill out a survey. It was found that the suspension bridge caused more anxiety naturally, and this heightened the attraction levels to the women standing there.

In another study, men had to cross a small bridge to speak to a female research assistant who gave her phone number for a follow-up on the study. The follow-up showed that of the sixteen men who crossed the secure wooden bridge, only two called, while nine of the eighteen men who crossed the suspension bridge called. The research further confirmed that the shakiness of the bridge played a major role. What both these studies suggest is that **attraction may be chemically stimulated in anxiety-provoking situations rather than in more normal circumstances.**

Phenethylamine

PEA decreases after dopamine does because the differences between masculine and feminine energies have decreased as well. When a man becomes more feminine, this leads to a reduction of the PEA in his system. It is interesting to note that after pregnancy, the woman shifts her oxytocin focus (nurturing/feminine) to the offspring (at the expense of her man). This explains why the connection is distorted after pregnancy and the relationship dynamic has shifted. Men and women need to be aware of this. It is not the woman's fault, but at the same time, this is when a compromise should be found.

At first, dopamine is in the driver's seat, but after pregnancy, oxytocin is in that seat. That is because women turn to their masculine energy to protect their offspring. As such, there is a lack of oxytocin (feminine energy) between the man and the woman since both are in their masculine energy. However, after the child grows up, the woman turns back to her feminine energy and expects her man to be there in his full masculine energy.

While differences were important before pregnancy, connection and nurturing are important in the early stages of pregnancy. In other words, the man must be emotionally intelligent and shift to his feminine energy "temporarily" to adapt to the current relationship dynamic and not withdraw emotionally in order to maintain the relationship. What could result is emotional withdrawal between the man and the woman. They both turn to different activities or partners to fulfill their emotional satisfaction.

Noradrenalin

The noradrenalin hormone, also known as *norepinephrine* or the "stress hormone," is a form of adrenaline that gets our hearts racing. It is a stress hormone that affects the brain where attention and action are stimulated, which in turn activates stimulation and arousal, affecting our reward systems. It also regulates our affective states, learning and memory, and hormone and autonomic functions.

The actions of noradrenalin are vital to the fight-or-flight response, whereby the body prepares to react to or retreat from an acute threat. Noradrenalin induces euphoria in your brain, exciting the body by giving it a booster dose of natural adrenaline. This causes the heart to beat faster and blood pressure to rise (due to a higher level of adrenaline and cortisol in the blood). This is why in the early stage of being attracted to someone (or what is called "falling in love"), your stress response is activated and you can experience a pounding heart or sweaty palms.

How to Increase Your Noradrenalin Level

1) Exercise

2) Cold exposure

3) Eat foods that taste bitter, such as oranges

4) Eat healthy food

Dopamine

Dopamine produces a goal-driven "must-be-with-them" attraction. It's commonly associated with the pleasure system of the brain, providing feelings of enjoyment and feeling good, motivating us to do certain activities. It is stimulated when we perceive a reward, and it stimulates gratification. When dopamine is released, we experience pleasure. It's the reason we can't sleep or always think of someone.

Oversleeping, a lower libido, procrastination, self-doubt, and lack of enthusiasm are the most important symptoms of low dopamine levels. This may be due to a deficiency in nutrients such as zinc, magnesium, and iron.

When dopamine is released, it can cause a state of infatuation (the second stage of attraction) and is due to a high energy rush. This is when we believe we are falling in love while we are in fact being chemically attracted. It is the effect of dopamine that makes us feel extremely happy and causes the butterflies in the stomach.

Biological anthropologist Dr. Helen Fisher published a study in 2002 where she recruited forty young people who considered themselves to be madly in love; they were in mutually loving relationships. She put each of the forty subjects in an MRI scanner with a picture of their lover and a picture of an acquaintance. They looked at the lover, then had a diversion task, and then looked at the acquaintance for thirty seconds. This whole cycle repeated for twelve minutes. The study showed that when the subjects looked at their sweethearts, dopamine released into other areas of the brain, including the posterior dorsal caudate and its tail, which are both central to the brain's reward-and-motivation system. When dopamine levels are high, the feelings of falling in love are fast and intense. This causes an obsession for the one in love and explains that we might crave a loved one because of the feeling we receive from him or her.

When a person is deeply in love, many regions of their brain show more activity involved in the dopamine reward system. The study also showed that the love of a parent activates almost all of the same areas except for the hypothalamus. This shows that the hypothalamus is responsible for the desire and sexual attraction with a romantic partner. Reduced activity in the amygdala (linked to fear and learning from mistakes) and the frontal and prefrontal cortices (both linked with analysis, judgment, delayed gratification, and predicting the outcomes of events) were also shown. The reduced activity in the amygdala and the cortices may explain why we lose ourselves in love.

How to Increase Your Dopamine Level

1) Discover new things.

2) List your small tasks; having a checklist boosts dopamine.

3) Break big goals down.

4) Create a series of little finish lines instead of just celebrating at one finish line.

5) Really celebrate (drink champagne, go to your favorite restaurants, etc.) when you meet a small goal.

6) Create new goals before achieving a current one; this ensures a continuous flow of dopamine.

7) Listen to music you love; even the anticipation of hearing the music releases dopamine.

8) Recognize the accomplishments of your partner; you will increase their dopamine level.

9) Exercise often.

10) Have a success journal.

11) Be creative.

12) Meditate.

Serotonin

The serotonin hormone, also known as the "happy molecule," makes us feel blissful. It is a neurotransmitter that is derived from tryptophan, which stimulates our moods and elevates them up or down in response to stimuli. Serotonin invites us to share and connect more, and it is responsible for the focus we have on, and preoccupation we have with, our partners. It is one of love's most important chemicals and one that may actually make us temporarily insane.

Donatella Marazziti, professor of psychiatry and director of the laboratory of psychopharmacology at the University of Pisa, found that in the early stages of romance, lower levels of serotonin exist. She also found that serotonin levels are depleted in people who suffer from obsessive-compulsive disorder. While both states are different in nature, they give feelings of anxiety and intrusive thinking. So, in the early stages of romance, it is fair to say that you become obsessed with the person of your desire while being a huge ball of uncertainty and anxiety.

Approximately 90 percent of the human body's total serotonin is located in the digestive system and impacts every part of your body, from your emotions to your motor skills. It controls impulses, unruly passions, obsessive behavior, and aiding the sense of being in control. Serotonin is considered a natural mood stabilizer. It's the chemical that helps with sleeping, eating, and digesting. Having a low serotonin level can result in mood disorders, such as anxiety or depression, as well as insomnia.

> **Tip 8**
> Low levels of serotonin are associated with an increased libido, while increased serotonin levels are associated with a reduced libido. This is why we have a low serotonin level in the attraction stage.

Remember: Our brains in lust and our brains in love act differently. You must dance between them. In other words, it is normal to dance between high and low serotonin when you're dancing between high and low noradrenalin. Older couples tend to complain about a lack of sex; this is because they have too much serotonin.

Serotonin is one of love's most important chemicals, which may explain why when you're falling in love, your new lover keeps popping into your thoughts. In the early stage of attraction, the levels of cortisol or noradrenalin (the stress hormone) increase and alert your body to be ready for the crisis at hand. The more noradrenalin increases, the more serotonin decreases. As a result of low-serotonin levels, people become borderline obsessed with their beloved and unable to focus or eat whenever apart. According to Dr. Schwartz, low serotonin levels precipitate intrusive, maddeningly preoccupying thoughts, hopes, and terrors of early love, and it is those obsessive and compulsive behaviors that are associated with infatuation.

Eventually, once a relationship solidifies, the raphe nucleus in the brain stem begins to cook up more serotonin, eliciting those warm and fuzzy feelings of togetherness that typify long-term attachment. The only downside of that serotonin upshot is the loss of excitement, also colloquially known as the end of the "honeymoon phase." Serotonin flows freely as you feel more connected and important. An indicator that serotonin is not present can be found in depressed or lonely people. Writer Thai Nguyen suggests that unhealthy behaviors can be related to a cry for more serotonin. Princeton neuroscientist Barry Jacobs explains that most antidepressants focus on the production of serotonin. Since the brain doesn't know the difference between what is real and what is imagined, adding gratitude during your day can help you feel more connected and give you a serotonin boost.

Low serotonin is expressed differently in men and women. Women are twice as likely to experience depression, anxiety, and other mood disorders as men. They're also more likely to exhibit carbohydrate cravings, binge eating, and subsequent weight gain. Overeating carbs is a way of self-medicating to raise serotonin levels naturally. Men, on the other hand, are more prone to alcoholism, ADHD, and impulse-control disorders.

How to Increase Your Seratonin Level

1) Exposure to bright light (go out in the sun)

2) Regular exercise (mood-boosting effect)

3) Healthy diet

4) Meditation can help relieve stress and promote a positive outlook on life, which can greatly boost serotonin levels.

5) Get a massage. A study conducted by the Touch Research Insti- tutes at the The Miller School of Medicine at the University of Miami showed that a massage increases se- rotonin by 28 percent and decreases cortisol (the stress hormone) by 31 percent.

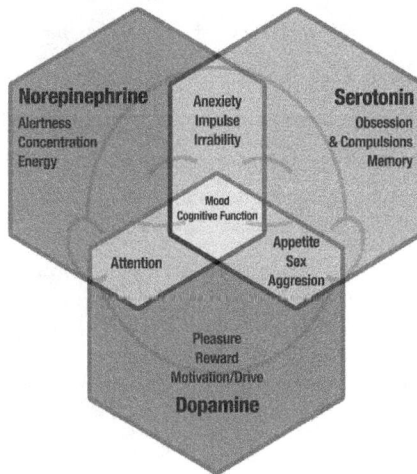

The Brain in Love

In stark contrast to the brain being in a state of lust, the brain in a state of love is distinctive and carries a special set of qualities and characteristics. Attachment can occur after the man has been depleted of his testosterone and filled with estrogen and the woman has been depleted of her estrogen and filled with testosterone. They'll find a meaningful attachment if the exchange of hormones between the man and the woman balances each other. If, on the other hand, the exchange of hormones is not regulated, then the long-term bonding will be affected. When tired or stressed, we tend to put out the opposite energy because we have spent all our natural energy and have no more (a man spending his testosterone needs to recharge, and during this time he only has oxytocin left).

The Brain in Love

Allan and Barbara Pease, authors of *The Mating Game* and *The Body Language of Love*, share with us that men's testosterone decreases and their oxytocin increases (to facilitate the bonding process) when they are falling in love, while a woman's testosterone rises when starting a new relationship. Biological attachment is often based on two categories of hormones:

1. The attachment hormones (vasopressin and oxytocin)
2. The addictive hormones (endorphins)

Let's take a closer look at each one.

The Attachment Hormones

The attachment hormones (oxytocin and vasopressin) are triggered when we are in love because of how well we connect. They are released in the bloodstream through the brain during sex and intimacy. Oxytocin strengthens bonds between people, and vasopressin strengthens the attachment between two people as well. According to Jed Diamond, we produce higher oxytocin and vasopressin levels as we trust more.

Mary Beth Bonacci, author of *Real Love: Answers to Your Questions on Dating, Marriage and the Real Meaning of Sex*, offers a great summary of the normal effects of oxytocin and vasopressin: "Oxytocin causes a woman to be forgetful, decreases her ability to think rationally, and causes an incredibly strong emotional attachment to form with the man she is with. While men also produce some oxytocin during sexual intercourse, their bodies also produce a hormone called vasopressin. Vasopressin, called the 'monogamy molecule,' kicks in after sexual activity, and its impact is to heighten a man's sense of responsibility. It encourages that part of him that says, 'My gosh, she may be carrying my child. I'd better get serious about life. I've got to get to work, to provide for this family.'"

Vasopressin

For men, in particular, this is a driver of faithfulness. According to Dr. Theresa Crenshaw, vasopressin is the "monogamy molecule" and can cause "aggression and territorial behavior." Vasopressin increases mental clarity, attention to detail, and short-term and long-term memory.

Vasopressin is among the hormones released during sexual activity. It initiates and sustains patterns of activity between pair-bonded and sexually active partners. This neurotransmitter induces male-to-male aggression. It is also noted that during the first year of a love relationship, the growth protein molecule NGF, or nerve growth factor, is found. This is what makes males territorial over their love interests.

How to Increase Vasopressin

1) Restrict water

2) Stand

3) Exercise

4) Visit a sauna

Oxytocin

Oxytocin is a neurotransmitter found in female reproduction but also in sexual orgasms and plays a role in social identifying and pair-bonding. It stimulates trust, love, and maternal instincts. This neurotransmitter is found in the plasma of men and women during orgasms, and because a response is enhanced by estrogen, women tend to have stronger reactions to oxytocin. It is believed that the more sex you have, the deeper your bond becomes.

Oxytocin invokes the feeling of contentment, reduces the feeling of anxiety, and promotes calmness and security in relation to a mate. It is released at childbirth and is partly responsible for the strong bond between the mother and baby.

Oxytocin is also known as the "cuddle" or "love hormone," which makes us grow attached. Kissing and hugging release oxytocin, which strengthens the bond between two partners and helps break down emotional walls. When the hormone is released in the brain, it results in feelings of attachment and bonding; this release explains why we listen more and why we get more attached. Oxytocin diminishes stress, lowers the blood pressure, reduces regular and social anxiety, boosts self-esteem, and helps us avoid and fight depression.

Tips to Increase Your Oxytocin Level

1) Listen with your eyes; make eye contact.

2) Give a gift.

3) Share a meal.

4) Meditate while focusing on others.

5) Soak in a hot tub or spa.

6) Get a pet.

7) Give eight hugs per day.

8) Engage in touching (hugs, kisses, cuddling, etc.).

9) Share words of encouragement.

10) Listen, be present, cry, connect, and talk.

11) Smile and laugh.

12) Make time for exercise.

13) Stop arguing, and find ways to apologize.

14) Seek out cute things and mention them.

15) Give her a foot massage; wash her hair.

Endorphins

Endorphins are biochemical compounds that enhance the immune system, block the passage of blood vessels, have antiaging, antistress, and pain-relieving effects, and help to improve your memory. They help regulate the pain and pleasure pathways associated with love, and this is what may be responsible for why we feel pain in a breakup. Endorphins are released in response to pain and stress and help alleviate anxiety and depression. Similar to morphine, they act as an analgesic and sedative, diminishing our perceptions of pain. Endorphins are also involved in the longevity of love. Love-related gestures, from holding hands to sexual activity, increase the production of endorphins, which, in turn, enhances the immune system.

How to Increase Your Endorphins Level

1) Sniff lavender or vanilla oils.

2) Engage in group exercise classes; in 2009, researchers found that college crews who rowed in synchronization had an increased rush of these feel-good hormones compared with those who rowed alone.

3) Laugh daily (the "inner jogging"), and anticipate laughter.

4) Have sex.

5) Eat dark chocolate.

6) Listen to music.

7) Eat something spicy.

The Grey Dance of Our Hormones Before, During, and After Sex

Dopamine is the reward hormone, noradrenalin is the stress hormone, and they are the strongest in stage one of relationships, where physical chemistry is dominant. Meanwhile, oxytocin is the bonding hormone, vasopressin is the attachment hormone, and they are the strongest in stage two of relationships, where intellectual chemistry is dominant. Finally, serotonin is the happy hormone, endorphin is the longevity molecule, and they are the strongest in stage three of relationships, where emotional chemistry is dominant.

Earlier in the book, I explained the Love Formula from an intellectual and emotional viewpoint; in this section, you will see the Love Formula from a biological viewpoint.

When we fall in love, we want to get closer and we want to connect, so we seek similarities (intellectual chemistry)—this is feminine energy. However, while oxytocin rises and vasopressin is released, dopamine and noradrenalin (differences) decrease. Moreover, dopamine and noradrenalin act in reverse by wanting to disconnect and be free—this is masculine energy. When we are "in love" or in lust, dopamine is at its peak and will start decreasing.

During sex, men release dopamine and take in oxytocin, because we merge, bond, or connect. Indra, a respected blogger, speaks about the rise and fall of dopamine during sex. For example, dopamine levels rise and climax during orgasm yet fall substantially immediately afterward. It has an almost hangover-like effect. She goes further, stating that it is immediate in males and delayed in females. This explains why men always need time after they ejaculate. They need to reinject dopamine in their systems after being depleted by it.

It is like an exchange of energy. During sex, a man releases dopamine inside his woman, and she, in turn, pushes her oxytocin toward him. This is why after orgasm, men feel more connected (in more feminine energy), which scares them away, but women feel more disconnected (in more masculine energy), which leads to them wanting to connect.

This explains why women want men to stay longer inside their vaginas even after ejaculation. Women crave connection; men crave disconnection. This explains why women love to cuddle after sex, while men love to sneak out after sex.

After having an orgasm, men and women feel depleted of energy. A man feels he is depleted of his masculine energy (because he released it into his woman), and a woman feels she is depleted of her feminine energy (because she disconnected with her man). So men want to do what men love to do, which is caving, and women want to do what women love to do, which is connecting. The solution is simply to take turns; you dance between cuddling or connecting and disconnecting. The result of the exchange of the dopamine and oxytocin has led to a decrease of testosterone in the man and an increase in testosterone in the woman.

> **Tip 9**
> Men need to disconnect. They don't do it because they don't love you, have another woman, just used you for sex, or there is something wrong or missing. They do it because they love you so much, and they want to come back stronger for you.

So you see why the Grey Dance of Love is crucial? Too much dopamine and there is no connection; too much oxytocin, and there is no passion. **Even biology is telling us to DANCE.**

On a side note, a reason the relationship dynamic changes after having a baby: The man and the woman start releasing more oxytocin to create a safe environment for the child. While this is great for the woman, it depletes the man of his strength. With time, he shifts to a more feminine energy, and this pushes the woman to turn to her masculine energy.

Why Attraction Fades and How to Rekindle the Sparks

So this is all fuzzy math, right? Well, not exactly. Surely we all have to give credence to the point that chemistry and biology are naturally occurring forces of nature, and we cannot necessarily fight to prevent their very existence. However, with knowledge comes power, and we can evaluate our chemistry and use it as a valuable tool to rekindle the sparks in any fading relationship. Dr. Becker-Phelps and Kaye wrote the following in their book *Love: The Psychology of Attraction:* "*We may remain passionately in love, or our feelings might cool a little as our sense of attachment grows, not because we've lost interest, but because oxytocin and vasopressin interfere with the dopamine and noradrenalin pathways in the brain. This doesn't mean you stop being attracted, just that you get better able to sleep, eat, and think straight. Your amygdala, which registers intense emotions like fear and desire, is now less overloaded, so it can process information more clearly. If you like a little madness in your romance, take heart: in long-term relationships, addictive hormones that are called endorphins act on your brain like opiates, you may be 'hooked on' your partner for real.*"

This proves that the brain processes differently during the attraction phase and the attachment phase. To go further, it also shows that while Mr. and Ms. Bad are good with the attraction phase and the Nices and Friends are good with the attachment phase, from a biological standpoint, they are incomplete. A relationship is about attraction and attachment; one cannot and does not work without the other.

Mr. and Ms. Bad have to learn more about the attachment hormones, while Mr. and Ms. Nice and Mr. and Ms. Friend have to learn more about the attraction and sex hormones. This shows that we indeed can create sparks by understanding how our attraction and sex hormones function, their processes, and how they marry with the attachment hormones. It is just a process to be followed.

Look at it like this:

> **Sparks = Sex Hormones + Attraction Hormones + Pheromones**
>
> **Connection = Attachment Hormones + Addictive Hormones**
>
> **Spark + Connection = Testosterone + Estrogen + Serotonin + Noradrenalin + Dopamine + Androstenone + Copulin + Vasopressin + Oxytocin + Endorphins**

The process of creating sparks is different from the process of creating attachment, which is also different from the process of creating connection. If you master those three processes, you will fall/be/stay in love forever after. This chapter shows you how to create those processes from a biological viewpoint.

This is why Mr. Bad is not enough, Mr. Nice is not enough, Mr. Friend is not enough, and Mr. Grey is the solution.

This is why Ms. Bad is not enough, Ms. Nice is not enough, Ms. Friend is not enough, and Ms. Grey is the solution.

Lust can be created, sparks can be created, and attraction is a process.

Attachment can be created. It is a process.

Connection can be created. It is a process.

Allan and Barbara Pease remind us in *The Mating Game* and *The Body Language of Love* that, *"Love can be a wonderful roller-coaster ride. The feelings come from the primary part of the brain known as the cerebral cortex, or gray matter, and overpower the rational, thinking part, making lovers behave in irrational ways. People in the falling in love stage say they can't eat, don't sleep properly, and show compulsive behaviors such as texting or calling. These behaviors have now been linked to the combination of low levels of serotonin and high levels of oxytocin. Serotonin is the neurotransmitter that gives us heightened feelings of awareness, sensitivity to our surroundings, and an overall feeling of well-being. Women naturally have around 30 percent more oxytocin than men, and this, combined with lower levels of serotonin, can explain why women are more inclined to become 'crazy' about someone, and even intensely obsessive."* [3]

Attraction and sparks are just a chemical reaction, and by following the process, you can create attraction with anyone.

Is It Possible for a Person to Be "In" Love with More Than One Person?

When your love needs are not met, you tend to cheat. For a man, not having your sexual needs met will lead you to cheat, and for a woman, not having your emotional needs met will lead you to cheat.

You can lust after or be attracted to more than one person, which explains polygamy. You can love more than one person at the same time—your parents, sisters, brothers, friends, and so on. However, you can never, ever, be "IN" love with more than one person—this is monogamy.

3   Allan and Barbara Pease, *The Mating Game* (Orion, 2010) and *The Body Language of Love* (Manjul Publishing House, 2012).

Lust or attraction is created when one person is masculine, the other is feminine, and they both do novel things together (release of dopamine), scary things together (release of noradrenalin), and have strong eye contact and presence (release of oxytocin). This can be done between any two people.

If you believe you love more than one person, this means that both partners are not able to be in full chemistry with you and that you are stuck in one of the three stages with each of them. Your relationship dynamic with both partners lacks one dimension of chemistry because being "IN" love requires the three stages to be in sync and compatible. You need lust, attachment, and bonding.

Nature made us with a powerful sex drive to be attracted to others; this was the time of physical chemistry and polygamy. Nature then evolved into nurture through romantic compatibility to help us focus energy on one partner; this was the time of intellectual chemistry and monogamy. And now, embracing nature and nurture gives us, through attachment, the feeling of security to build a long-term relationship full of passion and compassion with one partner to raise kids. Back in the day, we died young, so physical chemistry was enough. When we started to live longer, we started seeking companionship to share our lives, but with longevity and time came the lack of sparks. This is where emotional chemistry comes in to link both physical and intellectual chemistry to create magical love, and this is the best of times.

What Happens to Your Brain When You Fall in Love?

However, the question remains: What happens to your brain when you fall in love? Frankly, lots of really interesting and exciting things. Semir Zeki, professor of neuroesthetics at University College London, says, *"When you look at someone you are passionate about, some areas of the brain become active. But a large part is deactivated, the part that plays a role in judgment."*

Professor Zeki believes the brain may behave in this way for "higher biological purposes"; that is, it makes reproduction more likely. If judgment is suspended, the most unlikely pair can get together and reproduce. Someone in love will still be capable of making other major decisions in their life, from striking a business deal to choosing a new mortgage.

Brain scans have also shown one area of the brain that controls fear and another region involved in negative emotion, explaining why people feel so happy with the world and unafraid of what might go wrong when they fall head over heels. Studies have shown that dopamine is at higher levels in those in love. Dopamine is key to our experiences of pleasure and pain, linked to desire, addiction, and euphoria; a surge may cause such acute feelings of reward that it makes love hard to give up. A side effect of rising dopamine levels: a reduction in another chemical, serotonin, a key hormone that controls our moods and appetites.

Higher levels of adrenaline released when we are frightened means that two people going through a scary experience together can fall madly in love. Serotonin levels may fall in a similar way to those seen in people with obsessive-compulsive disorder, explaining why love can make us feel anxious and jittery.

The love chemical we are most familiar with is adrenaline. An increase in this hormone leads to our hearts racing, palms sweating, and our mouths going dry when we see the person we like. The same hormone is also released when we are frightened. This means that two people only vaguely attracted to each other can fall madly in love if they go through an exciting or scary experience together. It may also explain the lure of forbidden love.

A study led by Bianca Acevedo and Arthur Aron of Stony Book University proved that couples could stay in love for decades. In the study, they examined couples who were married for an average of twenty-one years and were still in love. The results showed that the dopamine region of their brains (associated with early-stage romance) was still very much alive; however, they were less obsessive than newlyweds, and the region of liking and attachment was very much alive as well! The main difference between the couples was the level of serotonin. New couples had low serotonin whereas more established couples had high serotonin.

Biological anthropologist Dr. Helen Fisher studied couples who claimed to still be in love with their partners after twenty- to forty-plus years of marriage. The results of her study showed what the brain says about long-term happiness. In those couples still in love after so many years, there was activity in the ventral tegmental area of their brains, which creates dopamine and gives them that elation and euphoria. There was also activity in the region of deep attachment, and the study showed that the deep attachment tends to grow. Dr. Fisher says, *"Romantic love can happen instantly, like a fear or anger system, but attachment grows."* Dr. Fisher linked the regions of the brain with positive illusions, or the ability to overlook what you don't like about somebody, with controlling stress and emotions and with empathy.

Tip 10
Studies have shown that the more you smile at your partner, the closer you will bond.

Once again, biology confirms the Grey Dance of Love: the dance between dopamine and noradrenalin; oxytocin and vasopressin; and serotonin and endorphins; or between attraction, connection and attachment. The brain in lust creates the attraction, and the brain in love creates the attachment. The magic is the connection between the brain in lust and the brain in love. That is where the Grey Dance of Love resides. This connection happens inversely for men and women; men connect sexually, and women connect emotionally. Understanding that distinction will help us all recognize the difference between what women need versus what they want.

CHAPTER 8
WHAT WOMEN NEED VERSUS WHAT WOMEN WANT

As YOU BEGIN TO GAIN a more insightful understanding of the chemistry and biology of love, you can take these valuable lessons and apply them to yourself and your better half. However, even then, there is great value in simultaneously developing a similar understanding of the difference between what your counterpart wants versus what your counterpart might need. After all, given their claims about wanting to be with a nice guy, their best friends, why are women constantly attracted to bad boys? Why do women say one thing and do its opposite? A discussion in the difference between wants versus needs can help explain this common phenomenon.

The biology of neither men nor women has changed since the beginning of time. However, they have tried to adapt throughout the centuries to the different circumstances and challenges they face within their lives. While unplanned, this adaptation has led to a contradiction with women. While women have been conditioned by society to think and behave differently, they are still biologically conditioned to feel and behave in the original way. This leads women to think one way and yet feel the opposite.

Women think they want the nice guy because he is perfect on paper, yet they feel an untamed lust for the bad boy. They cannot explain it, but they do know how they feel. Feelings can be a truly powerful force, overcoming even the most logical signals the mind sends. Women are now in a constant

149

battle between nature and nurture, genes and upbringing, and their sub-conscious and their conscious minds.

So should women choose the bad guy and live stuck in the past without evolving? Or should they choose the nice guy and slowly die without living? Isn't there a third option? Oh yes, there always is.

As women adapted to the new setting, they started thinking differently, and that is why they started wanting to find their equals. At the same time, women still have their biological needs or primitive instincts, which tell them that it is the strongest that will protect them and their children the best, so they need to be with the strongest.

This explains why women want to be treated as equals yet at the same time be treated as ladies. The equal part comes from nurture; the ladies part comes from nature.

The problem with women wanting to be equal to men is that by being so, women have become the same as men. It's like having sex with your guy friend, and this sameness has led to a turnoff of sexual polarity.

Nurture (What Women Want): Women want a man who is their best friend.

Nature (What Women Need): Women need a man who is their (polar) opposite.

What Are Women Craving for in the Bad Boy?

The truth is that women want a confident and assertive man who knows who he is and what he wants. Women want to get past the initial awkward phase of first dates to truly be vulnerable and surrender to a man's control of the situation. [1] Women want to experience the most passionate romance, just as in the movies. They need the magic; they need to feel that it's all destined. At the same time, they need to understand that this is just one part of the magic.

Ms. Bad craves a sexual connection with her ravisher, while at the same time, she fears emotional intimacy.

---

1   Tiffany Taylor, *The Attraction and Seduction Audio for Men*

Ms. Nice and Ms. Friend crave an emotional connection with their ravisher, while at the same time, they fear sexual intimacy.

Psychologists Gregory Carter, Anne Campbell, and Steven Muncer conducted a study on 2,000 females. They found that women find the three following sets of qualities particularly attractive in men:

1. **Machiavellian:** Machiavellian men are masters at the art of flirting.

2. **Psychopath:** Psychopathic men are masters of fearlessness (they don't care if they get rejected; they act on their desire), and they give out an element of arrogance.

3. **Narcissism:** Narcissistic men are masters at building an attractive image of themselves and their lives.

The results showed the following features: Machiavellian men are linked to dishonesty, psychopathic men are linked to aggressiveness, and narcissistic men are linked to masculinity.

Women (single and in a relationship) are attracted to Mr. Bad because he knows how to make them feel alive. He's a master seducer; he's masculine. He knows how to build tension, flirt, and be aggressive. However, those are the only things he knows how to do, which is why when single women cannot change Mr. Bad, they are then tempted by the nice guy, Mr. Friend. Inversely, when Ms. Nice is not feeling an emotional connection with Mr. Nice for a while, she is tempted by Mr. Bad.

What Do Women Crave in Mr. Bad Sparks?

Women love to be challenged. Because of their innate need for a relationship challenge, they try to change Mr. Bad into something worthy of a relationship. Even though they know that he is the wrong man, they pursue him anyway. They are intensely attracted to Mr. Bad because they believe they can change him. He's the guy that doesn't settle, and she makes it her mission to make him settle with her because if he does, she feels she has won the jackpot. This is exciting for women.

He also adds excitement to their lives. He lives focused on his purpose and adventurously, so she wants to tag along and be part of this magnificent adventure. This leads us to the third characteristic women find irresistible in bad guys: spontaneity. Women can't stand routine. They are multitaskers; they are life itself. After a hard day's work, women just want to be women. They don't want to lead, make a decision, or organize … they've done that all day. Coming home to the bad boy, she knows he will lead, decide the evening plans, organize the outing, and take care of her.

Women want to dance freely inside the strong bounderies of the relationship set by Mr. Bad. What women like about Mr. Bad, or rather what they seek, is his masculinity. They like the way he challenges her, excites her, surprises her, and shows how he is in control. The more feminine the woman, the more masculinity she craves in her man, which leads to more sexual tension and sparks. She is seeking those sparks that make her FEEL alive.

Women crave Mr. Bad because he projects his masculine energy on her. Wouldn't it be easier for you ladies if you stopped counting on external circumstances or people such as Mr. Bad and worked on being complete by yourself? On developing your underdeveloped masculine energy, which is calling you?

In his book, *Guy Gets Girl*, author Woody Wilcox did an interesting experiment with eighty-seven women, and here are the results: 44 percent of women want the good guy, while 56 percent of women want the bad guy. When asked what they looked for in a man and if they should give him a chance, these were the results:

Confidence: 61 percent
Looks: 7 percent
Signs of Success and Wealth: 9 percent
Nice Body: 4 percent
Nice Face: 6 percent
Nice Smile: 13 percent

When asked what is the first or most important thing they look for when determining whether a man has the level of confidence she finds attractive:

Acts in Control or Bossy: 1 percent
Seems Comfortable in His Surroundings: 53 percent
Able to Competently Engage in Meaningful Conversation: 44 percent
Displays Material Symbols of his Success: 2 percent
Dominates the Environment or Conversation: 0 percent

What do you find most attractive in a man?

Perfect Physique: 11 percent
Fame: 3 percent
Lots of Money to Spend on Her: 24 percent
A Man with a Plan; A Guy with the Balls to Just Go for It: 62 percent

Of the four categories, which do you find yourself most attracted to or turned on by?

The Kingly Conqueror: 11 percent
The Bad Boy: 27 percent
The Confident Charmer: 53 percent
The Playboy: 9 percent

Of the four categories, which do you find yourself most annoyed to be around or pissed off by?

The Kingly Conqueror: 34 percent
The Bad Boy: 29 percent
The Confident Charmer: 6 percent
The Playboy: 31 percent [2]

Bad boys turn women on but annoy them at the same time, with the same intensity and degree of effectiveness. This is why women can't make up their minds. This is why they keep sending mixed signals and aren't able to communicate what they want.

---

2   Woody O. Wilcox, *Guy Gets Girl: A Guy's Guide to: Meeting and Greeting, Dating & Mating the Various Women That You Desire* (Self-published ebook).

Can the Nice Guy Develop What Women Crave in the Bad Boy?

Women cannot feel attraction toward you if you are similar to them instead of being DIFFERENT and taking PRIDE in that difference. Otherwise, they'll just go out with one of their girlfriends. Mr. Bad has excess masculinity and lacks femininity. He has a lot of the negative masculinity traits, so it's all about developing the positive masculine traits to attract women without being a jerk. Moreover, if you are Mr. Nice or Mr. Friend, listen closely to what Neil Strauss, author of *Rules of the Game*, shares just for you: *"Women are drawn to men who demonstrate strength—not necessarily physical strength, but the ability to make them feel safe. So if you're a nice guy, you can still be nice. But you must also be strong."*

So here are the ten masculine traits women (or feminine energy) crave in the bad guy:

1) Women love to be challenged.

2) Women crave excitement in their lives.

3) Women relish spontaneity.

4) Women like to take on the feminine role in a relationship.

5) Women love it when they can dance freely inside strong bounderies.

6) Women are addicted to confidence (who you are, what you stand for, what you care about, what you're capable of, etc.), personal integrity, your ability to cope in difficult situations and not look to others for validation or approval, knowing that you are enough and capable, and showing authority.

7) Women want men that other women find sexually attractive.

8) Women want your masculinity (to protect them, emotionally support them, and give them strong genes and your appearance).

9) Women want to see your strength and dominance by your ability to be congruent between how you feel and how you act (acting on your feelings turns them on).

10) Women like it when you choose the woman you want because you have options and because you deserve the best.

Do you see any bad characteristics? I didn't think so. It is those exact characteristics from bad boys that turn women on. A big misconception exists that women are attracted to bad boys because they treat them badly; some women do enjoy that, but they are rare.

Tip 11
Women are emotional beings, and emotions are ruled by the moon. Just as emotions change around the moon, so do women's emotions. This means that if you change your opinion of yourself, you can convince her to believe in you too.

The Grey Dance of Want and Need for Women		
What Women Want	**What Women Need**	**What Women Want and Need**
Mr. Nice Mirror and Mr. Friend Amore	Mr. Bad Sparks	Mr. Grey Dance
They always want to please their women.	He always wants to challenge his women.	He balances between pleasing and challenging Ms. Grey Dance.
They are people pleasers and try to please their women all the time.	He is more authentic, and women love authenticity.	He balances between pleasing himself and pleasing Ms. Grey Dance.
They like to play it safe.	He likes to live on the edge.	He creates a safe edge for Ms. Grey Dance through strong bounderies.

Now that you know, you can master those characteristics and become Mr. Grey, which is an updated version of the nice guy. So, ladies, the next time you don't understand why you're always attracted to Mr. Bad (whether you're single or in a relationship), all you need to understand is that it is his masculinity you're attracted to.

Knowing that, if you are single, you can attract your best friend, the nice guy, or Mr. Friend, and help him develop that masculine edge and see how the sparks fly. If you are in a relationship, it is even easier. Remember that for energy to flow in a relationship, or for sparks to be there, you need to be in an opposite polarity.

In today's society, women tend to act more masculine at work but are still feminine at their core. So when a woman goes home, she likes to act as the feminine partner and expects her man to act as the masculine partner. This is because women want one thing but feel something else. They want to be seen as successful, and yet they want to feel feminine. That leads us to the realization that you have to supplement the notion of friendship with the excitement of being a lover. Let's take a look at how these qualities break down.

The Six Friendship Qualities of Intellectual Chemistry

1)   Loyalty

2)   Trust

3)   Sincerity

4)   Emotional Attentiveness

5)   Humility

6)   Appreciation and Love

The Six Lover Qualities of Physical Chemistry

1)   Mysteriousness

2)   Sexual Confidence

3)   Playfulness

4)   Apathy

5)   An Edge

6)   Power

The Six Connection Qualities of Emotional Chemistry

1)   Presence

2)   Grounding

3)   Setting Strong Bounderies

4)   Vulnerability

5)   Holding Space

6)   Intimacy

You might be friend-zoned because you have a lot of friend qualities and limited lover qualities. The same applies to long-term married couples that have lost that spark. They have developed the friend vibes and disregarded the lover vibes for quite some time. So they have become friend-zoned … and this is what leads to cheating.

Women end up with Mr. Bad because they find all the lover qualities in him, and this is what they NEED from a biological set point because it is how women are hardwired.

Emotionally intelligent women choose Mr. Friend because he has all the friendship qualities, and this is what they WANT from a nurture set point because it is how women's software is wired.

They then help him develop his lover qualities. They don't make long-term decisions based on sexual needs.

Mr. Nice and Mr. Friend, work on your playfulness, creating an edge to your demeanors, caring less what people think, becoming more mysterious and less privy to giving away information, more teasing, more sexually forthright, taking gambits, going for that kiss, and so on. At the same time, realize that you're performing a dance, something that should be fun for both parties. You are not changing; you are keeping your friendly qualities while discovering your lover qualities. Your woman will see you as more than a friend. It is the lover's qualities that will create your relationship and your friendly qualities that will keep your relationship. In reality, women want to test men to ensure they are strong, worthy, and will stand up for them as well as for themselves. This will show the true character of a man— when they can be the woman's rock and handle her raw emotions. This would mean that he can handle anything she throws at him.

What Do Women Really Want?

A couple of years ago, I came across this quote from an unknown author: *"A woman wants her man to observe and accept her feelings, insert his male strength and power, and give it back to her transformed into a new energy."* I never grasped the true sense of its meaning until quite recently. A woman wants her man to be present and grounded, to listen to her talk about her feelings without trying to fix them (that is how we accept their feelings), to insert his male strength (presence) and power (grounding), and to give it back to her transformed into a new energy. By letting her vent about her feelings in a safe and controlled environment, the energy has been transformed by the fusion of the feminine and masculine energies, and this helps her find the solution by herself.

> **Tip 12**
> Crying helps a lot in releasing stress for women. So, guys, don't take it the wrong way.

Before the 1960s, a woman had a husband to care for her basic needs (food, shelter, sex, etc.), and her friends cared for her emotional needs (communication, understanding, acceptance, etc.). This was the era of *physical chemistry.*

Today, this same woman is taking care of her own basic needs by working; however, since she is working, she doesn't get her emotional needs met from her friends during the day, which is why she now looks to her husband to care those needs. This is the era of *intellectual chemistry.*

Before the 1960s, a woman was happy when her man cared for her *basic needs*; today, this same woman is happy when her husband cares for her *emotional needs*.

Tomorrow, she will be happy when her husband cares for her *self-actualization needs*, but we are a long way from that kind of tomorrow (at least from a societal viewpoint).

She feels safe, secure, and protected when her partner takes care of her emotional needs. She knows she will be heard and understood, and this will make her feel cared for. So men, be present, listen, reassure her that she is making the right decisions, encourage her to have a girls' night out, and set strong bounderies, and she can be herself in a safe environment.

Go after your dreams, be a little dangerous, and take risks. This is when she will feel she can let go and trust you. Women believe that if men are passionately pursuing their dreams without ever giving up, no matter what obstacles arise in front of them, they can handle anything women throw at them and so will be able to lower their emotional barriers and let them in.

If you believe that Ms. Nice is complicated, then you are doing something wrong (and so is she). Ms. Nice will test you, become needy, and create drama when she doesn't feel secure or safe. Give her what she needs rather than what she wants or asks of you because until you give her what she needs, she will always have more wants.

The want part is in the conscious mind, whereas the need part is in the subconscious. In other words, all the drama and testing is just the effect. Her insecurity is the cause (physical insecurity or emotional insecurity); she is not feeling safe.

When you make her feel safe, all the drama and all the testing will go away. *It's not about giving her attention, which is what she wants, but rather it's about fulfilling her needs.*

How do you do that? Spend quality time with her. Connect with her. Be present. When you do that, she will feel secure and safe.

Note that if Ms. Nice has been high maintenance for a while, it will take time for her to trust you back. She will have to regain trust in herself, in you, and then in the relationship—it doesn't happen overnight. When a woman is under a lot of stress, the best thing you can give her is an opportunity to express herself. Empathize with her and be present. Once you give her that, she will love you in more ways than you can imagine. [3]

Because of today's expectations on women—that they have to be successful in their careers, families, and relationships—they have to overcompensate and put forward their masculine energy at the expense of their femininity.

Ms. Nice is only trying to compensate for what she is not able to get from you. When she claims that she needs to be independent, this is false. Yes, she wants to be independent (financially), but she still needs you (emotionally).

Having repressed her emotions for so long, Ms. Nice needs a man who is present and grounded, someone strong enough to handle her feelings. She needs a man who is going to protect her emotions, handle them with care, and make her feel safe. Once you set bounderies, are present and grounded, and listen to her at an emotional level, she will start to relax in her feminine energy and be more open. Yes, women love to be owned by their men.

With the rise of the feminist movement and with women putting their masculine hat on, they have developed a strong ego in order to control more. The more women are trying to control, the bigger their egos get and the more they believe they don't need men. This results in men feeling (yes, feeling, since the women are more masculine, the polarity has shifted and men have become more feminine) that their women don't need them anymore.

However, exactly the opposite is true. This is the time when your woman needs you the most. Many women are just putting on a mask and overcompensating with their masculine energy. When you step up with your masculine energy, your woman will then be able to relax into her feminine energy.

The more she is relaxed, the more she will open up and be feminine, playful, and girly. The more she becomes that, the more you will feel her

---

3   Jennifer Nielsen, *Hot Alpha Female*

needing and appreciating you. Be strong, set strong bounderies, be present, be grounded, and you will win her heart because that is what she is looking for in her man.

Women want to feel the attraction of a man. They are emotional beings and feel first before thinking, as it is in their nature. So, make her FEEL how YOU FEEL about HER. What she wants is someone who is comfortable with himself, has a purpose and follows it, is in control of his emotions, is not a people pleaser, and is the same with everyone.

The key to becoming more confident and sexually attractive: Follow your purpose passionately, be dangerous, be bold, and take risks despite the odds.

Tip 13

If a woman corners you, act emotionally cool and smooth, use humor, and tell her that you just want to have a good time.

Men often complain about women whining, bitching, moaning, and testing them. This is the nature of the feminine doing her job. A woman will push your buttons because she wants to help you grow so you can be an even stronger leader.

Why Women Keep Falling for the Bad Boys and How to Stop It

Do you now understand why a woman falls for the bad boy, even when it is unlikely to lead to a long-lasting and loving relationship? It's because it is a woman's current comfort zone. In his program *Winning the Game of Fear*, John Assaraf, entrepreneur and philanthropist, says that your current comfort zone creates security and predictability. Moreover, your brain's responsibility is to keep you alive, keep you secure, and create predictability for you. Your comfort zone may be limiting and even uncomfortable, BUT it's familiar, it's the default bottle, it's the go-to model for your brain, and you repeat it because you know how it will turn out.

What this does from a neuroscience and neuropsychology perspective is create the illusion of effectiveness, because it is predictable. As you change your new relationship story, here is what is going to happen:

A new relationship generates uncertainty and fear. The easiest and fastest way to end this discomfort is to go back to the familiar. People fail to change because they don't feel safe. Our brains always want to go back to their default modes (our home feelings, where it is safe, secure, and predictable). There is always the pole of the old versus the pole of the new. This is why change is difficult on our brains and emotions.

However, continuing to ring the changes within a familiar environment helps couples in love grow more in love. They know each other so they are familiar, and they do new things together. This is also why best friends are the best. You have to make a choice to change your internal relationship story. Your relationship story keeps repeating because it is your current comfort zone.

Why Women Reject Their Femininity

"If you are successful at making a woman feel comfortable and safe, there will not be a lot of times where she is doubtful of your future together. The more comfortable a woman feels with you, the less she will test you. The more she senses weakness and doubts your masculine core, the more she will test you."

—Corey Wayne, dating and relationship coach

"When a woman is stressed and feels that she cannot trust or rely on her partner—then she can sometimes assume the role of that partner. So, she has a 'let me handle it' attitude and while she does get things done—she secretly resents having to do these things and in the process suppresses her ability to be open, kind, and warm around her partner."

— Jennifer Nielsen, *Hot Alpha Female*

A woman often rejects her femininity because of you (the man). A woman might feel sad, insecure, and upset that you are not there for her. You are not present and grounded to listen to her emotions without trying to fix her; you are not setting strong bounderies; you are not fixing her problems; you are not the strong leader she wants you to be. She has to take the lead and assume the masculine energy (even though it exhausts the hell out of her), which leads her to shun her emotions. If she is rejecting her femininity because of you, then it's easy. You have been feminine in your relationship, and it is time for you to step up. Ravish her once again. Help her reconnect with herself before she reconnects with you.

Tip 14

"A man getting involved in housework and domestic duties has been shown to be the best aphrodisiac he can offer a woman."

—Allan and Barbara Pease, authors of
The Mating Game and *The Body Language of Love*

With a fundamental understanding of what women want versus what they need, we can turn our attention to the needs and wants of their counterparts—men.

CHAPTER 9
WHAT MEN NEED VERSUS WHAT MEN WANT

NOW THAT WE HAVE DISCUSSED in depth the difference between what women need versus what they want, we can turn our attention to the same analysis of men. Even after all their claims about wanting to be with a nice girl, their best friend, why are men constantly attracted to bad girls? Why do men always say one thing and do the opposite?

Since the beginning of time, men and women have not changed but rather tried to adapt throughout the centuries to different circumstances. However, this adaptation has led to an unusual contradiction in men.

While society has conditioned men to behave in a different way, they are still biologically conditioned to feel and behave in the original way. This causes men to think one way yet feel the opposite. Men think they want the nice girl because she looks perfect on paper, yet they feel a certain level of lust for the bad girl. This has created a battle for men between nature and nurture, genes and upbringing, and their subconscious and conscious minds.

So should men choose the bad girl and live stuck in the past without evolving? Or choose the nice girl and slowly die without living? Isn't there a third option?

As men have adapted to their new setting, they've started thinking differently, and this is why they started wanting someone who is their equal. Yet, at the same time, men still have their biological needs or primitive instincts, which tell them that the ones who nurture them the best will also praise them and their children the most. These are the women they feel the need to be with. This explains why men want to be treated as equals and yet want to be treated as gents too. The equal part comes from nurture, and the gent part comes from nature.

The problem with men's desire to be equal to women is that men have become the same as women by becoming equal to women. It's like having sex with your girl friend. This sameness can lead to a turnoff of sexual polarity. The best way to put it is as follows:

Nurture (What Men Want): Men want a woman who is their best friend.

Nature (What Men Need): Men need a woman who is their (polar) opposite.

What Men Crave in the Bad Girl

Men want to experience the most passionate sex. They need sex everywhere, anywhere, and anytime, as that makes them feel loved. At the same time, they need to understand that sex is just "one" part of the magic.

Mr. Bad craves sexual connection with his ravishee, but he fears emotional intimacy. Mr. Nice and Mr. Friend both crave an emotional connection but fear sexual intimacy.

Men are attracted to Ms. Bad because she knows how to make them "feel" alive. She's a master seducer who knows how to build tension; she's feminine. She knows how to flirt and manipulate. But these are the only things she knows how to do, which is why when men cannot change Ms. Bad; they are tempted by the nice girl, Ms. Friend.

What Do Men Crave in Ms. Bad Sparks?

Men love to be challenged. This is exciting for them. Ms. Bad adds excitement to their lives. She lives her life focused on him and seeks a relationship with him. She keeps her attention on him, so he wants to feed his ego from her. This leads to an irresistible attraction to Ms. Bad's spontaneity.

What men like about Ms. Bad, or rather what they seek, is her femininity. They like the way she challenges them, excites them, and surprises them. They like that she surrenders control to them and lets go. The more masculine the man, the more femininity he craves, and the more sexual tension and sparks there will be. He is seeking those sparks that make him FEEL alive.

Men crave Ms. Bad because she projects her feminine energy. Wouldn't it be easier for you gents if you stopped counting on external circumstances or people such as Ms. Bad and worked on being complete by yourself? On developing the underdeveloped feminine energy that is calling you? Women have reclaimed their rights at work; it is time for men to reclaim their rights in relationships.

Can the Nice Girl Develop What Men Crave in the Bad Girl?

Ms. Bad has excess femininity and lacks masculinity. She has a lot of the negative feminine traits, so it's all about developing the positive feminine traits in order to attract men without being a bitch. The following chart outlines what men (or masculine energy) are looking for in the so-called Bad Girl:

Here are the thirteen feminine traits men (or masculine energy) crave in the bad girl:

1) Being challenged

2) Excitement

3) Spontaneity

4) Allowing the masculine energy to take on the masculine role in a relationship

5) Allowing masculine energy to set strong bounderies where the woman can flow freely

6) Constantly praising the masculine energy

7) Being seen as sexually irresistible by other men

8) Being feminine, kind, and vulnerable (to praise them, emotionally support them, and give them strong genes and your appearance)

9) Self-confidence because it is sexy

10) Being present (your ability to live in the here and the now, especially during sex)

11) A good hostess (it shows that you can create an atmosphere of warmth and coziness)

12) Your smile

13) Authenticity

Do you really see any bad characteristic? I didn't think so.

You see, it is those exact characteristics from bad girls that turn men on.

The Grey Dance of Want and Need for Men		
What Men Want	**What Men Need**	**What Men Want and Need**
Ms. Nice Mirror and Ms. Friend Amore	Ms. Bad Sparks	Ms. Grey Dance
She gives him positive and constructive feedback in private.	She praises him.	She balances between praising and giving feedback to Mr. Grey Dance.
She is open for sex.	She initiates sex.	She balances between initiating and receiving sex.
She shares the power.	She gives him control.	She flows freely in the safe bounderies set by Mr. Grey Dance.

Now that you know what men are looking for, you can channel those characteristics and become Ms. Grey, which is an updated version of the nice girl.

So, gents, the next time you don't understand why you're always attracted to Ms. Bad (whether you are single or in a relationship), you just need to understand that you are really attracted to her femininity. Therefore, if you are single, you can attract your best friend, the nice girl, or Ms. Friend, and help her develop that feminine edge and see how the sparks fly. It is even easier if you are currently in a relationship. Remember that for energy to flow in a relationship, or for sparks to be present, you need to be in an opposite polarity to that of your partner's.

Understanding the Male Psychology to Dance Between Friendship and Lover

The Six Friendship Qualities of Intellectual Chemistry

1) Loyalty

2) Trust

3) Sincerity

4) Emotional Attentiveness

5) Humility

6) Appreciation and Love

The Six Lover Qualities of Physical Chemistry

1) Mysteriousness

2) Sexual Confidence

3) Playfulness

4) Apathy

5) An Edge

6) Power

The Six Connection Qualities of Emotional Chemistry
1)   Presence

2)   Grounding

3)   Setting Strong Bounderies

4)   Vulnerability

5)   Holding Space

6)   Intimacy

At this stage, you have a lot of lover qualities and rather limited friend qualities. Men end up with Ms. Bad because they find all the lover qualities in her, and this is what they NEED from a biological set point. Men are hardwired this way.

Emotionally intelligent men choose Ms. Friend because she has all the friendship qualities, and this is what he WANTS from a nurture viewpoint. A man's software is wired this way. They then help her develop her lover qualities, and they don't make long-term decisions based on sexual needs alone.

Ms. Nice and Ms. Friend, work on your playfulness, caring more what your partner thinks, becoming more mysterious and less privy to giving away information, more teasing and more sexually forthright, and so on. While at the same time, realize that you're just performing a dance, something that should be fun for both parties. You are not changing; you are keeping your friendly qualities while discovering your lover qualities. Your man will see you as more than a friend. Your lover qualities will create your relationship, and your friendly qualities will keep your relationship.

What Do Men Really Want?

Good question. When a man is stressed, upset, or emotional, sex can really help him. When a man ejaculates, he releases not only sperm but also stress. This can offer him a lot of relief, and at the same time, since it is an act of love, it will boost his ego. He will love you more for it.

Before the 1960s, a man's wife cared for his emotional needs and his friends/hunting companions cared for his basic needs. This was the era of *physical chemistry*.

Today, this same man is still taking care of his own basic needs by working, but because his wife is working too, she comes back home exhausted and cannot satisfy his emotional needs. If he doesn't get satisfied, he will shut down or look somewhere else. This is the era of *intellectual chemistry*.

Go after your man, be a little affectionate, and initiate sex. That is when your man will feel he can take control of the relationship and trust you. Men believe that if women are passionately pursuing them without ever giving up no matter what obstacles arise, they can handle anything they throw at them and so will be able to lower their emotional barriers and let them in.

How's It Going for Ms. Nice Mirror?

You are doing something wrong if you feel as if Mr. Nice is complicated. Mr. Nice will cut you off, become unavailable, and remove himself from the relationship when he doesn't feel secure or safe (loved and praised). If you can give a man what he needs, you can have anything and everything from him.

It's not about giving him attention, which is what he wants, but rather it's about fulfilling his needs.

How do you do that? Spend quality time with him. Don't criticize what you don't like; praise what you love. Sexually connect with him. Be present when having sex. When you do that, he will feel secure and safe to share his feelings (remember that men connect first sexually and then emotionally).

If Mr. Nice has been high maintenance for a while, it will take time for him to trust you back. He will have to regain trust in himself, in you, and then in the relationship; it doesn't happen overnight.

Because of today's expectation that a man must be successful in his career, family, and relationships, he has to overcompensate and increase his feminine energy, sometimes at the expense of his masculinity when at home. Be patient with him.

Having repressed his emotions for so long, Mr. Nice needs a woman who is present and grounded, someone strong enough to handle him. He needs a woman who is going to protect his penis, handle it with care, and make him feel safe. Once you give him oral sex, are present and grounded during sex, and listen to him at an emotional level, he will start to relax in his masculine energy and be more open. When you step up with your feminine energy, your man can then relax into his masculine energy.

The more he is relaxed, the more he will take charge and be masculine, playful, and manly. The more he becomes that, the more you will feel him needing and appreciating you. Be soft, be present, be vulnerable, and let go, and you will win his heart because that is what he is looking for in his woman. The driving force of masculine energy or the purpose of masculine energy is centered on feeling needed.

If you want something from the masculine energy, make requests based on trust and desire rather than criticize or manipulate. When you trust that the masculine energy is capable of handling your request (this can be sensed from the tone of voice), your wish will be granted. This is the highest form of influence the feminine energy can seduce the masculine energy. Transparency and vulnerability are the highest values in a relationship and will deepen it.

Men want to feel the desire of attraction from a woman. Men are sexual beings and desire physical expression first before feeling; it is in their nature. Make him FEEL how YOU DESIRE HIM. He wants someone who is comfortable with herself and follows him. It shows your man you're within your femininity when you follow him (you're trusting him and being vulnerable) and when he makes you come alive. Do that, and he will want you even more.

Why Men Reject Their Masculinity

Men often reject their masculinity because of you (the woman). A man might feel sad, insecure, and upset that you are not there for him. You are not present, you stopped having sex (which is love for him), you are not allowing him to set strong bounderies and flow, you are not flowing and letting go, and you are not vulnerable. So, he has given up on you and assumed the feminine energy (even though it exhausts the hell out of him), which leads him to shun the relationship.

If he is rejecting his masculinity because of you, then it's easy. You have been masculine in your relationship, and it is time for you to let go of the control. Give him the reins. Be vulnerable and trust him. Help him reconnect with himself before he reconnects with you.

Tip 15
When you try to change a man, you take on the role of his mother. This is a major turnoff.

While some women can interchange the masculine/feminine roles (at work and at home) with grace, men remain puzzled (because of their lack of understanding of women's wants and needs) about how to do so. Men hear women say they want a man who is more caring and understanding. In other words, they want their men to be more feminine. Yet, women don't know what they need, which leads men to disregard what women FEEL. Women feel for a masculine man. So, it's all about the balance.

Dancing between need and want, between nature and nurture, is how you're attracted to your partner and how you can deeply love him or her. It is also time for us to grow—for men and women to balance their masculine and feminine energies and dance. It is time to take our needs and bring them to the next level by adding the want and dancing in between the two.

PART II

The Step-By-Step Solution for Each
Love Problem to Get You from Where
You Are to Where You Want to Be

IN PART I OF THIS book, we enjoyed an important conversation about love, we were introduced to the Relationship Character Types, as well as the love formulas.

Now, in Part II, you will receive a step-by-step guide that will take you from where you are to where you want to be.

We will travel through each of the three stages of love. I highly recommend that you go through all of the chapters because in each of them you will learn something that you can apply to yourself, even if you are in a relationship.

The chapter entitled "From a Passionate Lover to a Passionate Relationship" will focus on the most important ingredient for the success of any relationship: your relationship with yourself.

The next two chapters will focus on physical chemistry (discovering your underdeveloped and repressed energies to balance your masculine energy with your feminine energy) and emotional chemistry (how to rekindle love and create stronger and deeper bonds). And finally, the chapter The Grey Theory will bring us to a landing.

Remember to visit www.greydanceoflove.com to claim two additional chapters. The chapter "Rational Love, Emotional Love or Magical Love?" which is written to make Feelers feel with Thinkers and Thinkers feel with Feelers. And the chapter The Secret to Successfully Dance Like The Greys will give you some additional tips to sparkle your life and relationship even more.

CHAPTER 10
FROM A PASSIONATE LOVER TO A PASSIONATE RELATIONSHIP

CONSIDER THAT YOU FIND YOURSELF stuck in stage one of relationships. You are a great player, but you aren't able to find someone to settle down with or, rather, you aren't able to connect with someone. Have you tried dating your best friend? Think about it ...

Here you have two scenarios:

First Scenario:
Mr. Bad is living in his natural masculine energy at the expense of letting nurture develop his feminine energy. This leads to an imbalance in the relationship since it is only about sex, sexual needs, sexual connection, ego needs, and ego boosts.

Second Scenario:
Ms. Bad is living in her natural feminine energy at the expense of letting nurture develop her masculine energy. This leads to an imbalance in the relationship since it is only about sex, sexual needs, sexual connection, ego needs, and ego boosts.

A relationship cannot survive over the long term if it is based solely on differences and Mr. and Ms. Bad only live in those differences. Even though they are both on the football field during the game, the quarterback will not have anything in common with the cheerleader except the sex and ego boosts. They don't think alike, they don't have common hobbies, they don't have common goals, they don't have common values, but they do have a common need for sex and ego boost.

At first, this intense polarity or physical chemistry sounds amazing because you develop a strong attraction to each other, but this is also dangerous because there is no stability or base for a long-term relationship.

In the first scenario, the woman living in her natural feminine energy will be attracted to Mr. Bad and want to be with him, but she needs someone who will also connect with her, communicate with her, and share hobbies with her. She needs someone more balanced. Therefore, Mr. Bad will keep on moving from one relationship to the next, changing to one feminine woman after another because he cannot satisfy his ego needs after some time.

In the second scenario, the man living in his natural masculine energy will be attracted to Ms. Bad. However, he will not want to be with her. He needs someone who will connect with him, share hobbies with him, and build a future with him. He needs someone more balanced. Therefore, Ms. Bad will keep on moving from one relationship to the next, changing to one masculine man after another because she cannot satisfy her ego needs after some time.

Simply put, what is the solution for the Bads to be in a relationship?

First Scenario:
In the first scenario, Mr. Bad should do the following:

Step 1: Mr. Bad must develop his feminine essence by working on his physical chemistry.

Step 2: He must calibrate and balance between his intellectual chemistry and physical chemistry.

Step 3: He must develop long-term emotional chemistry.

Second Scenario:

In the second scenario, Ms. Bad should do the following:

Step 1: Ms. Bad must develop her masculine essence by working on her physical chemistry.

Step 2: She must calibrate and balance between her intellectual chemistry and physical chemistry.

Step 3: She must develop long-term emotional chemistry.

Step One: Physical Chemistry

The first step to go from a lover to a relationship is to work on your own physical chemistry.

Where Are You Now?

First Scenario

Mr. Bad

Your Physical Chemistry: 50/100

Physical Chemistry = Masculine Energy + Feminine Energy
Mr. Bad's Physical Chemistry = 50 + 0 = 50

The reason: You have **excess** masculine energy and **lack** feminine energy.

The Excess Masculine Energy Characteristics: Supremacy, Hostility, Controlling, Unyielding, Competitive, Attached to Success, Detached, Moves Away From Love

The Lack of Feminine Energy Characteristics:
Overwhelming, Superficial, Rigid, Overthinking, Anxious, Emotionless, Dry or Blocked

The good part: Once you recalibrate your masculine energy (which is your natural predisposition), you will be healthier and more balanced. You need to move from excess masculine energy to balanced masculine energy and from lack of feminine energy to balanced feminine energy.

Second Scenario
Ms. Bad
Your Physical Chemistry: 50/100

> Physical Chemistry = Masculine Energy + Feminine Energy
> Ms. Friend's Physical Chemistry = 0 + 50 = 50

The reason: You **lack** masculine energy and have **excess** feminine energy.

The Lack of Masculine Energy Characteristics:
Fearful, Reserved, Weak-willed, Desperate, Inert, Low Self-esteem, Uninteresting, Naïve

The Excess Feminine Energy Characteristics:
Victimhood, Melancholy, Dreamy, Confused, Still and Motionless, Needy, Self-pitying

The good part: Once you recalibrate your feminine energy (which is your natural predisposition), you will be healthier and more balanced. You need to move from excess feminine energy to balanced feminine energy and from lack of masculine energy to balanced masculine energy.

In the next two chapters, you will see how you can develop your feminine energy if you are Mr. Bad and your masculine energy if you are Ms. Bad. After that, you will learn more about emotional chemistry. The reason: It will be easy for you to develop your masculine or feminine energies but only AFTER you have developed your self-love.

Mr. and Ms. Bad don't fall in love; rather, they fall in attraction. They are magnetized and sexually attracted. Their dopamine and noradrenalin levels are high, but it stops there. They don't know and never learned how to get past stage one of relationships; they couldn't get past the attraction stage or the brain in lust phase.

Look at it this way—Mr. and Ms. Bad's dance happens on the infinity stage. They are stuck in an eternal loop, and even though they keep on changing partners, they get stuck with the same type of relationship.

Stage One is where physical chemistry is dominant; this is where attraction happens.

Stage Two is where intellectual chemistry is dominant; this is where friendship or companionship happens.

Stage Three is where emotional chemistry is dominant; this is where connection happens.

Once you have mastered each of the three stages, you can then say you are in love.

Attraction is NOT love. Mr. and Ms. Bad do not know what love is, even if they claim they do.

You can never, ever "fall" in love with someone; you can only rise in love. If you want to rise in love with someone, develop daily rituals between the two of you. Routine, routine, routine. It creates safety and belonging-ness and drives up the oxytocin in the brain. After *rising* in love (which is still not love) with friendship and compassion, you can *become* love through connection. Being IN love happens in stage three of relationships. However, before we start with the step-by-step solution about how to go from being single to a relationship, there are four considerations of which you should be aware.

1.   You Must Heal Yourself First.

If you don't heal your wounded energy, whether masculine or feminine energy, you will remain in a victim mentality. You will always be in the state of mind that life happens to you rather than for you. The moment you stop being triggered and reactive, you will have healed your wounded self. The triggers and reactions will keep on coming from the outside until you heal yourself from the inside. Tracy Russell, relationship mastery coach, says, *"The balance of the feminine and masculine is likened to the in breath and the out breath. It is the receiving and the giving, the listening and the speaking, the content and the delivery—within ourselves and with each other."*

Living in my feminine energy for the majority of my life, I've always been a fountain of ideas and prepared master plans but never acted on any of my ideas or plans. It is only after reading the quote above that the light bulb came on and I realized that I have never trusted my masculine energy.

I've always had the content or ideas (feminine) but never trusted the delivery or action (masculine). I've always listened (feminine) but had never spoken (masculine) out of shyness.

I have always been told that I have an excess of raw, uncontrolled energy. Now, it makes sense. All this energy required some framework and bounderies to channel it, and this requires masculine energy to work.

2. You Must Love Yourself First

Finding "The One"

Seriously now, after all you've read so far, you are seriously still looking for The One? Well, I have to admit, you are persistent. I have a solution to satisfy your ego . . . You have to find The One inside you before finding The One who is right for you. I got you now, didn't I? When you find The One inside you or you become complete by balancing your masculine and feminine energies (a.k.a., Mr. or Ms. Grey), only then can you meet someone outside you who is complete (a.k.a., Mr. or Ms. Grey). A word of caution: Neither of you is perfect. You will learn and grow together, and you will make mistakes.

> **Tip 16**
> You will only encounter two types of relationship problems: when you and your partner become too different (you are in the fight zone) and when you and your partner become too similar (you are in the friend zone). Remember to always dance the Grey Dance of Love.

It is time for you to start looking for love inside yourself and to start healing yourself. The more you look inward and start loving yourself, the better quality people you will find. You will start attracting the right people.

Love yourself first. Otherwise, you cannot give what you do not have. How can you give love if you don't have or know what love is? Accept yourself, accept your weaknesses, and embrace your qualities. You don't need anyone to complete you. You are you, and you are amazing just the way you are. What you want is to seek a companion to share your completeness. When you start to look within, you'll realize that you and only you are the love of your life. You'll find unconditional love when you put your ego aside.

3. Why We Keep on Repeating the Same Relationship Mistakes Over and Over

The third consideration rests on why we keep making the same mistakes again and again. As Daniel Wile, relationship expert, says, *"Choosing a partner is choosing a set of problems."*

Humans are creatures of habit, so we keep on doing the same things over and over because this is comfortable and easy for us. We are afraid of change because we associate it with the unknown, and we fear what we don't know. We don't look for happiness but familiarity, at least in stage one and stage two of relationships.

Repeated patterns show us our needs. When the need is gone, you will have no desire for that negative pattern. When you remove these patterns, habits, and beliefs from thinking and behavior, either the other person will change, or he or she will leave your life. For example, on LifeAdvancer.com, Holly W. says: *"If one of your parents wasn't around or didn't give you much attention, you might end up with anxious or avoidant attachment. This could lead you to search for a partner who is emotionally unavailable. If you were abandoned as a child, you might look for love where you have to earn the other person's love. An anxious attachment person may need to be with their partner constantly. They might also need the frequent reassurance of their partner's feelings."*

It happens to us all. I had a belief that I didn't want a passionless and loveless marriage. That is why I needed to learn how to create sparks, first with my ex-girlfriend and then with my ex-best friend. I have finally learned this lesson. According to psychology, the way our parents treated us and how they treated each other will form our ideas of how a relationship should be.

4. Recognizing the Purpose of a Relationship

When you understand that you come into relationships to heal your emotional wounds and that we all have problems that we project, you stop all the blaming, criticizing, and resentment. You grow up. You become mature and talk about how you feel with your partner to heal and let go of the hurt. You realize that your partner is as scared as you are, and instead of increasing the fear in each other, you show love, you accept each other, and you understand each other. Susie and Otto Collins, authors of *The Relationship Attractor Factor*, say, *"What we know to be true is that we all come together in relationships to heal, learn, and grow and to experience more joy and love in our lives."*

> **Tip 17**
> Do you know that fear leads to baldness and ulcers? Or that criticism leads to arthritis? Or that resentment leads to cancer? These are, according to author Louise L. Hay, all results of patterns that manifest physically.

Problems in your relationship are often the result of an emotional thought pattern that stems from your childhood. The good news: You can change patterns. Author Louise L. Hay claims that all problems come from a lack of self-love and that loving the self is the cure to all problems. She suggests that repeating for a month the phrase, "I approve of myself," will bring all the unhealed parts from your subconscious to the surface.

Studies show that one of the major ingredients in marriage is that happy couples love themselves while unhappy couples don't. This is because happy people learned to love themselves and take care of their ego needs to then truly connect with their partners from a place of unconditional love (not the, "I love you if …").

Rhonda Byrne, the author of *The Secret*, shares with us that, *"You can't receive love before giving love yourself. Whatever you give, you receive. This means that it has nothing to do with the other person but with you. You can change any relationship right now by searching in the other for what you love and appreciate, and for that, you're grateful to them."*

Look at your partner as your emotional guide to how you feel. Know that good relationships don't just happen but take time, patience, and two people who truly want to be together.

A friend of mine best summarized the purpose of a relationship: *"Relationships are playgrounds where we come and play with our emotions to heal our wounds."* I will add: *And to learn unconditional love and grow.* In a relationship, your inner child comes to the surface, and he or she WANTS TO PLAY.

To illustrate further how each character likes to play, concerning the three stages of relationships:

> Stage One: When the "car" breaks down, Mr. and Ms. Bad are already long gone.

> Stage Two: Mr. and Ms. Nice and Mr. and Ms. Friend run away from their challenges and grow apart.

> Stage Three: Mr. and Ms. Grey face their challenges and grow together.

The Power of Self-love: Some of the Rituals
That Helped Me Love Myself

As much as it might make sense to turn your love inward and focus on yourself, it isn't always that easy. Louise L. Hay offers great insight into self-love. She also outlines some of the most valuable steps we can take to find it. I am still in awe with her magnificence. In this section, I am skimming over the basics, but I highly recommend that you read her books.

Affirmations

An affirmation is a statement that you repeat to yourself. It is like a seed that you plant in the garden of your mind, and the repetition is the water that you give to that seed for it to grow. So, while at first an affirmation might not be true, as you plant it in your mind and you repeat it consistently (with emotions; the emotions are the vitamins) it will become true, but you have to be patient during the sowing season. When you plant a seed in the ground, the tree doesn't appear immediately; it needs time and care. However, for an affirmation to work, you must remove any limiting beliefs as well, as these can block your progress.

To help you along the way, here are my top affirmations:
"I like myself."
"I can do it."
"I love my work."
"I feel good."
"I am more than I appear to be. All the world's strength and power rest inside of me. All the stars of the galaxy are in me."
"I believe in myself."
"I believe in my success."
"I believe I am phenomenal."
"I believe I am moving mountains."
"I believe I am achieving the impossible."

Also, my personal favorite: *"I love myself. I am so passionate, charismatic, confident, I FEEL good, I am enough, I am smart enough, I am loved and lovable. I am living an abundant life full of love, prosperity, health, and happiness. I am guided and protected by (what you believe in). I am receiving abundant gifts, tools, and techniques to manifest my vision from (what you believe in). I feel so grateful and blessed to have been bestowed this vision by (what you believe in)."*

I repeat my favorite affirmation every morning in front of my mirror seven times by looking into my left eye and then seven times by looking into my right eye. Peggy McColl taught me this powerful exercise. I have added the superman power pause while doing that, and I have to say that this is one of the most powerful exercises I do for self-love.

Visualization

I visualize my daily successes ahead so that they will come true. Visualization helps create the feeling of having what you visualize. I have studied a lot of successful people across history and found that while most did not seem to have anything in common, they all used visualization. Of course, hard work is necessary too, but if you work hard on your visualization to close the gap between where you are and where you want to be, you will get there faster. The same is true of relationships. You can try to make a relationship work with forceps or try this method:

Visualize yourself problem-free. Better yet, visualize yourself with your partner having the type of relationship you dream of. Picture all the sparks, the sex, the trips, anything you want—visualize it.

Just like affirmations, after a period of time (depending on how far you are in your spectrum of where you are and where you want to be) you will get there.

Do you know that Napoléon Bonaparte imagined himself a commander many years before he ever stepped on a battlefield? So, start writing the movie of your life with your partner the way you want it.

Gratitude

Albert Einstein, theoretical physicist, said, *"A hundred times every day I remind myself that my inner and outer life depend on the labors of other men, living and dead, and that I must exert myself in order to give in the same measure as I have received and am still receiving."* [1] I start my day with gratitude so I may focus on the positive in my life. It's probably worth noting that I still struggle to write ten things I am grateful for (but I am getting there).

I use two types of gratitude. One of them is about what I have (such as "Thank you for my education"), and another type is about what I will have (such as "Thank you for the incredibly successful meetings today"). The reason: Your subconscious doesn't know the difference between what is real and what is imaginary. I do keep it a little realistic. For example, I won't say,

---

1   "Full Text of 'Albert Einstein: The World as I See It'": https://archive.org/stream/AlbertEinstein TheWorldAsISeeIt/The_World_as_I_See_it-AlbertEinsteinUpByTj_djvu.txt *

"Thank you for receiving one billion dollars today." And I use many forms of gratitude journals: love gratitude, work gratitude, abundance gratitude, happiness gratitude, health gratitude, and so on.

Meditation

For fifteen minutes every morning, I listen to Esther and Jerry Hicks's Vortex application on relationships, finance, health, and physical strength. It is by far the most powerful guided meditation I have come across.

Habits

Discover yourself. It wasn't until I started discovering and loving myself that my life started to slowly but gradually change. Some of the best habits you can form to love yourself are:

- ✓ Read the list of your qualities and strengths.
- ✓ Read the list of your successes.
- ✓ Develop a passion for something, and do it daily.
- ✓ Develop your receiving power by celebrating every time you receive something.
- ✓ Sing in the shower.
- ✓ Create a song based on the opposite of your limiting beliefs, and sing it.
- ✓ Laugh and smile.
- ✓ Take care of your body (such as having a massage).
- ✓ Walk in nature.
- ✓ Play childish games with your partner.
- ✓ Choose a feeling you want to change, and work on it.
- ✓ Do what you love. Don't let love only come from your spouse, or else you are depending on her or him.

As you develop self-love, you will find yourself better positioned to search for the love of another. You can share, become one, and rise in love together.

The Law of Love

I was inspired by the Babylonian law of success and developed my own Law of Love: I imagine receiving my salary at the end of the month, but instead of money, I receive my own love check. So here is what I suggest you do:

Start by giving yourself the first 10 percent of your love (and save it).

Give 50 percent of your love to your partner.
Give 20 percent of your love to your family.
Give 10 percent of your love to your friends.
Give 10 percent of your love to strangers.

This can be done through activities, rituals, or any of the practices previously mentioned.

Seventeen Things You Should Do When Searching for Your Partner:

1. Manifest in the now (present tense).

2. Create a life partner list. List all their qualities but don't focus on a particular person; it removes their free will.

3. Create a list of what you have to offer.

4. Create a list of the things you are going to do together.

5. Manifest from a deep state. If you talk about it, it will happen 5 percent of the time. If you visualize it, it will happen 50 percent of the time. If you use a deeper state, it will happen 80 percent of the time.

6. Specify the race, ethnicity, and age range if they are important to you.

7. Specify the availability of your soulmate.

8. Specify that you have a high degree of intellectual chemistry.

9. Specify that this person is romantically interested in you.

10. If you are in a period of change, it might be best to wait.

11. Make space (sleep on half the bed, have time to spend with them, etc.).

12. Show appreciation and gratitude for other couples (to remove jealousy and resentment).

13. Get into shape.

14. Become the ideal person that your ideal partner would be attracted to.

15. Clear your subconscious blocks to intimacy and romance.

16. Find gratitude and perfection in all your past relationships.

17. Don't think there is only one perfect match for you (it creates attachment); trust that an abundance of partners exists for you.

The Biggest Relationship Problem: Lack of Self-love

A lack of self-love is often the backdrop for almost all our relationship challenges. Because of the gap between our internal and external images, we have been conditioned for love. We reject a part of us and accept another, and this leads to not fully loving ourselves and not loving ourselves unconditionally.

This conditional love will keep on attracting situations that will confirm our conditioned lovability for us to heal our childhood traumas, or close the gap between our inner and outer selves, or be balanced between our masculine and feminine energies, and finish our unfinished business with our caretakers.

In other words, if you are single and don't love yourself and you unconsciously believe that you are not worthy of love, you will attract a partner who doesn't love himself or herself.

The lack of self-love will reflect as neediness in a relationship. For Ms. Nice, for example, being critical is a sign of insecurity and lack of self-love; for Mr. Nice, withdrawing is a sign of insecurity and lack of self-love.

We pretend to be what we're not because we are afraid of being rejected. The fear of being rejected becomes the fear of not being good enough. Eventually, we become someone who we're not, and we play the victim because of the fear of being judged.

So, because of this gap between our internal images and the images we want to project to the world, we develop feelings of lack of love that we keep on having because we relive them every time our partners trigger them.

By accepting yourself for who you are, by becoming balanced (masculine and feminine), you close the gap between your internal image and the image you project to the world. You start loving yourself more and feeling more complete. You start loving yourself unconditionally. In the end, you don't want to replicate someone else's life, right?

Why Relationships Die and Why You Should Develop a Sense of Direction in Your Relationship

Often, people die shortly after retirement because they have nothing to look forward to. The same applies to relationships; they die if there are no goals or purpose to look forward to. Fixed-mindset people (those looking for The One to save them) have only one goal. They are looking for The One (a finished product) to get married (another finished product since marriage is their end goal), and this can only lead to a disaster. Relationships often die when marriage is the goal. When lovers come to face reality, instead of challenging themselves and growing together, they see that as The End. Yes, The One leads to The End.

Do you know that Michelangelo created some of his best paintings after he turned eighty? That Thomas Edison was still inventing at ninety? History is full of examples of people who, because of their productivity beyond their sixties, lived longer. And so it is with relationships. You can see that people are happily married for years when they make a relationship their priority and set relationship goals. They accomplish this because they made, and committed themselves, to a pact to improve together.

A Brain in Lust Leads Us to Think We Are in Love

Danger! Be careful! Lust can mislead us, making us think we are in love when we truly aren't. When we are at opposite poles, we keep on thinking about them because we believe that the difference in our partners can solve our problems. So, just as a masculine man wants a feminine woman, a feminine woman wants a masculine man. As mentioned previously, we want the other person because they reflect our internal image externally. The masculine man lacking feminine energy inside him seeks it in the feminine woman. Similarly, the feminine woman lacking masculine energy inside her seeks it in the masculine man.

The attraction is nothing but the wanting to complete ourselves. Seeing this part of us that we believe will complete us makes us go gaga over another. We believe they are the solution to our problems (oh, how disappointed we will be once the PEA dissipates).

Also, guess what? The more you think about someone, the higher the frequency of your thought for that person becomes. The more you think of that person, the more energy and focus you start giving that person, and the more importance you start giving to that person, the more emotion starts to gather. The more emotion starts to gather, the more feelings you develop for that person.

So what happens?

1. We keep thinking about them.
2. We keep thinking about our differences and how they can solve our problems.

"Emotion is energy in motion," which leads us to develop more feelings for that person.

According to one of my mentors, Bob Proctor, the author of *You Are Born Rich*, a feeling starts with a thought, which consistently turns into emotion and then feeling. However, feelings and emotions are just a process; you can trigger your feelings for anyone by choosing a particular thought and focusing on it over and over.

So you want the sparks? Easy. Be their polar opposite, and keep on thinking about that person (and let that person think about you). To make sure they are thinking about you most of the time, create problems. I am not talking about psychopathic problems. The sparks come from a place of ego, and ego craves drama, so create some drama. It's easy, right?

See how easy the primitive part of the brain fools us into believing we have fallen in love? Now, if you want to rise in love, then it's a different story. The friendship part will help you rise.

First Scenario: Love at First Sight

As Mr. and Ms. Bad, learn how to love yourselves, be more stable, commit to someone you like, value your friends, develop deep bonds, and develop deeper relationship values.

Mr. Bad: discover your feminine side, connect with it, and show it to your partner. If you don't want to be perceived as a jerk and for the relationship to end shortly, then show your woman your softer side (women find it sexy after you have shown her—your masculine side, that is).

Ms. Bad: discover your masculine side, connect with it, and show it to your partner. If you don't want to be perceived as a bitch and the relationship to end shortly, then show him your stronger side (men find it sexy after you have shown him—your feminine side, that is).

You should be working on your intellectual chemistry. Develop your integrity in relationships and friendships, develop new sets of values, and build long-term projects with your friends or partners. Remember, getting married isn't sacrificing or giving up; instead, it is investing and gaining. Getting married is knowing that there will be a season to sow and a season to reap. Getting married is knowing that when you're sick, your partner will take care of you and you will return the favor. The sowing season isn't a sacrifice but rather an investment in yourself for the next season to reap. It is a gift from you to you.

It is time to build the building blocks of a relationship in order to transform the sand castle into a concrete one. And mostly remember, as Rumi says, *"Your task is not to seek for love, but merely to seek and find all the barriers within yourself that you have built against it."*

CHAPTER 11
FROM FRIEND ZONE TO A PASSIONATE RELATIONSHIP

COREY WAYNE, DATING AND RELATIONSHIP coach, might have put it best when he said, *"Men often fall in love through their eyes and can instantly feel like they want a woman they just met or started dating as a girlfriend. Women on the other hand, tend to fall in love slowly over time through their ears."* It is a far too common occurrence for men and women to find themselves dancing in the friend zone, the inevitable place where they live in *connection* but not in *love*.

Every person starts a relationship as a lover or a friend; however, all relationships will pass through the three stages of love. These stages are never static, and you will always dance between the three unless you get stuck in one stage. If you do get stuck, you will want to get out as soon as possible or else your relationship will die. Are you stuck in the second stage of relationships? Congratulations, you have been friend-zoned. This chapter will help you better recognize it, avoid getting stuck, and even get out of the friend zone. We usually see this in two scenarios.

First Scenario:
Mr. Friend has nurtured his feminine energy at the expense of letting nature take its course with his masculine energy, while the woman is living in her natural feminine energy. This leads to having two feminine energies, so the relationship flow dies.

Second Scenario:

The man is living in his natural masculine energy, while Ms. Friend has nurtured her masculine energy at the expense of letting nature take its course with her feminine energy. This leads to having two masculine energies, so the relationship flow dies.

This means that best friends can remain best friends even if one of them falls for the other. If Mr. Friend is in love with his best friend and she doesn't want to date him, she needs to be more masculine with him. If Ms. Friend is in love with her best friend and he doesn't want to date her, he needs to be more feminine with her.

Best friends can remain best friends, even if one of the best friends is in love. All it takes is a shift in polarity.

Once the polarity shifts, the relationship dynamic changes, and the attraction will gradually dissipate.

If you insist on remaining friends, here are six techniques to help you overcome seduction temptation:

1. Don't push your friend away; instead, ignore their attitude.

2. Act normal around him or her, and act as if you don't know what he or she is trying to do.

3. Don't avoid the person; make the person your friend.

4. The more he or she gets to know you, the less mysterious you appear.

5. Never be alone with him or her (seduction flourishes in secrecy).

6. Let someone know what you are passing through (to remove the secrecy).

While at first this intense compatibility or intellectual chemistry sounds amazing because you develop a strong bond and relationship with each other, it can also be quite dangerous.

In the first scenario, the woman living in her natural feminine energy will love Mr. Friend and want to be with him, but she needs someone who will protect her, challenge her, and make her feel safe—that is, someone more masculine.

If Mr. Friend keeps pushing for a relationship with the feminine woman, this will push the woman to act more in her masculinity with him. The more he pushes, the more she will pull. The more he wants to connect with her, the more she will disconnect from him.

In the second scenario, the man living in his natural masculine energy will love Ms. Friend. However, he will not want to be with her because it would feel like sleeping with a guy friend. He needs someone who will cherish him (not compete with him)—that is, someone more feminine.

If Ms. Friend keeps pushing for a relationship with the masculine man, this will push him to act more in his masculinity with her. The more she pushes, the more he will pull.

Simply put, what is the solution for best friends to be in a relationship?

First Scenario:
Take the following steps if you find yourself in the first scenario:

Step 1: Mr. Friend has to revert back to his core masculine essence (with or without the help of his friend, depending on the friend-zone stage they are in). He does this by working on his physical chemistry and by developing his underdeveloped or repressed masculine energy.

Step 2: Mr. Friend has to calibrate and balance between his intellectual chemistry and physical chemistry.

Step 3: Mr. Friend has to develop short-term emotional chemistry.

Second Scenario:
Take the following steps if you find yourself in the second scenario:

Step 1: Ms. Friend has to revert back to her core feminine essence (with or without the help of her friend, depending on the friend-zone stage they are in). She does this by working on her physical chemistry and by developing her underdeveloped or repressed feminine energy—that is, by dropping her masculine mask.

Step 2: Ms. Friend has to calibrate and balance her intellectual chemistry and physical chemistry.

Step 3: Ms. Friend has to develop short-term emotional chemistry.

Before we start with the step-by-step solution for how to go from the friend zone to a relationship, I would like to clarify five points.

1. Why Being Friend-zoned Is the Worst Type of Rejection

From my experience, the friend zone is by far the worst type of rejection. Let's be honest, you know you'll never see again a stranger at a bar that rejects you. He might have been handsome, or she could have been pretty, but you rationalize that maybe you weren't compatible after all and that "there are plenty of fish in the sea."

However, it is terrible when a friend or even a best friend rejects you.

You know you have a lot in common, and yet …

You don't understand WHY.

You start overanalyzing the reasons (which, by the way, is feminine energy).

Things like, "She likes everything about me, so why doesn't she want to be with me?"

In my case, my ex-best friend and I had a magical friendship. My problem? I was too much in my feminine energy.

2. Should You Let Your Friend Help You?

If you are the one on the other side of the friend zone and want to help your friend because you see the potential, here is how you can do that:

First Scenario:

Having a feminine essence at your core, you can increase your positive feminine traits, be very feminine (not the needy part), and you will then inspire the lead in your friend to be more masculine. By being very feminine, you are surrendering and letting go, which helps the masculine man take the lead since you have removed your resistance. (When you surrender and stop trying to control, Mr. Friend will step up, and he will feel encouraged because by surrendering, you trust his masculinity. So when you stop controlling, he will feel safe to be more masculine.)

Second Scenario:

Having a masculine essence at your core, you can increase your positive masculine traits, be very masculine (not the jerk), and you will break the masculine mask of Ms. Friend (which is what she has been craving all along), and this will inspire her to follow your lead and relax in her femininity. By being very masculine, you are taking the lead and showing who the real man is. This will help her relax and trust your masculine energy. Ms. Friend will feel encouraged to be pampered and let go of trying to compete with you.

This would be the ideal scenario, but sometimes your friend will not be willing or able to help you out. In that case, it will take you more time, but you can still work it out. Being in a relationship with your friend will depend on how well you master your core essence, how you mix it with your intellectual chemistry, how you integrate emotional chemistry, and the timing and level of emotional maturity of your friend.

So if you are not too deep into the friend-zone stage, take advantage of the fact that you are friends since your potential partner already trusts you and this is huge. Not only will it help you change much faster, but it will also be fun for both of you to experiment together and see the changes. This will lead to strengthening your bond much more because you will have experienced change together.

Remember that friendship (which comes from the things we have in common) is one-third of the relationship. When you say that you don't want to be friends, you're saying that you don't want one-third of the relationship and that you're rejecting one-third of the relationship.

Certainly, you shouldn't stay in the same dynamic, and if your friend doesn't want to help you or you both believe it is best if you work on yourself, then a couple of months of disappearance to work on yourself should be good to get back with a new dynamic. When you're back, all you need is to balance the other part of the relationship.

3. Does Your Friend Really Care About You?

You must listen to your friend if and when he or she tries to explain what is wrong with the relationship. This is often a sign that your friend likes you and has a high degree of interest in you. This occurred to me. I tried listening, but at the time, I didn't know how or what she meant by that. Now that you have this book, you don't have that excuse.

She told me I wasn't listening; I was trying to make her understand or rationalize love. Then she told me it would be a good idea to take some time apart and that it might work without having any expectations. Since I didn't listen then either, she probably thought I didn't care enough or didn't understand her; it was the latter.

My ex-best friend also played her part in this. I believe she gave up on me and our magical friendship, and she made sure to disappear as if we had never been in each other's lives. I felt that she had deleted three years of our lives. Sadly, at that time I felt I could no longer call her a friend.

She will say that she tried. I say trying is not good enough. That's because I come from a school of thought where a solution always exists when you stay long enough and you both want to find a solution. You don't just throw away a friendship because there is a problem; you stay with it until you find a solution.

4. Why Aren't There Sparks?
Why Have You Been Friend-zoned?

If you are a man and keep on being friend-zoned then, like me, you have been repressing your masculinity. If you are a woman and keep on being friend-zoned, then you have been repressing your femininity.

This is one of the reasons I could not create sparks or sexual tension with my ex-best friend. However, there is no need to worry if you are in this situation. All you need to do to ignite the sparks and sexual tension: Develop the energy you have been repressing within this particular relationship. When you are friend-zoned, you are stuck between the friendship and the relationship, or more like the purgatory phase. Why? You have not built the attraction. Work on the attraction and things will change for the better.

You have shown your potential partner that you have many similarities. Now, it is time to show him or her your differences or how you complement each other for a short period before then dancing between the two. The key is always to flirt and be playful.

5. Why Do We Need to Change the Relationship Dynamic?

For a new relationship to happen, you have to let the old friendship die; that is why transformation is a must. It would be a symbolic death for change to take place.

In the old dynamic, you saw your friend as your lover, and you put him or her on a pedestal. The dynamic wasn't equal, and your friend was dominating or controlling the dynamic. In your friend's mind, it is clear that you two are friends and nothing more.

When your friend tells you that he or she doesn't feel this way about you, your friend really means that he or she doesn't see you as a sexual being. And this is great news. We are all sexual beings. However, being Mr. Friend or Ms. Friend, you have been repressing your sexual energy (or natural energy).

You have tried to mask it, and you did it so well that your friend couldn't pick up on it.

This is because you have been spending too much time acting as a friend. The relationship dynamic is too feminine if you are Mr. Friend and too masculine if you are Ms. Friend.

Now, it is time for your friend to see you in a new light. Changing the relationship dynamic is the only way for your friend to see you in a new light and fall in love with you.

Now, let us begin.

Step One: Physical Chemistry

The first step to go from a friendship to a relationship: work on your own physical chemistry.

Where You Are Now

First Scenario:

Mr. Friend

Your Physical Chemistry: 50/100

$$Physical\ Chemistry = Masculine\ Energy + Feminine\ Energy$$
$$Mr.\ Friend's\ Physical\ Chemistry = 0 + 50 = 50$$

The reason being, you **lack** masculine energy and you have **excess** feminine energy.

Lack of Masculine Energy Characteristics: Fearful, Reserved, Weak-willed and Confused, Desperate, Inert, Low Self-confidence and Self-esteem, Uninteresting and Naïve

Excess Feminine Energy Characteristics: Victimhood, Melancholy, Dreamy, Confused, Still and Motionless, Needy, Self-pitying

Now for the good part: Once you recalibrate your masculine energy (which is your natural predisposition), you will be healthier and more balanced. You need to move from lacking masculine energy to balanced masculine energy, and once you do, your feminine energy will automatically be balanced and move from excess feminine to balanced feminine.

Second Scenario:

Ms. Friend

Your Physical Chemistry: 50/100

$$\text{Physical Chemistry} = \text{Masculine Energy} + \text{Feminine Energy}$$
$$\text{Ms. Friend's Physical Chemistry} = 50 + 0 = 50$$

The reason being, you have **excess** masculine energy and **lack** feminine energy.

Excess Masculine Energy Characteristics: Supremacy, Hostility, Controlling, Unyielding, Anxious, Pushy, Detached

Lack of Feminine Energy Characteristics: Overwhelming, Superficial, Rigid, Overthinking, Anxious, Emotionless, Dry or Blocked

The good part is that once you recalibrate your feminine energy (which is your natural predisposition), you will be healthier and more balanced. You need to move from lacking feminine energy to balanced feminine energy, and once you do, your masculine energy will automatically be balanced and move from excess masculine to balanced masculine.

Eighteen Mistakes I, Mr. Friend Amore,
Made with My Ex-best Friend

The friend zone is certainly not comfortable for the person on the other side who sees it as awkward and uncomfortable. My ex-best friend knew I wanted her, and she did want me, but the thing is that I put myself there in the first place by being in a feminine energy with her. I was always waiting for her to be ready, waiting for her to give me a sign, and overanalyzing her every move; this is all wrong. We were two people waiting for the other to make a move, and she certainly wasn't the one who would. Twice, I had a perfect opportunity to kiss her, and I wanted to, but I didn't so as to "protect our friendship." They say hindsight is 20/20, and here are the nineteen mistakes as a result of excess feminine energy I made that kept us in the friend zone:

1. I was too nice to her all the time.

2. I was a people pleaser and not authentic to myself and to her.

3. I texted too much (with lots of emoticons), and my messages were too long all the time.

4. I overpursued her and insisted on having closure, while she was still questioning whether we would be a match. Still, I kept pushing.

5. I acted needy and insecure at the end, which showed my unworthiness.

6. I acted shy and lacked confidence.

7. I was unsure of myself and my potential.

8. I waited for her to give me the green light instead of taking the reins (in other words, I expected her to lead).

9. I did not escalate things physically when I had the opportunity.

10. I sought her approval all of the time.

11. I gave presents even when it wasn't a special occasion.

12. I pushed her for a commitment.

13. I was always indirect.

14. I didn't go after what I wanted.

15. I shakily asked her out.

16. I always needed to know where we stood.

17. I was always available whenever she needed me.

18. I acted like a friend.

Also, here are nineteen more mistakes (just for fun):

1. I didn't look into her eyes. Yes, I was too shy.

2. I didn't make enough body contact (touching hands).

3. I agreed to everything (even when deep down I didn't agree).

4. I would diffuse tension whenever it appeared.

5. I always tried my best to please her in each and every way.

6. I was always there for her.

7. I became an open book toward the end. She knew almost everything about me.

8. I was too predictable.

9. I was too cheesy.

10. I was always making long statements. We talked for several hours per day.

11. I was always asking for permission rather than taking the initiative.

12. I was a problem-solver.

13. I always called back and replied in less than two minutes.

14. I was indecisive.

15. I wasn't assertive.

16. I wanted to be her savior.

17. I kept on talking and talking, opening up new subjects because I was afraid of running out of things to say.

18. I never stopped to breathe because I always hated the silences; they made me feel so uncomfortable that I would laugh.

19. My energy was all over the place, and I had uncontrolled passion.

This shows that our relationship dynamic was purely feminine and that I was acting out of my feminine energy. There was no semblance of masculine energy, and I wondered why she didn't have THOSE feelings for me.

This is why she didn't trust me. I always believed that trust was about not hurting or cheating, but women have a different definition of trust. When a woman says she wants to trust you, she means she wants to feel comfortable with you. She wants you to be someone she can count on, a confident and assertive man who is direct, takes what he wants, and so on. She wants a masculine man; she wants to trust his masculine energy so that she can relax into her feminine energy.

In short, I wasn't masculine enough. I didn't lead, and I wasn't confident. I was unworthy, uncertain, unsure, and didn't know what to do or how to lead. I put her on a pedestal, made her superior, and downgraded myself.

What was the solution to getting out of a friend zone? Just do the opposite of what I did (I'm half joking, of course). Some dating experts would say I was totally wrong; others would say I was half wrong. I believe the latter. My reaction to my ex-best friend shows excess feminine energy and a lack of masculine energy. (Note that my excess feminine energy started growing more and more at the end.)

If I had to do it all over again, I would be more masculine while keeping a balanced feminine aspect. This means that it is important to have long conversations, even go shopping, but if you do so, you have to balance it with masculine activities.

If you spend long hours talking, you have to balance this time by doing something more masculine together, such as going out on an adventure and discovering something new together. You can develop attraction with anyone because attraction has nothing to do with how much you have in common but rather how much you stand at polar opposites. You talk to your friend logically (intellectual chemistry), listen to your best friend emotionally (emotional chemistry), and are present for your lover physically (physical chemistry).

Remember, women are always attracted to the bad boy (and they usually have nothing in common with him). Women like their friends but rarely date them; they date the bad boy. They just feel secure around the bad boy.

When I started to develop my masculine energy, I started to feel better, and people around me started to see me differently. I started being more present, talked less, and listened more. Although I still need to work on my tone of voice, breathing, and pausing when I talk, I have overcome one of my biggest problems: my presence, or lack of it.

Because of the fear of running out of things to say, I used to think of the next question while people were answering or talking. Working on my presence was a big challenge for me. Something else that I learned: Sexual tension develops in silence and anticipation, so I began to shut up during conversations, and the tension and the conversation around the energy took on a whole new dimension.

How to Develop Your Masculinity (For Mr. Friend Amore)

What are the steps we can take to develop our masculinity and avoid the friend zone? Leadership in relationships is quite different and more challenging than traditional leadership. While traditional leadership expects you to lead others by putting intelligence before emotions, relationship leadership is all about leading emotionally and putting emotions before intelligence. If you want to conquer your lady, start by conquering yourself and then lead her.

The five masculine traits that you **MUST** adopt and cultivate:

1. **Have a purpose in everything you do (always know what to say and do).** Masculine energy is all about having a purpose for everything. It's about having the right attitude. When you have a purpose, the way you walk/talk/project yourself is different. When your friend feels you are committed, focused, persistent, and consistent with your actions, she can relax and be more intimate.

2. **Act with integrity (act on your feelings).** The more masculine you are, the more the woman will feel safe and the less she will test your integrity. A woman will keep on testing, nagging, and teasing you until she feels safe with you. Her tests and nags are a call for attention; she is trying to tell you that she doesn't feel safe. It's about how easily you can act from a place of authenticity rather than insecurity.

3. **Use your caving to restore equilibrium.** From a biological standpoint, the cave time allows you to increase your testos-

terone level by disconnecting, gives you space, and provides clarity of mind, which will help you know what you want. This will increase your confidence, which your friend will find irresistible, and help you regain your focus from stress.

4. **Take action.** Nature has created women to talk and men to act. You can talk as much as you want, but remember that communication is a feminine trait. So, Mr. Friend, you can promise your friend the moon, but unless you are figuratively able to bring the moon to her, you will remain, now and forever, her trusted friend.

5. **Set strong bounderies (be in control).** Women love it when you set strong bounderies, and they will test those bounderies. Masculine energy sets the bounderies of a relationship in order for the feminine energy to flow smoothly between them. If you are both flowing, then no one is controlling the ship, and we all know that a ship without a captain will get lost at sea (i.e., there is no safety). Mr. Friend, it is time to man up.

I lacked all five traits. I talked about my purpose (but I didn't act on it), which means I wasn't acting with integrity nor being responsible. By writing this book, I have reclaimed my integrity; I have taken responsibility and action by solving my problems in relationships. Over the past few years, I have developed strong bounderies for myself and others. I am now congruent with myself, I take action, and I have shown emotional maturity.

Are You Rejecting Your Masculinity?

Still not feeling masculine enough? Take a closer look, as there are times when a man inadvertently rejects his masculine energy. I know I did. I have been living on my feminine side for most of my life. I have been daydreaming a lot. I've always had plans to conquer the world but never implemented them (perhaps because I wasn't inspired by the right woman). I always had a lot of drive and purpose but never seemed to act upon it. I always waited for women to approach me.

All this feminine energy inside of me was screaming, and I was looking for a way without finding it until, thanks to my ex-best friend, I started to develop my repressed masculine energy. Now I can tell you, this book is just the beginning for me. All my ideas (feminine energy) needed strong bounderies in order to flow safely and be structured, and now I have that through my masculine energy. Let's explore this a little deeper.

<u>The Eleven Routines That Will Help You Claim Your Masculinity</u>

Taking this one step further, here are the eleven routines any man can fold into his life to claim a greater sense of masculinity:

1. **Physical activities.** Exercise regularly, whether it's going to the gym, practicing martial arts, attending boot camps, or playing extreme sports.

2. **Breathing.** Take deep breaths. Breathing is important since it will help you develop a deeper and lower voice, which women find very sexy. It will also help you get out of your head and develop a strong presence because you are living in the now, which women crave.

3. **Spend time with male friends.** They will help you engage in conversation about business and goals instead of gossip and complaining. They will challenge you when you lack integrity, and they will be direct with you.

4. **Watch your sports team.** According to Dr. John Gray, a man tends to project his own life on his team. Watching your team is a way to escape from your daily problems and

project your problems on to it, which explains why you get happy and excited when your team wins and angry and sad when your team loses.

5. **Focus on your life purpose.** Create daily goals that will help you get closer to your purpose, and work on them.

6. **Practice clarity.** Try to express your thoughts and desires in fewer words. Make it a game, and challenge yourself.

7. **Challenge yourself.** Face a fear, and/or do something new every week. This will strengthen you and help you grow.

8. **Cave time.** It will help you get clear, focused, and increase your testosterone level, which lowers during the day.

9. **Watch action movies.** These can help increase your testosterone level.

10. **Have a hobby.** Spending time alone on a project can help create valuable me time.

11. **Practice self-control.** Restrict by delaying short-term gratification.

I particularly enjoy cave time. I never engaged in it before, but I now realize how important it is. For a long time, I felt low, tired, unfocused, and unclear. I started to get irritated, and I didn't know why. After I cave, I feel so energized, like the world is in the palms of my hands.

Five Ways to Increase Your Dopamine Levels (Adrenaline Rush)

These five ways are important to help Mr. Friend develop his masculinity and, at the same time, look more attractive to women:

1. **Exercise:** raises serotonin and endorphins

2. **Listen to or Perform Music:** it will make you smarter

3. **Organize Your Life:** gives you masculine energy as you tick off boxes by giving a feeling of accomplishment

4. **Be Creative:** participate in creative activities

5. **Engage in Meditation:** it literally rebuilds your brain's gray matter in eight weeks, according to Harvard MRI studies

How to Develop Your Femininity (For Ms. Friend Amore)

Femininity requires strength and maturity to surrender and let go. If you fear to appear weak, foolish, or being taken advantage of, you are resisting your femininity. When you surrender, it exposes your fears about losing control, which makes your ego go crazy. If you are not willing to surrender, your partner will not be able to lead you.

The four feminine traits that you can adopt and cultivate:

1. **Be radiant and nurturing.** This is what feminine energy is all about. When you are radiant and nurturing, the way you walk/talk/project yourself is different, because you are connected to yourself. When your friend feels you are beautiful from the inside out, at peace with yourself, and full of love and praise, he will feel more confident and want to ravish you.

2. **Be loving and receptive.** Feminine energy is focused on relationships and love. Today, however, women tend to put their masculine masks on (even after work), and they block their receptivity. If you want love, you have to be receptive to it.

3. **Be playful and flow.** When you are playful, you are being light. You are adding fun to your relationship dynamic and making it more pleasant. It also removes the heaviness of daily tasks and helps your partner shift his heavy thoughts

and decompress. You are allowing the relationship to flow between the rigid masculine bounderies. Feminine energy flows smoothly between the bounderies set by the masculine energy.

4. **Be vulnerable and surrender.** Men love it when you surrender control to them. It shows that you are vulnerable with them, and they will test you for it. If you are both controlling, then no one is allowing the dance to happen, and that means the energy of the relationship gets stuck (i.e., there is no flow). Ms. Friend, show us your beauty already.

Are You Rejecting Your Femininity?

It happens, and you might not even realize it. If you had a bad experience with a very masculine man or with your father, it could lead you to repress your femininity to protect yourself so you can survive and feel safe. As a result, you may shun men and not allow them to see your feminine side. You don't feel comfortable enough to be vulnerable. You would rather do everything on your own and not ask for advice or help.

Do you feel depressed, anxious, or helpless? Are you adopting an "I-don't-care" attitude or always claiming that you are career-oriented? Then, Ms. Friend, you are wearing your masculine mask to perfection. You are living in your nurture side a little too much, and this is making you miserable.

Society has taught you that to be enough and feel important, you need to be more masculine—independent, tough, thriving at work, and so on. That is all good, but when you come home, drop your masculinity. Remember, nature made you a woman for a reason, and it is certainly not to act like a man.

Keep in mind that most men will not commit to a woman who is not feminine enough.

If you are still not sure if you are rejecting your femininity, here are a couple of questions you can ask yourself:

1. What type of men are you attracting?

2. Are you the one controlling the relationship?

3. When a man gives you a gift, do you feel uncomfortable or embarrassed?

4. Do you feel you have to pay back the favor to the man who offers you something?

5. Are you uncomfortable crying in front of men?

6. Do you love being in control?

7. Do you have activities that you do just for fun without controlling or rationalizing?

The Thirteen Routines That Will Help You Claim (and Nurture) Your Femininity

Just as a man can take meaningful steps to develop his masculine energy, here are some routines a woman can engage in to increase her femininity and avoid the friend zone:

1. **Engage in Physical Activities.** Yoga, meditation, and dancing can help you regain your femininity.

2. **Breathe.** Breathing helps you relax and get out of your head, be in the moment, and feel life. When you feel life and express it through your body, you will radiate and become irresistible as a woman.

3. **Meditate.** It will help you reconnect with yourself.

4. **Spend Time with Female Friends.** Spending time with like-minded females will give you the opportunity to share your deepest desires without fear of judgment, celebrate each other, cry with each other, and enjoy life together by going shopping; these women will also help you reflect on your problems by talking about them.

5. **Write in Your Journal.** Spending five minutes doing this each day allows you to release your emotions and feelings.

6. **Practice Gratitude.** You might like to set aside a regular time to remember everything that you feel grateful for, as this can help build self-appreciation and confidence.

7. **Express Pleasure.** Studies have shown that women who experience more pleasure in their lives enjoy greater physical, mental, emotional, and even spiritual well-being. Pleasure is also the quickest and easiest way for a woman to get out of her head and into her body, which means it's a powerful way to relax into her feminine side. When a woman experiences pleasure, her body relaxes, her heart opens, and her inner radiance is revealed.

8. **Be a Radiant Woman.** Wear earrings and shop for shoes and handbags; this will connect you with your femininity.

9. **Use the Mirror Exercise.** Look straight into your eyes and appreciate yourself.

10. **Relax and Be Receptive.** This helps you be more open to receiving (which is one of your weak points since you are Ms. Friend). Smiling more often and playing with kids helps.

11. **Practice Self-care.** Share, touch, go shopping, pamper yourself, have beauty rituals (spa, massage, or a warm bath), daydream, and so on.

12. **Create a Better Work Environment.** Add some family pictures and a plant to your desk and talk during breaks.

13. **Be a Wife or Lover, Not a Mother, to Your Partner.** Replace your demands and judgments with your desires and emotions; for example, if your partner is driving fast, tell him "I feel scared" rather than "Slow down." Do not rescue him; be willing to let things fall apart a little.

Each of these routines is traditionally feminine in nature and will help you develop your femininity.

Eleven Ways to Increase Oxytocin (the "Bonding" Hormone)

It is not an anomaly to feel this disconnect with your femininity. However, when it does happen, you must look toward your chemical makeup and consider taking valuable steps to increase your oxytocin, which is your "bonding" hormone. These steps might include:

1. Engage in Physical Touch

2. Share Words of Encouragement

3. Listen (Everyone wants to feel acknowledged. We all want to know that we are being heard and accepted. When you are present with another, you can feel the connection.)

4. Smile and Laugh

5. Meditate and Pray (Oxytocin increases when you are not under the fight or flight mode. Prayer and meditation allow the mind to detach from stress.)

6. Exercise

7. Cry (Studies have shown that suppressing your emotions lowers oxytocin levels.)

8. Give

9. Get Creative

10. Get a Pet (Research shows that just touching your pets lowers your blood pressure and increases your oxytocin levels.)

11. Hug for Twenty Seconds (This releases oxytocin, which can make you trust someone more.)

Step Two: How to Change Your Friendship Dynamic

Once you have mastered your physical chemistry and are ready to make your friend your partner, you are ready to change your friendship dynamic. To do that, you have to go from changing your physical chemistry to changing the physical chemistry of your friendship; at the same time, you have to keep the intellectual chemistry at bay. In other words, it is time to take one step forward toward the Grey Dance of Love and start dancing between physical chemistry and intellectual chemistry. It is time to create desire.

Please note: You must give time for the change in the dynamic, and for your friend, to change their mind. This specifically applies to Mr. Friend, as research shows that a woman requires around seven weeks to fall in love. And never drop your expectations; just shift your current reality.

Here is how I shifted my expectations of being with my ex-best friend:

I believe people have a wrong definition of expectation. For most, when they expect something or someone, they just rely on faith and say, "Okay, I let it go and let it be, and if it's meant to be, it will happen" (and sometimes it does, but most of the time it doesn't). I look at expectation the same way I look at a goal. When I expect something, I first look at where I currently am with regard to my expectation and where I want to be. I then set up a plan of action and work on it until I close the gap between where I was when I started and where I wanted to be.

When I expected to be with my ex-best friend, I looked at where I was (I found out I was in feminine energy) and understood that to be with her I needed to be masculine. I set up a plan to become more masculine, and I acted on it. You see, to reach your expectation, you must close the gap between where you are and where you want to be.

Prior to changing the dynamic, you must bring your friend down from the pedestal. Being in a friend zone, you are very much in a state of infatuation. That is why to be on the same playing field as your friend; you need to have a pit stop or a time-out to work on your nature energy. You are putting your friend on a pedestal because you believe he or she has something that you don't have in you, and you believe that you are incomplete.

After regaining your nature energy, you will realize that you are complete from within and that all those traits that you love in your friend are inside of you; you were projecting the traits onto her or him. This will help you bring your friend down from the pedestal so that you are both at an equal level.

How to Change the Friendship Dynamic
The logical first step: Work on your physical chemistry to regain control and equilibrium. If you are still talking to your friend, the next step is to start blurring the lines of friendship. This will confuse your friend, and she or he will start to think.

If you are no longer in regular contact with your friend and worked on your physical chemistry, or if you are still in contact but feel stuck in your nurture energy, then start by cutting contact for a few weeks or months (no contact at all whatsoever) to change the dynamic. During this time, work on your masculinity or femininity by experimenting with other people. I practiced my masculinity with six to eight women every week. They helped me a lot with my eye contact, body language, grounding, presence, and more. I am forever grateful to 'My Ladies'. When you see your friend again, don't, I repeat, *don't* sit with them to discuss your feelings or have dinner. This is what friends do. Start acting less friendly and more teasing.

Let the sexual tension increase as much as possible without talking about it. Provoke your friend to start thinking about you differently and more often. The more they think about you, the more they will overanalyze, and the more they do that, the more they will develop feelings for you. Yes, "those" feelings. This is the best way for your friend to start thinking that they are falling for you until they really do.

When your friend sees the new you, the dynamic will automatically shift, and you will be in control. Your friend will be intrigued and will want to know more.

Eight Steps to Get out of the Friend Zone If You Are Not Talking to Your Friend (For Mr. Friend Amore)

Now that you have regained your repressed masculine side and are more complete, learn and apply masculine energy in a relationship, and, more particularly, learn how you can add masculinity to your friendship to transform it into a relationship. Assuming, of course, that you are still interested in your friend and that you have other common friends and activities, then note the following:

1. Back away and become scarce—make her miss you.

2. Now that you are more in your natural masculine element, date other women until your friend shows interest.

3. Become busy with other women; you will be perceived as a catch.

4. Be the same with all women; flirt with all of them even when your friend is around.

5. Let your friend seek approval from you (for a change).

6. Act like you are bored with and disinterested in your friend.

7. Set rules and bounderies.

8. Start asking questions and let her do the talking and pursuing (to remain mysterious and interesting).

Remember, women are attracted to men whose feelings for them are unclear. In other words, don't show her your feelings and keep sending mixed signals. That doesn't mean you can't be a good friend, but don't say yes to everything and do whatever she wants, and don't drop everything for her. Instead, create experiences that bond you (do stimulating activities together to increase her dopamine and oxytocin levels) such as watching action/horror movies, going to concerts, or riding on roller coasters (physical touch helps release oxytocin, the "bonding" hormone).

Play hard to get. Tell your friend that you shouldn't date her, and state the reasons why you shouldn't. She will perceive it as a challenge to overcome. If she is still in stage one and doesn't have a balanced masculine/feminine energy, then you can feign interest in someone else.

By acting as her friend, you are allowing her to be vulnerable, and you are building trust. Next, when you are creating bonding experiences, you are releasing dopamine and oxytocin in her brain and it will get you closer. By saying you're not interested, you are creating a challenge for her and making her work to have you.

Eight Steps to Get out of the Friend Zone If You Are Not Talking to Your Friend (For Ms. Friend Amore)

Now that you have regained your repressed feminine side and are more complete, learn how you can add more femininity to your friendship so that it can transform into a relationship.

1. Back away and become scarce—make him miss you.

2. Now that you are more in your natural feminine element, date other men until your friend shows interest.

3. Become busy with other men; you will be perceived as a catch.

4. Be the same with all men; flirt with all of them even when your friend is around.

5. Let your friend seek approval from you (for a change).

6. Act like you are bored with and disinterested in your friend.

7. Breathe, relax, and have fun.

8. Start asking questions and let him do the talking and pursuing (to remain mysterious and interesting).

Once again, remember that men are attracted to women whose feelings for them are unclear. In other words, don't show him your feelings and keep sending mixed signals.

Twelve Steps to Regain Your Masculinity in Your Friendship (If You Are Still Talking to Your Friend)

What if you are still talking to your friend but find yourself locked into the friend zone? It happens all the time. Some of the best practices to regain your masculinity include the following:

1. Take ownership of the friendship.

2. Put your purpose and drive in front of your friendship.

3. Foster her respect by respecting yourself first.

4. Set strong bounderies.

5. Reward her and give her approval so that she feels more secure.

6. Make the decisions, plan, determine what is acceptable in the relationship, set the tone, and take charge; she's craving your leadership.

7. Appreciate her and give her affection.

8. Cultivate your own confidence. Your inner strength in navigating life's pleasures and challenges will help her relax into her femininity.

9. Reward her for sexy behavior, and she will give you more of it.

10. When you are living your mission, she will want to participate in it too. Women like playful adventures and they want to be transported erotically.

11. Have an abundance mindset instead of a scarcity mindset.

12. Be playful, and tease her while being romantic.

Twelve Steps to Regain Your Femininity in Your Friendship (If You Are Still Talking to Your Friend)

What if you are still talking to your friend but find yourself locked into the friend zone? It happens all the time. Some of the best practices to regain your femininity include the following:

1. Let go of trying to control the friendship.

2. Focus on your friendship, and make it a priority over your career.

3. Foster his respect by respecting yourself first.

4. Go with the flow.

5. Reward him and give him approval so that he feels more cherished.

6. Let your friend make the decisions, plan, determine what is acceptable in the relationship, set the tone, and take charge; be feminine and inspire his leadership.

7. Appreciate and praise him.

8. Cultivate your own confidence. Your inner strength in navigating life's pleasures and challenges will help him relax into his masculinity.

9. Reward him for the small things he does for you, and he will give you more of them.

10. Support his mission, participate in playful adventures with him, and he will feel like your hero.

11. Have an abundance mindset instead of a scarcity mindset.

12. Be playful, and tease him while being romantic.

Four Ways Your Friend Can Help You Develop Your Masculinity or Femininity and Add More Sparks

1) Affirmations are powerful. Your friend can repeat an affirmation that will help her or him love you more, such as, "I find you very attractive and sexy." Affirmations are similar to seeds that you plant in your mind. The more you water them (by repeating daily), the more they will grow, become real, and transform into a belief.

2) Do stupid things together (laughing and seduction), and you will be able to drop the guard in your conscious mind. This will help the message pass right through to both your subconscious minds.

3) If your friend is interested in you for your personality and needs a boost in the physical attraction department, he or she can boost the attraction by focusing on the positive and writing it down in a gratitude journal.

4) Do something new together; start a new project together.

Building Sparks and Creating Attraction

Now that you are polarized (balanced masculine and feminine energies), you are ready to play at an equal level with your friend; you even have an advantage because you are now balanced.

The following section is all about building sparks and creating attraction. I won't delve into commercial seduction techniques, such as hypnosis and neuro-linguistic programming (NLP), as I believe those are short-term seduction techniques. They are powerful and they do work, but I'm not a fan of them because to produce an emotional bond between two people, they use, for example, fractionation. This is a two-step system that makes your target move through an emotional roller coaster by recalling equally happy and depressing memories. By making them emotional, you will make them feel a deep rapport with you.

Now, let's turn our attention to the classier side of seduction by exploring some of the following powerful techniques.

The Eight Attributes That Will Flip Attraction and Desire [1]

1. **Looks:** Grooming, Posture, Eye Contact, Standing Out, and Style

2. **Adaptability:** Adventurous, Spontaneous, Independent, Risk-taking, Social Intelligence, Flexible, Ability to Handle New Situations

3. **Strength:** Effective Communicator, Powerful Frame, Living in Your Own Reality, Ability to Take Care of Others; Criteria: Assertiveness, Leadership, Courage, Loyalty, Decisiveness, Self-assurance

4. **Value:** Leader of Social Circle, Admired, Teach People Things, High-Status Behavior. Criteria: Intelligence, Interesting, Talented, Entertaining, Successful, Self-sufficient, Creative

5. **Emotional Connection:** Creating Deep Rapport, in Touch with Your Feelings, Listening

6. **Goals:** Clarity of Goals, Dreams, Hunger for Life; Criteria: Stability, Efficiency, Perseverance, Learn Quickly

7. **Authenticity:** Actions Matching What You Say

8. **Self-worth:** Self-confidence, Self-esteem, and Self-care

Be sure you speak loudly, slowly, clearly, and dynamically. To further hook your target, stress key words and insert pauses to build suspense or humor.

---

1   Influenced by Neil Strauss

Fourteen Things That Will Create Attraction [2]

1. Be the person giving validation, not the one needing it.

2. Make it a privilege to talk to you.

3. Challenge your friend.

4. Be the snob.

5. Be the authority figure.

6. Reverse roles; tell him or her to stop flirting, using pick-up lines, and treating you like a piece of meat.

7. Give your friend points for good behavior and subtract points for bad behavior (push and pull).

8. Teach her or him something about herself or himself; this is one of the best and most efficient ways to make an impression.

9. The more yes responses your friend gives, the more their subconscious will accept you as an authority; get him or her to say yes a couple of times on small things.

10. Make your friend feel good about themselves.

11. Practice casually pausing at the climax of the story to build suspense.

12. Let unfinished stories dangle; this will make your friend think.

13. Seeding (planting a thought and repeating it regularly) helps to increase the odds of your friend saying yes by avoiding putting the pressure on.

14. Elicit jealousy, give mixed messages, and/or disappear for a while.

---

2   Influenced by Neil Strauss

Twenty-four Ways to Develop YOUR Mystery
Side and Seduce with Panache

Mystery is important because it keeps your partner intrigued, and he or she will want to know more about you. By being mysterious, you can be sure that you will stay in their mind.

1. Display different sides of you (the lover side of you and the friend side of you, not a different personality).

2. Develop something new that your friend doesn't know about, something that sets you apart.

3. Ask a lot of questions (run the conversation) and listen attentively.

4. Demonstrate sticky and unwavering eye contact.

5. Be random; create patterns and break them.

6. Play with your friend's emotions (tease them).

7. Give the image that there is always something in your mind.

8. Come across as if you have absolutely no need of other people's company and you're totally fine on your own.

9. Talk and cut off the rest of your speech.

10. Don't tell your friend everything you do during your free time (for example: Mystery Monday).

11. Spend a lot of time alone; convey the message that you are self-sufficient and that you don't need attention or approval from anybody.

12. Be very quiet; speak the least, and show that you don't need the attention.

13. Wear dark-colored clothing.

14. Talk in theories.

15. Ask your friend to guess.

16. Be unpredictable and contradictory; be a tough guy or girl

with some traits of innocence, and get lost for days so that nobody knows where you have been.

17. Don't show emotions verbally, and be stoic. Only show emotions with your eyes (never yell, look excited, or angry; never be affected). This shows you are in control of your emotions.

18. Be charismatic.

19. Cultivate your intellect in many areas.

20. For masculine energy: Find a purpose and stick to it; know what you want and have a strong opinion.

21. Use humor to mask your feelings.

22. For masculine energy: Feminine energy want to work for you, so let them.

23. Rarely joke and rarely laugh.

24. Embrace the power of touch.

Ten Behavioral Secrets of Seduction

Seduction is building temptation or attraction. It can feel mysterious, but it has a resounding impact on connecting you to your mate. Here are some of the best practices to help you create sparks through seduction:

1. It's all in the mind.

2. Set the scene.

3. Be interested (in your friend).

4. Be interesting.

5. Dare to say it; it's the way you say it.

6. Embrace change; suggest new experiences.

7. Roll out the compliments.

8. Show vulnerability; be impressed and give compliments.

9. Don't always be available.

10. Be mysterious.

The Twenty-Five Qualities of Mr. Bad that Mr. Friend Can Incorporate to Seduce Any Women (Including His Friend) Successfully
We should all work to have a little Mr. Bad in us. He is seductive, mysterious, and rarely gets friend-zoned. Taking a page out of his book, here are some of the best practices to help you (Mr. Friend) seduce any woman:

1. Don't give a damn about what people think about you, and be spontaneous. If you are cautious, conservative, and follow the rules that people and society expect you to follow, women will see you as safe or boring. Make no excuses for your desires; have the bad guy attitude. Show outrageous balls or guts (for her).

2. Be socially dominant, and be in control; this will show your high value.

3. Treat women like they are little girls (from time to time) who need teasing, and play with them.

4. Expand your body language to create more space, which shows your high status (swagger when you walk, lean far back on your seat, stretch your legs far), and project a deep and low tone of voice.

5. Set the rules and bounderies (set your own rules, not society's rules) so that women will follow you.

6. Make her feel safe—that is, be in control of everything and everyone; be present and grounded.

7. Have a strong sense of identity; know yourself and be comfortable with who you are.

8. Make people feel good about themselves; let them talk, especially about themselves, and guide them with questions.

9. Show confidence. Have an "I-don't-give-a-damn" or "I-don't-care" attitude until your friend really demonstrates why she is a catch; women are addicted to confidence. Be a man she can never hope to control.

10. Challenge your friend. Women love to be challenged; they don't want to be placed on a pedestal; they want to be treated as equals intellectually. Physically, however, they want you to be sexually secure and dominant. Make her do things she wouldn't dare.

11. Take risks and be adventurous, even sexually. Women crave excitement in their lives; they see that if you have many sexual partners, that you are desirable to other women.

12. Take the lead. Be assertive and domineering; women like to be feminine in a relationship. Don't ask for permission. Tell her what will happen (she loves a good story), and by telling in advance, she can trust and let go.

13. Send mixed signals. This will stop you from seeming too clingy, needy, or available; it will give her the drama she biologically craves. Her mind will start going in all places, and she will build an addiction toward you. It will make her assume that you have other options; again, she will perceive it as a challenge if you have other women around you.

14. Uncertainty creates tension and chemistry, so when your friend can't figure you out, that is when she will start to chase you, and she will work harder to get you interested in her, which means she will start to think more and more about you. This will lead her to unconsciously think that since she is putting out so much effort, she must really like you, and so this is the start. She will overanalyze every action you make to figure you out.

15. Don't show her your emotions. When you have a poker face, she will start doubting whether you like her, and this will build tension. She will start to anticipate and want to see you more because she will be afraid of losing you.

16. Be authentic.

17. Create sexual tension; create anticipation and add excitement to the conversation by flirting and pausing for two seconds while looking into her eyes before replying; create a fantasy in her mind, letting her imagine that you are hard to get; tease her, disagree with her, use intense eye contact, be playful and carefree; "forget" to call back, be late for dates, mix pleasure with pain, stir up taboo subjects, create temptation, insinuate things without being clear and create confusion; create a need and stir anxiety and discontent, create a love triangle, be a problem creator, play with her emotions (provoke her), don't be available, confuse desire and reality.

18. Appeal to her ego; attraction happens in stage one.

19. Be indifferent until she has earned something more; maintain control and create mystery.

20. Don't talk personal (talk in theories); this shows that you are not infatuated by her and creates mystery.

21. Use time limitations with your friend, as this will show that you have other things to do and that you are not overly interested. It also shows your value and dominance.

22. Use silence in conversation, pause for two seconds, and look in her eyes.

23. Use time breaks in the middle of conversations; she will want more.

24. Focus on your purpose. When you do this, you can *give* something to the woman; whereas, when you pursue the woman, you are *getting* and so they feel used.

25. Flirt with all women, and it will remove the weight, anxiety, heaviness, and expectation of being with one woman.

How Women Are Physically Attractive to Men [3]

Most of what immediately follows are things that women can strive toward and would dramatically impact their attractiveness to men.

1. Waist-to-hip Ratio (7:10)

2. High Voice (signifies youth and a smaller body)

3. Healthy Hair (signifies health and fertility)

4. Smiling

5. Using Less Makeup

6. Wearing Red

The Five Proven Things That Make a Man Fall in Love [4]

1) Make him feel that you are his home, his safest place.

2) Make him feel like a hero; by surrendering to his strength, you trust him.

3) Praise him; reward the good behavior, and ignore the bad behavior.

4) Have sex with him often; even better, take the initiative.

5) Share your feelings.

Taking this one step further, let's look at how to increase attraction with our non verbal communication.

Albert Mehrabian, a professor of psychology at the University of California, Los Angeles (UCLA), conducted research in 1967 that demonstrated communication based on feelings and attitudes makes up only 7 percent of the words we use, while the remaining 93 percent is divided between 55 percent body language and 38 percent vocal tone. This is very important for couples in long-term relationships to understand.

---

3   Influenced by Dr. Midge Wilson

4   Based on Annie Lalla

$$\text{Magical Love} = \text{Physical Chemistry} + \text{Intellectual Chemistry} + \text{Emotional Chemistry}$$

$$\text{Magical Love} = 55 \text{ Percent} + 7 \text{ Percent} + 38 \text{ Percent}$$

I have generalized this equation to show you that by being Mr. and Ms. Nice or Mr. and Ms. Friend (even if you are a prolific speaker and you always have interesting topics), you will only appeal to your partner or friend up to 7 percent of your message (again, the figures are exaggerated).

Let's unpack this at length.

Body Language: Increasing Your Attraction Level by up to 55 Percent

The best way to attract the opposite sex is to emphasize the masculine and feminine energy differences. It would be interesting for both of you, Mr. and Ms. Nice and Mr. and Ms. Friend, to read the body language of both to not only improve yourselves but also to understand your partner and friend better.

How Mr. Friend Amore's Body Language Can Help Him Be More Masculine

1. Stand straight, walk tall, act assertively, and wear dark-colored clothing to gain perceived height.

2. When a man mirrors a woman's facial expression, she will describe him as caring, intelligent, interesting, and attractive.

3. Economy of movement; too much movement shows anxiousness and insecurity. Don't touch your face, fidget, show unnecessary facial expressions, or play with objects.

4. Walk like you are going somewhere (with a purpose and no rush).

5. Dominate and control; the more space around you, the more dominant you are.

In a TED Talk on body language, Amy Cuddy, a social psychologist, showed how a two-minute Superman power pose increases your confidence as well as your testosterone level. I am a particular fan of this pose, and it helped me a lot in both my posture and confidence. Another exercise I found interesting and that works is to open your hands and chest while you are sitting.

From an evolutionary viewpoint, space is status. When you look at high-status men, they spread more. One reason why it is counterintuitive and against nature to have a closed posture is that our bodies think we are under stress, which decreases testosterone and increases cortisol.

> **Tip 18**
> The best way to master body language is to master your feelings. Your body language and tone of voice are but a mirror of your emotions. As such, by becoming conscious of your feelings, you can control your body language and tone.

Twenty Ways Ms. Friend Amore's Body Language Can Help Her Be More Feminine

1. Emphasize your breasts, tilt your head, touch your hair, and expose your wrists; you will appear submissive.

2. Increase eye contact, smile more, nod more, talk, touch (your hair, your clothing, etc.), place your hands on your hips, lick your lips, and point your foot or body toward your friend.

3. Fondle a cylindrical object; finger and play with your jewelry (especially a necklace).

4. Touch yourself. Slowly and sensually stroke your thigh, neck, or throat; you are implying that he can touch you.

5. Point your knee at your friend; you are signaling that he is the most interesting person.

6. Do the face platter: present your face to be admired.

7. Your handbag is an extension of your body; put it close to your friend, and slowly fondle and caress it; you are signaling that you are interested in him.

8. Women tend to keep their arms open when they are around men they find attractive and are likely to fold their arms across their breasts around aggressive or unattractive men.

9. Tilt your head to one side to show you are listening and show your neck; you are being vulnerable, and this appeals to his masculinity.

10. Tilt your head down a little, so your chin touches your chest.

11. Sideways glances create sexual tension by signaling your friend to chase you.

12. Rub your face, head, or neck; this raises your hands and breasts.

13. Blink more often.

14. Remove physical barriers between you and your friend.

15. Stroke the back of your hand to draw attention to the softness of your skin and the idea of him caressing it.

16. Pull your upper arms tight, and this will emphasize your breasts.

17. Play with your wrists or brush your thighs up against your friend more than once.

18. Touch him while you talk.

19. Cross your legs (while pointing at your friend), and recross your legs.

20. Move closer to him.

You will notice that most of the body language actions are centered on breasts and lips, and this is because men are attracted visually first. As Ms. Friend, you have not emphasized your physical appearance enough; it's not about the clothing, it's about your attitude and behavior. You have been behaving like a man.

> **Tip 19**
> *"Studies suggest that before a man speaks, his posture accounts for up to 55 percent of a woman's first impression of him."*—Dr. Leslie Becker-Phelps and Megan Kaye, authors of *Love: The Psychology of Attraction*

Remembering that body language is 55 percent of communication, you can use this to your advantage by using silence and not always answering questions, as this can be more powerful than words. You can respond with a look, a touch, a smile, or a wink. The more you say with your body, the less you say with your words, which leads people to wonder more and it triggers an intense sense of curiosity, an anticipation of wanting to know more. This creates tension—sexual tension.

Tone of Voice: Increase Your Level of Attraction by up to 38 Percent

Neil Strauss, the author of *Rules of the Game*, says: *"Your voice is your identity; it can tell people everything about who you are, how you feel about yourself, and what you believe in."* Just as body language can have a tremendous impact on your perceived attraction level, your tone can accomplish a similar advantage for you. Here are some of the most valuable ways to use your voice tone to appear more attractive:

1. Stress important words, and subordinate unimportant ones.

2. Change your pitch.

3. Vary your rate of speaking.

4. Pause before and after important ideas.

5. Don't apologize (unless you really messed up).

6. Match the other person's speed and tonality.

Studies show that the same voice qualities attract men and women regardless of the gender of the speaker. Tony Robbins, author, entrepreneur, philanthropist, and life coach, discusses a recent study examining hundreds of conversations from couples in therapy. The study found that how you say things is just as important as what you say. Your tone of voice can make a big difference in the success of your marriage. Here are some steps you can take to assist with your tone:

1. Effect a low pitch (a deep voice).

2. Effect a soft, quiet timbre.

3. Slowly pronounce and enunciate.

4. Talk from your heart not from your nose, by visualizing your words coming out of your heart.

To develop a seductive voice, try deep breathing exercises from below the diaphragm.

Breath and Posture

In his book, *The Relationship Cure*, Dr. John Gottman reveals that when it comes to assessing the meaning of what their partners are saying, only 7 percent of that meaning comes from the spoken word, while 38 percent comes from tone of voice and speech patterns. Words that may seem neutral can become incendiary if spoken with a sarcastic, demeaning, or contemptuous tone, causing the listener to feel hurt and disrespected.

Bad posture can restrict your diaphragm and breathing, effectively neutering your vocal power, while a calm and slow voice commands authority. Experiment with changing the volume, pitch, speed, timbre, rhythm, and flow of your voice. Try emphasizing different words by creating pauses where they don't normally belong; shortening or elongating words; and speaking in different voices and accents.

How to Create Sexual Attraction

This is important for Mr. and Ms. Friend to learn. Because they had associated the feelings of shame with love when they were small, this led them to reject sex or believe that sex is bad or taboo.

You have a masculine body language and tone of voice if you are Mr. Friend and a feminine body language and tone of voice if you are Ms. Friend. It's now time to learn some little tricks to increase the tension and create sexual attraction to create THE SPARKS.

Physical touch, eye contact, and showering her with words that she is sexy are not enough. Sexual attraction is more like a state; it happens in the pauses. It is a desire that is not acted upon. Rather, it creates anticipation, and it is this anticipation, this moment of "what's going to happen now" that creates anxiety. It's about this adrenaline rush. Recall Dr. Helen Fisher's study on how fear and love are associated. This is what you are creating; this is sexual attraction, the state of anticipation that links fear with love.

One of the most powerful ways to increase tension and create sexual attraction as you have never experienced is to let your eyes linger on someone for a second or two before you reply. This creates anticipation in your friend's mind. The mind doesn't do well with emptiness—it needs to fill the void; otherwise, your friend's subconscious will start going in all directions to fill the emptiness.

Seduction happens in the pauses. It is in the pauses where the attraction is built.

However, remember:

- The less healthy you are, the less horny you are.
- Low testosterone levels lead to low sexual desire.
- The more you masturbate, the lower your sex drive is.

Taking this one step further, let's look at how to increase sexual desire.

Seven Keys for Sexual Tension

The longer you hold back before making a move, the more the sexual tension will grow. The trick to building incredible tension and anticipation: Do not give them what they want. Here are some other steps you can take to stay out of the friend zone:

1. Remain calm in tense situations.
2. Don't spill your beans; it's the guy who's the mystery which makes women's hearts beat faster.

3. Use strong eye contact.

4. Keep talking to a minimum, and sit there quietly but listen intently while she talks.

5. Employ the power of suggestion.

6. Use touch well.

7. Keep her guessing.

One of the reasons your friend is not feeling attracted toward you is because she lives in fear and fear blocks her from feeling. She fears that life with you will be boring or safe; but if you are both willing to build it and proactively work on it, you can create attraction. When you understand that chemistry happens in the moment and you start being present, the sparks will start to fly.

Chemistry is the polarity between your masculinity and her femininity. **You feel sparks because her femininity makes you FEEL more masculine, and she feels sparks because your masculinity makes her FEEL more feminine.** Chemistry is how you make him or her feel emotionally—how he or she feels when they are around you.

> **Tip 20**
> A person's name is the sweetest word they can hear, so keep using it. At first, it will draw their attention, but if used consistently, it will engage them and stimulate feelings for you.

Step 3: Emotional Chemistry

After you have worked on your physical chemistry and reclaimed your natural energy, and now that you have changed your friendship dynamic, it is time to start connecting deeply. Emotional chemistry is the glue that will hold your physical chemistry and intellectual chemistry together. It will fortify your love and transform your journey into a passionate and magical forever-after beyond what you ever thought was possible.

How to Create More Intimacy and Connection

One of the most important ways to increase emotional chemistry with your partner is through creating more intimacy and connection. Here are some of the best ways to do that with her:

1. Declare your love for her.

2. Create rituals, symbols, and traditions; create that solid foundation of love.

3. Do things that remind her of consistency; show her the consistency of your love.

4. Always take a shower together on date night; this will show her that you will take care of her, so she can let go.

5. Reward her, appreciate her, and approve her.

6. Be certain. Be responsible for her. When she perceives your inner strength, she will let go into the feminine. If she is masculine at work, she wants to be feminine at home.

7. Let her feel her emotions; she is the river, and you are the riverbank. Let her river of emotions flow without fixing it (unless she asks), and allow her to feel. When a woman feels anger, she also feels passion.

8. Be her tree of emotion while her hurricane of emotions surround you. Stand firm and hold her without always wanting to fix something; this is a way a woman can feel safe and allow herself to be feminine.

9. Reward her, and approve of her sexually.

10. Have a fun life, and let her participate in your life. Women want to be transported on erotic adventures, exciting life adventures, hot monogamy, and playful adventures.

11. Understand her feelings. Her chemistry or desire comes from your understanding of the feelings she is trying to feel to be attracted.

12. Make yourself trustworthy. She will want you if she can trust you with herself, her emotions, and her body; and if she knows that you will take care of her and keep her safe, she can fully express herself.

13. Be willing to listen to her without judgment, without making her feel inadequate, without trying to fix her or her problems, and without trying to impact the outcome.

14. Just be present for her, open your heart, let her in, and offer her unconditional support without judgment or control.

15. Provide a secure and safe place for her to feel stable and relaxed.

16. Connect with her emotionally; let her talk about her emotions, listen without trying to fix her, and be grounded and present.

And here are some of the best ways to create more intimacy and connection with him:

1. Declare your love for him and if applicable praise his sexual exploits.

2. Create rituals, symbols, and traditions; create that solid foundation around sex.

3. Do things that remind him of consistency; show him the consistency of your willingness to explore sex with him.

4. Initiate sex from time to time; this will show him that you will take care of him, so he can let go.

5. Reward him, appreciate him, and approve him (especially his sexual prowess).

6. Be patient. Be understanding with him. When he perceives you are foreplaying to communicate with him, he will appreciate you and love you even more. Be and act feminine with him (don't boss him around).

7. Teach him about emotions (not like a teacher or a mother), tell him how you feel but don't overwhelm him all at once. Be willing to be very vulnerable, this will help him open up (gradually).

8. Allow him to be masculine, to have his cave time. Don't try to control him, criticize him, or bring in the comparison game. Praise him for what he is doing good.

9. Motivate and encourage him to follow his passion. Be his first and most avid cheerleader.

10. Accept him for who he is without trying to change him.

11. Make yourself trustworthy. He will want you if he can trust you with himelf, his and his penis and sexuality; and if he knows that you will take care of him and keep him safe, he can fully express himself.

12. Be willing to listen to him during sex without judgment, without making him feel inadequate, without trying to fix him or his problems, and without trying to impact the outcome.

13. Just be present for him during sex, open your heart, let him in, and offer him unconditional support without judgment or control.

14. Provide a secure and safe place for him to feel stable and relaxed during sex.

15. Connect with him sexually; let him express himself, listen without trying to fix him, and be grounded and present.

The Four Magical Ingredients to Create an Even Deeper Intimacy and Connection

1. Presence is a very important practice to create intimacy and a deeper connection. It is important for the man to be emotionally present when the woman is talking or sharing her feelings, while at the same time it is important for the woman to be emotionally present when they are having sex or being intimate.

2. Another powerful intimacy practice that will deepen your emotional connection and, according to Nicholas Boothman, "create immense rapport and sexual intimacy," is eye contact.

3. Vulnerability is another crucial ingredient that helps develop deep emotional chemistry—understanding each other's imperfections, what makes and breaks each other, and accepting each other. Vulnerability requires courage and openness rather than shutting down or shunning your partner. In times of conflict, vulnerability is most important as it can either deepen your connection or completely distort it. Be vulnerable (share your feelings, your fears, etc.) without being needy. This will deepen the bond and create the trust for her to surrender in your arms.

4. Hold space for her (listen without trying to fix her; be grounded and present). She will feel safer, protected, and secure, which will lead to great intimacy and connection. By holding space, you are creating trust. Holding space also allows her to be vulnerable without fearing being judged. Empower your partner by allowing her to make her own decision; don't overwhelm your partner with knowledge, make her feel enough to fail. As Heather Plett puts it, *"Create a container for complex emotions, fears, trauma."* Similarly, hold space for him (be present and grounded during sex). He will feel safer, protected, and secure, which will lead to great intimacy and connection. By holding space,

you are creating trust. Holding space also allows him to be vulnerable without fearing being judged.

Develop an emotional fitness program. Identify, generate, and regulate emotions that you and your partner have to promote emotional and intellectual growth.

How to Make Your Man Commit (For Ms. Friend Amore) or Recommit (For Ms. Nice Mirror)

Even with all of this good advice and these practices in place, you still might find a lapse in your connection. In that case, you have to either commit or recommit to the relationship. To connect with your man, he must value you and your relationship. In other words, what added value do you or the relationship bring to him?

If a woman can show a man that she adds greater value to him than his fear of freedom, he will commit.

Freedom for men is like commitment for women. Just like a woman loves when a man is the bank of her emotions and creates space for her to feel her emotions, a man loves when a woman is the bank of his freedom and creates space for him to feel his freedom.

You see, both men and women feel; they just feel differently. Feminine energy wants connection, while masculine energy wants separateness or disconnection. The Greys have learned that the best way is to balance between both.

Tip 21

Before going into your cave, reassure your woman that you will be back and that you love her because for a woman if you don't explain why you need space, she will assume she did something wrong.

Creating a Passionate Relationship

The next time your best friend tells you that he or she is not attracted to you or doesn't feel any sparks, tell your friend that friendship is the foundation of love and that can't be found on every corner; attraction, on the other hand, can be created at will. Tell him or her that you are a master of relationships but a novice in attraction. Further, impart that you are a great relationship communicator but a novice dating communicator and that once your friend gets tired of the mystery, you are their rock that will keep their feelings and emotions safe. Impart that your type of love is unconditional. As Dr. Helen Fisher, biological anthropologist, said, *"If you really want to fall in love with someone, do novel things together – take a hike, ride your bikes out to dinner rather than take the car, go to the opera, go skiing, take a trip to Paris for the weekend, have sex in a different room. Novelty, novelty, novelty. It drives up the dopamine in the brain and can push you over the threshold into love."* So take your friend on a journey of discovery and develop new common activities.

Love is about making all the small daily moments magnificent, while sparks are about making all the random big moments magnificent. That's why we need love and sparks to have a balanced life to dance the Grey Dance of Love.

Dr. Sue Johnson, author, clinical psychologist, researcher, professor, popular presenter, and speaker, as well as a leading innovator in the field of couples therapy, says, *"We know from all the hundreds of studies on love that have emerged during the past decade that emotional responsiveness is what makes or breaks love relationships. Happy stable couples can quarrel and fight, but they also know how to tune into each other and restore emotional connection after a clash. Our loved one is our shelter in life."* Dr. Johnson goes a step further by claiming that the real problem when people fight is not about money, the kids, or sex, but rather that both partners feel emotionally disconnected. To that end, let's all move in the direction of building a strong foundation for that home.

CHAPTER 12
REKINDLING THE SPARKS
IN A LOVELESS MARRIAGE

YOU PASSED THROUGH THICK AND thin together, from the magical honeymoon period to more challenging times in your relationship. Your rose will always be your rose; you will never find another one quite like it. If you choose to seek another rose, you may find that you're only happy with it for a while before moving on to the next one. Even when times are tough, the best shortcut to finding love, in your case, is to fix the problems you currently have and tend to your rose with the most loving care.

Rekindling the sparks in a loveless marriage is something most couples deal with over the course of their relationships.

During the second stage, Mr. Bad often becomes Mr. Nice and Ms. Bad becomes Ms. Nice. While this might work in the short term, this reversal of energy creates a depolarization and kills all sexual tension. A masculine woman turns off the man, and the feminine man turns off the woman. This may work for the short term, and Mr. and Ms. Nice can still have sex to please each other. However, this is a Band-Aid on a bigger problem and in the long run will lead to cheating, separation, or divorce. When Mr. Nice or Ms. Nice find someone they feel attracted to or more polarized with, they may naturally think they are in love with this new person, while it is just polarity.

From Stage One (Mr. and Ms. Bad Sparks) to Stage Two (Mr. and Ms. Nice Mirror)

Mr. Bad loved Ms. Bad because she wanted him and needed him. Ms. Bad loved Mr. Bad because he wanted her and didn't need her. This is how their love grew. Then Mr. Bad's love grew so much (because he became too much in his femininity at the expense of his masculine side) that he started needing her love. He became Mr. Nice when he started to need her love (remember that feminine energy is focused on love), and she, being feminine, started doubting him and, as a result, rejecting him.

They then got married, but as the years passed, Mr. Bad became more feminine (a.k.a., Mr. Nice) and Ms. Bad became more masculine (a.k.a., Ms. Nice), so the sparks started to die. This led them both to friend-zone each other. Mr. Nice stopped listening to Ms. Nice, and he became emotionally absent. Ms. Nice, to take her revenge, withheld sex from him. This led to one of two challenging scenarios.

First Scenario: The newly married couple enjoyed spending their honeymoon period in la-la land:

Mr. Bad gave all his masculine energy to Ms. Bad. Now depleted of his masculine energy, his only remaining energy is feminine energy. Mr. Bad, therefore, becomes Mr. Nice, the feminine man. At the same time, Ms. Bad, after giving all her feminine energy to Mr. Bad, was depleted of it. Being depleted of her feminine energy, her only remaining energy is her masculine energy. Ms. Bad, therefore, becomes Ms. Nice, the masculine woman. Since both are not living in their natural energies, they become depolarized and, as such, the physical chemistry dies and the sparks die. They start thinking that they have fallen out of love, when in fact they have just fallen out of sparks.

Second Scenario: The couple has been married for many years and is stuck in stage two:

Life has gotten in the way, and Mr. and Ms. Nice resigned after initially trying to rekindle the sparks. This stage happens around the midlife crisis when they start to wake up and wonder where their lives have gone. At this stage, Mr. or Ms. Nice regain their natural energy, and since they have tried inserting their core energy into the relationship once and this failed, they start looking elsewhere. This is how cheating starts. The man acts like Mr. Nice at home and like Mr. Bad outside home and has an affair; similarly, the woman acts like Ms. Nice at home and like Ms. Bad outside the home and has an affair.

While at first, the intense physical chemistry is amazing, it's also easy to mistake this for love, which is also dangerous.

Why?

In the first scenario, if Mr. Bad is not receiving feminine energy from his partner, he will look for it inside of him, and if Ms. Bad is not receiving masculine energy from her partner, she will look for it inside of her. This is a great step forward, as biology ensures that after discovering their core natural energies in stage one, both men and women become complete from inside by discovering their opposite nurtured energies in stage two. Mr. Bad and Mr. Nice and Ms. Bad and Ms. Nice will stop looking for their partners to complete them; they will stop loving from the ego ("Give me. It's all about me, me, me.") and start looking for unconditional love ("I love you no matter what.").

In the second scenario, Mr. and Ms. Nice are well into their nurtured energies, and they completely forgot about their core energies. They got stuck in stage two and just gave up. If Ms. Nice keeps pushing for talking, this will push Mr. Nice to disconnect emotionally. The more he disconnects, the more she withholds sex. Simply put, what is the solution for the couples to rekindle the sparks and live a second honeymoon forever after?

In the first scenario, they can take the following steps:
Step 1: Mr. and Ms. Nice have to revert to their core essences. They do this by working on their physical chemistry and by redeveloping their repressed masculine energy (Mr. Nice) or feminine energy (Ms. Nice).

Step 2: They must calibrate and balance between their intellectual chemistry and physical chemistry.

Step 3: They must develop short-term emotional chemistry.

In the second scenario, they can take the following steps:

Step 1: Mr. and Ms. Nice have to revert to their core essences. They do this by working on their physical chemistry and by redeveloping their repressed masculine energy (Mr. Nice) or feminine energy (Ms. Nice).

Step 2: They must calibrate and balance between their intellectual chemistry and physical chemistry.

Step 3: They must develop short-term emotional chemistry; this is the most important part.

Before we start with the step-by-step solution towards how to go from a passionless relationship to a passionate one, a few important points must be clarified:

Why Being Friend-Zoned Is a Good Thing.

This is simply biology and evolution (a.k.a. nature and nurture). You can see that in the yin and yang of relationships. However, we have to pass through two stages to be balanced. In stage one, the man experiences his masculinity, and the woman experiences her femininity; in stage two, the man discovers his femininity, and the woman discovers her masculinity. Only then, in stage three, once they are complete from within, can they blossom and fulfill their potential. The only pitfall found in this stage is that Mr. Bad or Ms. Bad lose themselves and cannot dance back and forth, or they discover that they have nothing in common and no intellectual chemistry. This is often the result of a lack of emotional chemistry. When you are friend-zoned as a couple, you are stuck between the friendship and the relationship because you have stopped being playful, stopped courting, stopped building attraction, and let yourself go. You have stopped dating, and you have stopped connecting emotionally. Remember your inner child is screaming for playtime. You are neglecting him or her and need to refocus on that.

Should Your Partner Help You?

By all means, *yes*. This is a no-brainer. By helping your partner, you are helping yourself. Not only will it help you improve much faster, but it would be fun for you both to experiment together and see the changes. It would strengthen your bond much more since you have experienced change together. Of course, you shouldn't stay in the same dynamic; and if your partner doesn't want to help you or you both believe you should work on yourselves alone, then a couple of months away from each other to work on yourselves should do the trick. When you are back, all you need to do is balance the other part of the relationship and start working on your emotional chemistry.

The Entitlement of Your Partner's Feelings and Attraction

Being in a relationship with someone (even if it is for years) doesn't entitle you to his or her feelings or attraction toward you. You can't just expect your partner to feel for you or be attracted to you; it doesn't work that way. If you want your partner to be more attracted to you or feel more for you, you have to trigger the feelings by shifting your polarity and going back to your core energy. You can always ask your partner to go back to his or her core energy to help you create or recreate the attraction faster. Feelings and attraction will decrease when you stop polarizing yourself and your relationship. A lack of attraction means that the man has become more feminine and the woman more masculine. Since you are already in a relationship, you need to help each other out and revert to your core energies.

This sense of entitlement is one of the reasons the dance stops and the sparks die. This is why it is important never to assume you know your partner's feelings and never take your partner for granted. The dance of polarity should always be present, until death do you part. Remember always to do the Grey Dance of Love. Attraction, sparks, and emotions (or feelings) are pure biology. The good news: Now you know how to have fun with biology and trigger the sparks anytime you want.

Finally, Remember the Eight Reasons People Fall Out of Love [1]

1. Lack of communication. According to John Gottman, communication is affected in four ways: criticism, contempt (sarcasm and name-calling), defensiveness, and stonewalling (the silent treatment that is caused by the other three).

2. Feeling invisible. Never take each other or the relationship for granted.

3. Magnifying insecurities. Once the PEA (the love hormone) dissipates and the feelings of attraction are gone, we start to see our partners with different eyes. As a result, our insecurities start to show up and we start to be needier. Since we are not blind or focused only on our partners, we start to notice that our partners act differently with others. We just want to feel like we used to in the beginning.

4. Boredom sets in, and we settle into a boring routine.

5. Holding on to grudges.

6. Dishonesty.

7. No one wants to compromise.

8. Believing that the fairytale is over, love wasn't *really* love, and it was just an attraction (and now it's gone).

This list shows that the relationship dynamic is a reverse in polarity. Ms. Nice is bossing around, giving orders, holding grudges, and criticizing, while Mr. Nice is being dishonest and doesn't want to compromise or communicate.

Understanding each of these points will help you work toward rekindling the sparks within your relationship. The rest of the chapter will outline the steps you can take to turn your relationship from a passionless one into a passionate one.

---

1   "10 Reasons People Fall out of Love," *Power of Positivity:* https://www.powerofpositivity.com/people-fall-out-of-love/.

Step One: Physical Chemistry

Working on your physical chemistry is the first step to reclaiming the sparks in your relationship.

Where You Are Now

Mr. Nice

Your Physical Chemistry: 0/100

$$\text{Physical Chemistry} = \text{Masculine Energy} + \text{Feminine Energy}$$
$$\text{Mr. Nice's Physical Chemistry} = 0 + 0 = 0$$

The reason being, you have a **wounded (or lack)** masculine energy and lack feminine energy.

Wounded Masculine Energy Characteristics: Fearful, Reserved, Weak-willed and Confused, Desperate, Inert, Low Self-confidence and Self-esteem, Uninteresting and Naïve

Lack of Feminine Energy Characteristics: Overwhelming, Superficial, Rigid, Overthinking, Anxious, Emotionless, Dry or Blocked

The good part: You will be healthier and more balanced once you recalibrate your masculine energy (which is your natural predisposition). You need to move from excess masculine energy to balanced masculine energy and from lack of feminine energy to balanced feminine energy.

Ms. Nice

Your Physical Chemistry: 0/100

$$\text{Physical Chemistry} = \text{Masculine Energy} + \text{Feminine Energy}$$
$$\text{Ms. Nice's Physical Chemistry} = 0 + 0 = 0$$

The reason being, you **lack** masculine energy and have **wounded (or lack)** feminine energy.

Lack of Masculine Energy Characteristics: Fearful, Reserved, Weak-willed and Confused, Desperate, Inert, Low Self-confidence and Self-esteem, Uninteresting and Naïve

Wounded Feminine Energy Characteristics: Overwhelming, Superficial, Rigid, Overthinking, Anxious, Emotionless, Dry or Blocked

The good part: You will be healthier and more balanced once you recalibrate your feminine energy (which is your natural predisposition). You need to move from excess feminine energy to balanced feminine energy and from lacking masculine energy to balanced masculine energy.

How to Regain Your Masculinity (For Mr. Nice Mirror)

In the previous chapter, you learned how to develop your masculinity. I encourage you to dig into it and refresh your memory as it is part of regaining your masculinity. Once you do that, we can turn to the different scenarios we often see for Mr. Nice and how we can help him regain his masculinity.

Scenario 1: Starting to feel comfortable in a relationship is a clue for you to increase the sparks. It is time for the man to shift into his masculine energy to keep the relationship dynamic healthy. If the man doesn't dance back to his masculine energy, he will become more feminine and this will lead the woman to become more masculine. Remember, the masculine energy leads the relationship (no matter if it's the man or the woman who is masculine), and since it is the man who is naturally masculine, it is up to him.

Scenario 2: If you are in the stage where you are fighting all the time or barely talking, the first thing to do to reclaim your masculine energy is to take some time apart. Having space is important; it will increase the tension, create a separation, and will make you stronger and more willing to see your woman. At the same time, your woman will want you more and will want to connect with you more.

If you are in stage two, check out the twelve steps to regain your masculinity section in the previous chapter.

How Ms. Nice Mirror Can Help Mr. Nice Mirror Regain
His Masculinity and Love Her All over Again by Being More Feminine

Ladies, if you feel the relationship is starting to be too comfortable and you see that your man has sunk too deeply into his feminine energy, then work to save your relationship by using your feminine leadership to inspire his masculine energy.

1. When you make him feel like a hero by surrendering to his strength, you are showing Mr. Nice that you trust him and his masculine energy.

2. When you appreciate and acknowledge the hero in him whenever he does a small or big act for you, he feels valued.

3. When you let his wisdom and power guide you, he feels strong and powerful.

4. When you let him support you and protect you, he will feel unstoppable.

5. When you focus on the positive of what he is doing for you and you are praising that (instead of focusing on the negative or what he is not doing for you and criticizing), he will want to do more (and even the impossible) just for you (sometimes even without you asking, just because he wants to be praised).

6. When a man feels safe in your presence—that is, NOT JUDGED OR CRITICIZED (yes, I am typing it that way on purpose)—then Mr. Nice will feel that YOU are his home.

7. When a man has sex, he feels loved; don't deprive him of love, or he will deprive you of emotional connection.

8. Teach him about the world of emotions and how to express his feelings (most men are clueless.).

9. Wear skirts and dresses, high heels, paint your nails, smile, give compliments, speak with a soft voice, move your hips when you walk, etc.

10. Be soft, nurturing, open, accepting, and responsive. Leave your masculinity at work, and be more seductive.

11. Let your man take the lead, flirt, wait until he asks you out, let him ask you out, pay the bills, ask for your drink, accept his help, and thank him.

12. Don't criticize or argue with him. Respect and admire him openly, and be vulnerable.

13. Be his lady, not his guy friend.

Remember that men think first (nature) before feeling second (nurture), while women feel first (nature) before thinking second (nurture). Therefore, Ms. Nice, leave your ego aside and be emotionally mature. If you cannot get your way, change the dynamic of your relationship or just leave it; don't suffer and make your man suffer for it. Remember, for Mr. Nice to become Mr. Bad once again, you need to act as you did when you first started dating—that is, empower him with praise rather than criticism. Give him feedback (don't play cold war on him and stop talking; tell him what you want). Don't be a bitch.

When you nag and complain, Mr. Nice runs away and stops listening; try the opposite, and you will see miracles. Be nice and loving, and give an A-to-Z explanation, and you'll have everything you want. Mr. Nice wants you to be his cheerleader, not his mother.

When you are wearing your masculine mask, you don't show appreciation for your man's masculinity. When Mr. Nice is giving you compliments, you are not being receptive but resisting him, and he interprets this as you resisting his masculinity. You are telling him that he is wrong.

And, Ms. Nice, sex is important. It's how Mr. Nice feels connected and loved. Initiate sex from time to time, as it will show Mr. Nice that you really love him.

One more important thing to consider, which Annie Lalla, speaker and thought leader, says is the following: *"Many men don't know how to feel their feelings, and they're unconsciously looking to their woman to teach them. [...]*

Learn to identify, map, and name your emotional states, then practice sharing them. This can be scary but it's a crucial skill, if you want to connect with your partner's heart."

How to Regain Your Femininity (For Ms. Nice Mirror)

In the previous chapter, you learned how to develop your femininity; I encourage you to dig into it and refresh your memory. Once you do that, we can turn to the different scenarios we often see for Ms. Nice and how we can help her regain her femininity.

Scenario 1: Feeling comfortable in a relationship is a clue for you to increase the sparks and to shift into your feminine energy to keep the relationship dynamic healthy. If you don't dance back to your feminine energy, you may become more masculine; this will lead your man to become more feminine. Remember, feminine energy leads the relationship, and since women are more naturally feminine, it is up to you to lead. And men, if you feel the relationship is starting to be too comfortable and your woman has sunk too deep into her masculine energy, then use your masculine energy to ravish her.

Scenario 2: If you are at the stage where you are fighting all the time or barely talking, the first thing to do to reclaim your feminine energy is to take some time to love yourself. Reconnecting with yourself is important and will increase your charm, radiance, and make you more lovable, caring, and more willing to see your man. At the same time, your man will want you more and will want to connect with you more.

If you are in stage two, check out the twelve steps to regain your femininity section in the previous chapter. And consider those additional points:

1. Let go of the need to control the relationship, and trust, and surrender to, Mr. Nice's leadership. Allow him to make mistakes and learn from them; trust him that he is doing his best for you, because when you do, he will do the impossible to become better just for you.

2. Learn to flow and relax within the bounderies set by Mr. Nice.

3. Provide a secure and safe place for Mr. Nice to feel stable and relaxed.

4. Give Mr. Nice the opportunity to support and protect you (learn to receive).

5. Dance, sing, cook, paint, garden, decorate, do yoga, swim, go to beauty spas, get massages, go flower picking, sew, sunbathe, wear fashion and makeup, go shopping (especially clothing that will make you feel sexy), talk with female friends, and/or play with children.

6. Initiate sex; it shows your vulnerability (which is one of the best feminine features).

Do everything to connect to your own femininity before connecting with your man. Regain your femininity; you have been in your masculine energy for far too long. When you connect, you will become radiant and open to receive. When you are open to receive, your man will feel it and, as such, regain his masculinity and give.

How Mr. Nice Mirror Can Help Ms. Nice Mirror
Regain Her Femininity and Love Him All over Again

Gents, if you feel your relationship is starting to be too comfortable and your woman has sunk too deep into her masculine energy, then use your masculine energy to ravish her.

If Ms. Nice is being too masculine, it's because she is protecting her emotions. But putting on the masculine energy is exhausting her; all she wants is to relax into her feminine energy. The masculine energy is pushing her not to love herself (feminine energy is about love), and this is depleting her. Her love for herself is diminishing, and her love for you is diminishing as well. This is killing the attraction of the relationship. Mr. Nice, if she is buying clothes, wearing beauty products, or getting Botox, it doesn't mean she is being feminine; this can only be a mask.

> **Tip 22**
> You can help encourage her femininity by helping her feel beautiful and sexy. Buy her a sexy outfit, notice the things about her, touch her, hug her, make eye contact, and/or use a voice of authority.

Now that your woman is bathing in her masculine energy, that automatically means that you, my friend, are in your feminine energy. The poles of the relationship have shifted. Your woman is now controlling the reins. It's time for you to man up. To melt her heart, you must stop playing small and flirt with all you've got. You've been nice for too long, and she's now controlling you. You have to show her a different person, one she will respect. Start by setting some bounderies and taking the lead.

- **Hold space for her.** When you hold space for her without judging or trying to fix her, you allow her to be honest about her emotions and delve into her feminine energy.

- **Be very strong.** Give her time and space to relax. In return, she'll become more relaxed and feel you needing and appreciating her.

- **Set strong bounderies for her; be grounded and present.** If Ms. Nice is being controlling, you have to understand that she is feeling insecure, and her self-controlling behavior is a result of her insecurity and an effort to gain some control back. This insecurity can come from you (she doesn't trust you), or it can come from her (she doesn't trust herself) in a particular situation. There is an unmet need somewhere. The best way to help Ms. Nice be less controlling is to set bounderies for her. She is testing you with her controlling behavior to see where you will set your bounderies and potentially give in. She is testing your self-respect. Another powerful way to calm her down is to be more grounded and present with her. She feels misunderstood, and by being present, you are listening to what she is saying.

Step Two: Changing the Relationship Dynamic

The second area of focus in rekindling the sparks is an effort to change your relationship dynamic. Women should change their focus; instead of doing more stuff and complaining, they should ask for more from their men and respond appropriately. Men need to feel appreciated, so the more a woman does to show gratitude and appreciation when he does something for her, the better he feels. [2] Once you have mastered your physical chemistry and are ready to make your partner love you again, the next step is to change your relationship dynamic. For that, you have to go from changing your own physical chemistry to changing the physical chemistry of your relationship while at the same time keeping the intellectual chemistry at bay. In other words, it is time to recreate desire. Be patient, and give time for the change in the dynamic (and for your partner) to change his or her mind.

But First ... Why Do We Need to Change the Dynamic?

Simply put, your relationship was thriving when you were Mr. and Ms. Bad, and it went haywire after you became Mr. and Ms. Nice. Yes, life did get in the way, but that is an excuse, and we are here to remedy it. In the old dynamic, Mr. Bad was masculine, and Ms. Bad was feminine; in the current dynamic, Mr. Nice is feminine, and Ms. Nice is masculine. In the new dynamic, Mr. Grey is masculine first and feminine second, and Ms. Grey is feminine first and masculine second.

In step one, you worked on your physical chemistry to regain self-control and the equilibrium of the relationship. The next step would be to start healing the rift between you and learn new techniques that will create a stronger bond between you. However, before that, please check again steps one and two of the previous chapter to master every aspect of physical chemistry.

---

2   Dr. John Gray, *Men Are from Mars, Women Are from Venus* (Harper Thorsons, 2015).

The Ten Steps to Bridge the Gap and Create a Stronger and Deeper Bond for Greater Intimacy

The following steps will help you bridge the gap and create a stronger and deeper bond with your loved one.

Step One: Understanding How to Fight and Argue in a Way That Will Bring You Closer

There is certainly an art to fighting. Remember that both of you are trying to figure things out, so instead of bashing each other and letting your egos talk, join forces and try to figure things out together. Try to look at things from your partner's perspective. I love the way Rob and Kristen Bell, authors of *The Zimzum of Love* express it: *"When you get married, you get another set of eyes. Instead of seeing with two eyes, you're now seeing with four."*

You are two individuals who speak eleven languages (physical chemistry, intellectual chemistry, and emotional chemistry), and additional languages if you have spiritual chemistry. You are similar and yet opposite, and that means there will come a time when you will argue and have different opinions on some subjects. To say you will not fight is like saying you can see a pink elephant fly. Fighting is simply part of any relationship.

Arguing can be very healthy when it helps you express yourself and your feelings to the person you care about the most, your partner. You both must, however, have a set of rules and preset bounderies to safely argue without harming your partner or the relationship. This will lead to good arguments, which also leads to a deeper connection with your partner and more sex.

Why and When Does Arguing Start?

Arguing typically starts in stage two of relationships. In stage one, the masculine man kept releasing his testosterone into the feminine woman, while she kept releasing her oxytocin with the masculine man. After giving and giving and giving, you become empty and need to replenish. After the PEA (the love hormone) dies, the man is depleted of his masculine energy, and the woman is depleted of her feminine energy. Both will then revert to their polar opposite energies, and this is when arguing will start. Both partners will be more irritated (not living in their core energies) and therefore triggered more easily. This is why it is important to have healthy arguments.

You must not keep things inside, or else they will bottle up and explode. This being the independent stage for the woman, she wants to be heard, understood, to follow her passion, and be acknowledged for who she is. She needs to express her needs healthily.

Remember that needs come from nature and wants come from nurture. Therefore, nature is about polar opposites, and that means masculine versus feminine. Masculine being different from feminine means they are bound to have different viewpoints and perspectives on different subjects. It is important to respect your partner's viewpoint and yet be vulnerable even if you don't agree.

As Elizabeth Gilbert, the author of *Eat, Pray, Love*, says, *"You can measure the happiness of a marriage by the number of scars that each partner carries on their tongues, earned from years of biting back angry words."* Remember that arguing is a sign of passion and increases the dopamine hormone in your blood, which is a good thing because it can lead to makeup sex.

By remembering that you're both simply trying to resolve an issue, you can fight and argue in a way that will bring you closer. You can take the passion out of a fight with the following:

1. Count to ten.
2. Have a special "stop sign."
3. Don't try to win.
4. Understand that some issues aren't worth fighting for.
5. Hug your partner.
6. Do something impossible; try to understand your partner's feelings—this will change the dynamic.
7. Bring in some humor.
8. Provide a dose of pleasure.

You can also use the six commandments for a great argument. [3]

1. Don't insist on being right (that is your ego), insist on keeping the relationship right (unconditional love).

2. Speak up as soon as you feel anger rising; anger builds up into resentment, which is a major cause of divorce.

3. Listen to your partner's viewpoint.

4. Stick to the topic at hand (that applies especially to women who tend to connect everything and all the problems).

5. Don't say something you will regret.

6. Discuss, don't argue.

If all else does not work, try the **Three Ways to Stop Arguing**. [4]

No one wants to be in a relationship clouded with intensive and never-ending arguments. We all want to avoid them as much as humanly possible. However, they are bound to occur, and how you deal with them can be the difference between a strong relationship and one that needs work. Here are three ways to reduce your arguing and create an honest and connected relationship:

1. Get back into connection with each other. Because you are both in opposite energies (masculine and feminine), you see your partner as an enemy. Drs. Katie and Gay Hendricks of the Hendricks Institute suggests touching each other gently or breathing together. All the books and poems you read will mean nothing during the heat of the moment. When that moment comes, exaggerate your body posture or voice. When you exaggerate these, you ridicule the situation, and it bypasses your conscious and makes you laugh and ease the tension.

2. Tell the truth, or else you won't orgasm. In other words, keeping the truth under wraps blocks intimacy. Drs.

---

3   Influenced by Dr. Gail Saltz

4   Based on Drs. Katie and Gay Hendricks

Hendricks and Hendricks had a patient who hadn't had an orgasm for seven years. When asked, "What was the thing you didn't tell the truth about seven years ago?" she answered that she had had a one-night stand with her husband's best friend. Always tell the truth.

3. Exaggerate what you are doing; it breaks the pattern. When you turn conflict into play, you shift the fight dynamic. Start doing faces, use the fight energy, and transform that energy into something creative to solve the problem. Remember that words (or what you say) are only 7 percent of communication, so focus on your tone and body. According to Drs. Hendricks and Hendricks, any relationship struggle or problem you have is because creativity is not being expressed (look at the patterns of your fights). Conflicts and arguments are opportunities to become creative together, to grow closer. I will go even further by saying that if you fight from an ego or from a stage one or two viewpoint (you want to be right more than you want to save the relationship), you believe love is a compromise. If, on the other hand, you fight from a place of love or stage three, then you find creative ways to be passionate and learn new things together.

Tip 23

The best way to disrupt a heated argument: create a humorous interruption through a private joke you both share.

Why Arguing Is Important [5]

One of the reasons Mr. and Ms. Nice love each other but are not "in love" anymore (the correct words would be "are not attracted to each other") is that they do not argue and, as a result, they don't understand each other anymore. Relationships are often impacted when one partner cannot voice his or her feelings. [6]

Friction and arguments happen because of the opposite or physical chemistry, while understanding and compassion are about similarities or intellectual chemistry. The physical chemistry helps you keep your individuality, while the intellectual chemistry helps you keep your unity as a couple. You must dance between the two.

The most common diagnosis for why people fall out of love: They are not arguing enough. Remember that friends don't argue and lovers do. If you believe that arguing is not nice, then you are not being authentic. We are different, and that's why we argue. When you argue, you are not arguing for the sake of being right; you are arguing because you want to feel accepted for who you are. There is one rule to avoid fallout: Provide safety nets such as time limits for arguments. Richard A. Luck, love and relationship coach, reminds us that no one is wrong inside their own head. You can learn something and make your partner feel honored by saying this one simple thing: *"I'd never seen it that way. Can you please explain to me how you came to that conclusion?"*

We talked about Maslow's hierarchy of needs in Part I. Even emotional needs have their own ladder. Until the 1960s, the forbidden basic feeling was sex. It was considered something that should only be discussed behind closed doors. Since Mr. and Ms. Nice took over from Mr. and Ms. Bad, the taboo has moved from physical chemistry and basic sexual need to intellectual chemistry, and the forbidden emotional feeling is now anger.

If you're angry, then you're bad; that is what society has taught us. Incredible, isn't it? Why should you repress your anger? Do you know that anger is unrepressed emotions?

---

5   Influenced by Andrew G. Marshall

6   Marshall, *I Love You, but I'm Not in Love with You*

Therefore, we learned to avoid anger by getting detached, rationalizing, and repressing our emotions. What is the problem with these strategies we have been taught? They freeze every emotion, disconnect us from each other, and with time, even the positive emotions will subside. They don't tackle the real issue; it's like a mask. Should you not argue, then you will simply keep all that negative energy inside. What happens with all this unprocessed anger? You get sick.

To deal with our emotions and process them correctly, Andrew G. Marshall, marital therapist and the author of *I Love You, but I'm Not in Love with You*, proposes a simple statement that would remove all assumptions and keep things specific. He calls it the 3 Part Statement: *"I feel (x) when you (y) because (z)."* This is called being vulnerable, and this is powerful.

See the importance of arguing? It is not only healthy but absolutely essential to voice your emotions and prevent the negative energy of not arguing from building up inside of you and then coming out in very harmful ways. Conflict is part of any relationship, so you will have to accept it and deal with it or sink in the process.

Step Two: Forgiveness

Now that you have learned how to argue and understand why your partner is acting the way he or she does, it is time to consider forgiving him or her. When you forgive each other, you can liberate the stuck energy that flows between the two of you. Forgiveness is a decision and a process. However, the more you do it, the better you will become. [7] It is not about keeping a tally or determining who wins and who loses. Forgiveness is win/win in the sense that you grow and forge a deeper bond that is the base of a very powerful connection that moves you toward a stronger relationship.

Step Three: Regulate Your Emotions to Fall in and out of Love

A study by Dr. Sandra Langeslag, of the University of Missouri in St. Louis, and Nicolaas Jan van Strien, of Erasmus University in Rotterdam,

---

7   Rob and Kristen Bell, *The Zimzum of Love: A New Way of Understanding Marriage* (HarperOne, 2016).

on learning how to regulate positive emotions such as love revealed that an individual can indeed learn to up-regulate and down-regulate and that when they up-regulate, they feel more love.

"The idea that we can regulate love makes a lot of sense, because we can regulate every other emotion," says Dr. Holly Parker, a lecturer in psychology at Harvard University, where she teaches a course on the psychology of close relationships. There is plenty of evidence, she says, that *"we can dramatically change how we see something, how we see someone, based on how we frame our perspective."*

This is a very important step to learn.

Step Four: Dealing with Tough Times

Always remember your "why" in your relationship, and keep reminding yourself about it when times get tough. When they do and you can't see the big picture, work on small successes. Since love can be hard, you can look at the small love rather than the big one. When the big love seems far away or lost in a fog of uncertainty, try to refocus on the small love. You need small love and big love to achieve success. Feminine energy thrives on small love, and masculine energy thrives on big love.

The fourth step to creating a strong bond: deal with conflicts in your marriage. Here are some of the best ways to face conflict head-on and overcome it:

1. **The Month "Focus" Exercise.** When William James, a well-known philosopher and author, was young, he was very depressed and contemplated suicide. Today, he is recognized as a very positive philosopher who has written many books. How did he do that? How did he go from a depressed young man to a positive philosopher? He came across a quote from a French philosopher, who stated, *"Make a wager with the universe and give yourself a month to live as if everything had meaning."* How can you apply this to change your relationship? Live one month as if everything in your relationship had meaning. Focus on the positive (of your partner, your relationship, and your surroundings), be playful, and have fun as much as you can.

2. **The "Clarity" Exercise.** Are you focusing on all the bad things in your relationship?

Adjust your focus from everything that is wrong with your relationship to everything that is "right" by using the followings steps:

1. Write down all the things you want to experience or have in your relationship.

2. Co-create the movie of what you want with your partner, and live it daily.

3. Be clear with what you want from your partner; as time passed, you and your partner both changed, and so did the expectations; don't expect your partner to always read between the lines.

4. Model yourselves after Mr. and Ms. Grey. Look for three qualities that they have and emulate them. Look for three keys that make their relationship successful and implement them in yours, and find three ways you can improve your relationship.

5. The key to improving your relationship is to improve yourself. What is this one area you are blaming your partner for that you are not taking responsibility for? Replace controlling your partner with controlling yourself.

Step Five: Learning the Value of Giving Positive Attention

Hannah Fry, the author of *The Mathematics of Love*, says, *"Human emotion isn't neatly ordered or rational, and easily predictable, but Love is full of patterns, and mathematics is all about the study of patterns. Patterns from predicting the weather to situations in the stock market, the movement of the planets or the growth of cities; and none of these are neatly ordered or easily predictable either."*

Dr. John Gottman, a professor of psychology at Washington University, observed hundreds of couples having a conversation. The results showed that one of the most important predictors for whether a couple is going to get divorced is how positive or negative each partner is in a conversation with each other. Dr. Gottman teamed up with James Murray, a mathematician, to understand what causes the negativity spirals and how they occur. They predicted within 94 percent accuracy whether a couple would divorce or not within four years. Dr. Gottman found that positive attention outweighs negative attention by a factor of 5 to 1. [8]

Now for the fun part. Would you like to know how your partner will respond to you? These equations predict how a wife or husband is going to respond in the next turn of the conversation and how positive or negative they are going to be.

$$W_{t+1} = w + r_W W_t + I_{HW}(H_t)$$

$$H_{t+1} = h + r_H H_t + I_{WH}(W_t)$$

[9]

Where,

$W_{(t+1)}$: Wife's Reaction

w: Wife's Mood When Alone

$r_{(w)}W_{(t)}$: Wife's Mood When with Husband

$I_{(HW)}(H_t)$: Husband's Influence on Wife

$H_{(t+1)}$: Husband's Reaction

h: Husband's Mood When Alone

$r_{(h)}H_{(t)}$: Husband's Mood When with Wife

$I_{(WH)}(W_t)$: Wife's Influence on Husband

---

8   Marshall, *I Love You, but I'm Not in Love with You.*

9   John Gottman, Catherine Swanson, and James Murray, "The Mathematics of Marital Conflict," *Journal of Family Psychology:* https://www.johngottman.net/wp-content/uploads/2011/05/The-Mathematics-of-Marital-Conflict-Dynamic-Mathematical-Nonlinear-Modeling-of-Newlywed-Marital-Interaction.pdf.

Once again, Fry, the author of *The Mathematics of Love*, helps to explain this: *"These exact equations have also been shown to be perfectly able to describe what happens between two countries in an arms race. So that, an arguing couple spiraling into negativity and reaching the brink of divorce is actually mathematically equivalent to the beginning of a nuclear war."*

Tip 24

"Science is now confirming the wisdom of the great sages of the past, with research studies showing people who practice gratitude have closer relationships, are more connected to family and friends. Gratitude makes relationships flourish. As you increase your gratitude for any relationship, you will magically receive an abundance of happiness and good things in that relationship. The little irritations you once felt and the complaints you had in your relationships will disappear. You won't criticize, complain about, or blame them, because you're too busy being grateful for the good things about them."—Rhonda Byrne, author of *The Magic*

Step 6: Dealing with Conflicts

It is important to understand the role conflict plays in your relationship. As Dr. Leslie Becker-Phelps and Megan Kaye, authors of *Love: The Psychology of Attraction*, say, *"The most common times for a marriage to end are either five to seven years, due to a high level of conflict, or at fifteen to sixteen years, due to a lack of emotional connection."* Once the couple enters stage two, and Mr. and Ms. Bad become Mr. and Ms. Nice, they stop living in their natural energies and, as such, they become very irritable at the smallest things. This increases their fights, and the conflicts will rise tremendously at first because each of the partners wants to be accepted but they end up attacking each other. What started as a call for help turns into a misunderstanding? If Mr. and Ms. Nice continue with the conflicts without dealing with the true cause (returning to their core energies), then two scenarios will emerge: Either they will get divorced, or they will bottle up their feelings and resent each other. Then, as time passes, they will lose all their emotional connection.

However, even with the helpful steps just outlined, conflict is coming. Renee Wade, a dating and relationship expert, shares with us that a woman's feminine energy can help fuel a man's masculine energy, and this especially helps when there is a lot of tension and resistance in the relationship. They are connected and intermingle, and by going back to your core energy, this is how you can ease the tension. With that said, here are some important steps you can take to resolve conflicts with your partner:

1. Remember it's not about who is right but what is right (don't shoot your partner) by focusing on the solution, not the problem.

2. Write down how you feel about your partner. Put all your emotions down, and then go and face them. Put yourselves in a loving place (restate that you love each other), and then discuss.

3. When you are in conflict, ask your partner to share with you their deepest personal value to help shift the dynamic of the current energy. This helps strengthen the motivation for conflict resolution between the two of you.

4. Dr. Eric Berne, a psychiatrist dealing with human behavior, wrote about the three stages we can have: parent state (concerned with external rules, stage two of relationships), child state (concerned with feelings, stage one of relationships), and adult state (decision-based on observation, stage three of relationships). The best way to deal with a conflict is adult to adult (conflict resolution).

Tip 25
Multiple relationship experts have found that money and sex problems in relationships are often more about control issues.

It's Also Vital to Avoid the Three Long-Term Relationship Killers [10]

1. **Blame.** This is all about the other person. It's their fault, if they'd just change, if they weren't so this or that, then you both would have a wonderful relationship. Blaming is putting attention on all the things you don't like about your partner. What do you think happens when you do that? You see more and more of their faults and the things that bother you about them. Sooner or later, the relationship isn't any fun anymore, or even worse, it becomes daily torture.

2. **Shame.** This is blame directed at yourself. Instead of blaming your partner, you're blaming you. Blame is just as destructive, no matter whom it's aimed at. When you see the worst in you, where do you think your partner's attention goes? That's right—to all the worst in you. This is not the basis for a loving, long-term relationship.

3. **Justification.** This is another form of blame, but now you're blaming your situation or circumstances. If things were different, the relationship could be wonderful. Just like blame and shame, justification is a subtle way of putting attention where what you don't want, and it's a very effective long-term relationship destroyer. All of these "killers" arise from our culture's focus on looking for things outside of us to make us happy.

Dr. David Niven, the author of *100 Simple Secrets of Great Relationships*, says: *"Couples who talk to each other about how they disagree, and not just about the disagreement, spend less time arguing."* Since the single most important predictor of the success of a relationship is how a couple deals with conflicts, it is important to learn the strategy to navigate them. To do that, let's look at how happy couples argue and deal with the problems they face: [11]

---

10   Influenced by Chris and Janet Atwood
11   Based on Whitney Anthony

1. **They commit to deal with the problem.** This is especially important for people who have avoidant personalities; remember that the problem will not go away.

2. **They attack the problem, not the person.** This is especially important for people who have anxious personalities; remember that your partner is not your enemy.

3. **They listen.** Really listen to your partner to understand him or her and what they are trying to say; this is not a reference to the words they are saying. By listening to their tone and body language, you will know their deep message, that they are seeking love and attention.

4. **They are honest and transparent.** The more honesty and transparency you convey, the more trust will grow between you, and, as a result, the intimacy will thrive.

5. **They stop trying to mind read.** You and your partner have grown and changed over the years; stop the mind guessing and simply put everything out in the open.

6. **They list all their options.**

7. **They together choose the best solution for the relationship.**

8. **They look for growth opportunities** and what you can learn from the conflict instead of focusing on the negative.

9. **They are gracious.** Let your partner save face sometimes; it is good for the ego.

10. **They never withhold love.** Especially during a conflict, you can disagree with grace.

What Does All That Mean to You?

The truth is that resentment and bad conflict management will kill your relationship. *Moreover, there is nothing that can create resentment like endless arguments.* Your negativity threshold will influence your partner and how you react in conversations. The more you build things up by repressing your thoughts and feelings, the more resentment you will have toward your partner. The more resentment you have toward your partner, the more annoyed you will become at your partner.

The negativity threshold pushes this question: How annoying can the husband be before the wife gets really pissed off, and vice versa? A lot of misconceptions exist today that say a good marriage is about compromise, understanding, and allowing space. You must not let resentment build up. The happiest couples don't let that happen; they deal with situations as they occur. They trust each other to handle the other's emotions and find a way to work on things together. They are in it as a team and continually work on their relationship. If you are repressing, then you are NOT exhibiting trust toward your partner, which questions the very foundation of your relationship. Good partners don't let things go and don't let small things build up. This leads to divorce. The more you repress, the higher your negativity threshold; happy couples are the ones with the low negativity threshold.

Research by the HeartMath Institute showed the physiological and psychological effects of compassion and anger on people. According to the research, *"Heart-focused, sincere, positive feeling states boost the immune system, while negative emotions may suppress the immune response for up to six hours following the emotional experience."* [12]

> **Tip 26**
> The key to improving your relationship is NOT better communication (although body language and tone of voice do help slightly). What will dramatically improve your relationship is your CONNECTION (i.e., emotional chemistry).

Sometimes, conflict can truly take over your life. When it does, you might find that there is love lost and a disconnect between you and your partner. Don't give up when that occurs. Here are some steps you can take to make your partner fall in love with you again:

---

12 The HeartMath Institute

Twenty Ways to Make Your Partner Fall in Love Again [13]

1. Tell her she looks good in her jeans.

2. Catch her eye across the room at a party and wink.

3. Do the dishes while she takes a bath.

4. Gaze into her eyes.

5. Ask about her day, and then don't interrupt as she tells you about it.

6. Listen to her problems without trying to fix them. Sometimes, women just need to vent. Let her know that you hear her and that you will always be there for her.

7. Encourage her to take a night out with the girls.

8. Buy her something in which you know she'll look good.

9. Ask her opinion.

10. Give her a neck massage without expecting it to go somewhere.

11. Rent a chick flick, and snuggle while you watch.

12. Leave a love note on her pillow.

13. Kiss her goodbye before heading to work.

14. Encourage her dreams. Don't let her abandon them because she's a wife and mother.

15. Read to her before bed.

16. Appreciate her, out loud and often.

17. Buy her roses or chocolates on a day that is not her birthday or a major holiday.

18. Call her and let her know you've been thinking about her all day. Tell her you just wanted to hear her voice.

19. Book a hotel and take her away for the weekend, just the two of you.

20. Wash her car—preferably without a shirt.

---

13   Reference quote (TED Talk)

What is the main problem? You don't feel connected, and this connection creates the fights and the problems. One or both of you are trying to connect. Try to act the same way you were acting when you first started dating. Do new activities, and create dopamine in your brains.

Step 7: Learn How to Add Humor and Playfulness to Build a Deeper and Stronger Bond [14]

Sam Keen, an author, professor, and philosopher, says: *"We come to love not by finding a perfect person, but by learning to see an imperfect person perfectly."* People expect the person not to change or, if they grow, expect that they should adapt to them. In her book *Wabi Sabi Love*, Arielle Ford talks about an ancient Japanese method of finding beauty in imperfection, and she explains the art of loving your partner's imperfections. Once you learn to accept, embrace, and find the gift in your partner's imperfections, your life will never be the same. This exercise will create a deeper and stronger bond that will help you commit for your happy forever after.

In Japan, they use gold to fill the cracks in a vase because they believe the cracks are what make the vase look more beautiful. It is the cracks or the imperfections that allow love to come in. Ford goes on to talk about her imperfections and how she started feeling lighter when she saw them as more valuable than her perfections. She decided to make it a new lifestyle. *"The mess of papers on my desk was no longer evidence of my disorganized mind but rather a testament to my creativity and hard work. The stain on my skirt, obtained at a lunch meeting, was no longer embarrassing proof of my klutzy cutlery skills, but instead proof of my strong appetite for nourishment and for life."*

Learn to apply humor, listening, intimacy, and generosity at precisely those moments when you would normally retreat, says Ford. In the spirit of doing that, she started playing a game with her husband, Brian. Whenever she was acting strong and opinionated like her mom, Brian would say, "Is Sheila in the room?" referring to her mother. This reference is playful, adds humor, and directly eases the tension between the two. Similarly, whenever Brian was giving the silent treatment like his father used to, Arielle would call him "Wayne" playfully.

---

14   Based on Arielle Ford

I cannot stress enough how important this exercise is and how it can change your relationship dynamic. It helps you celebrate your imperfections rather than tolerate them. Isn't it more fun to play instead of fight? This is why adding in humor and playfulness builds a deeper connection and rekindles the sparks in your relationship.

Psychology teaches us that the best way to diffuse tension and to face fear is to use humor and make the tension ridiculous. Try it on your partner the next time he or she is being difficult or a pain in the ass. Humor bypasses the conscious, and all logic will break down and the pattern of thoughts will be disrupted. The more ridiculous or humorous, the better. Ford says, *"A key aspect of Wabi Sabi is learning to move our focus from what makes our partners so annoying to what makes our partners so unique. At its heart, this transition is about gratitude."*

The next time you get annoyed at your partner's habits and you want to change your partner, try changing your perception of the habit instead. If, for example, you get annoyed because your partner is overprotective and suffocating you, rather than seeing him or her as insecure and needy, look at your partner as someone who truly loves you and realize that there is no one else who cares so much about you. This overprotection represents your partner's love for you. Learn to embrace it rather than reject it. You cannot and will not change your partner; you can, however, change your perception.

Remember that Japanese vase? Your partner is the vase, and his or her imperfections are the cracks. By adding humor and being playful, you are painting the cracks (their imperfections) with gold and making your partner more lovable. You both will enjoy the process so much. One of the key secrets of couples that last for more than twenty-five years of marriage: They turn their fights into fun.

Step 8: How Difficult Emotions Can UNLOCK Intimacy [15]

According to Drs. Katie and Gay Hendricks, when you get angry with your partner, you must address your anger right away to prevent resentment from building up. What is the worst thing you can do? Ignore it because you are scared of how your partner might respond. When you don't express your emotions, they will come out and be expressed anyway. The worst part is that you will not be able to control them or anticipate them. Drs. Hendricks and Hendricks say, *"How you express them makes all the difference in building an intimate, supportive, honest connection, or an escalating series of fights, passive-aggressive encounters, or distant relations."* When you deny your feelings (even if you are fooling yourself), they will come out as a sickness and you will try to cure it, whereas the most effective way would be to acknowledge and express your emotions. *"In addition to freeing up all of your energy to create the relationship you want, sharing your emotions is also the most powerful way to open the flow of intimacy between you and your partner."* [16]

However, the second you unlock those difficult emotions, you will find a deeper connection. The resentment can act as a limiter to intimacy and love. It is like poison, and talking about your feelings is the antidote. Anger is a natural emotion, but not dealing with it head-on is a dangerous practice.

---

15   Based on Drs. Katie and Gay Hendricks.

16   Drs. Katie and Gay Hendricks, The Hendricks Institute.

Step 9: Avoid Cheating and Being Cheated On

There is a big misconception today that men and women can't stay in a relationship or with one partner for the rest of their lives. I believe they absolutely can, so long as men feel physically fulfilled and women feel emotionally fulfilled. If not, this can lead to cheating. While completely unjustified, it often happens when a man doesn't have sex, or a woman finds that she cannot vent and her feelings are not prioritized.

The First Reason People Cheat (Unmet Need: Biology)

Yes, this is true, especially if you don't satisfy the need of your man or woman. This happens when the man doesn't make the woman feel safe, secure, and protected, and the woman doesn't have sex and take care of her man's penis. Just like you ladies love to vent and talk about your emotions (that is how you feel loved, cherished, understood, and accepted), men love to have sex (that is how they feel loved, cared for, accepted, and validated). Those emotional needs are biological, and there is nothing we can do about it. The only thing we can do is understand each other's needs, embrace them, and create strategies around them. Masculine energy connects through the penis, while feminine energy connects through the heart.

Cheating occurs when the couple gets stuck in stage two. Ms. Nice is wearing her masculine mask (at home, with her partner), and Mr. Nice is acting feminine with his partner. Biology eventually takes over. Mr. Nice has replenished his testosterone and now wants to empty his hormones. After getting sexually rejected by Ms. Nice two or three times, Mr. Nice feels it's time to start looking outside for a feminine woman who will appreciate him, love him, and accept him for who he is. Mr. Nice doesn't mind having multiple partners since sex is his way of connecting and feeling loved (the more, the better).

At the same time, Ms. Nice has replenished her oxytocin and now wants to connect emotionally with Mr. Nice. After being emotionally rejected by him, Ms. Nice feels it's time to start looking outside for a masculine man who will cherish her, make her feel understood, and love her. Now, when Ms. Nice cheats, it is usually after a very long period of resentment, and she takes her time to build up a new relationship again. She will have one or two love affairs that will last since an emotional connection is her way of connecting and feeling loved.

Mr. Nice starts acting like Mr. Bad outside the house, and Ms. Nice starts acting like Ms. Bad outside the house. They become egocentric. They have this deep want to be needed again, and because they feel incomplete, they will seek that validation or need somewhere else because their biological and emotional needs are not being met by their partners. Mr. and Ms. Grey, who are in stage three of their relationship, know that monogamy is the only way.

The Second Reason People Cheat (Lack of Creativity: Biology)

Renee Wade, a dating and relationship expert, says, *"Boredom in having sex with the same person comes when one or both of you just don't make an effort to constantly find new ways to fill up the other person, and to grow, contribute and give more to your spouse."* While the first reason was that the partners are not present for each other, the second reason is that they lack creativity and have the same type of sex over and over.

What's the secret to monogamy? Always and consistently satisfy the needs of your partner, and be creative in doing so, especially when times are hard. You'll find a multiplicity of love if you can satisfy your partner's needs when times are hard (for example, when you are fighting or they feel weak). It's like the saying, "Everyone can love when it is easy; it is when it is hard that you know who really loves you."

Mr. Nice wrongly believes that he needs more than one woman to fulfill his sexual urges. He believes that Ms. Nice cannot fulfill him, so he goes through life cheating and yet still feels empty. If only he knew that by being present, grounded, and listening to Ms. Nice venting, he could have Ms. Nice and want only her for the rest of their lives.

Ms. Nice wrongly believes that by going out and having an affair, her needs will be fulfilled. If only she knew that by being present, supportive, and having sex with Mr. Nice, she could have Mr. Nice and want only him for the rest of their lives.

Nature has created men to be polygamous (you can see that by studying history). Mr. Bad always cheated when he went on long quests because he needed to feel loved. He connected through sex.

Nature has created women to be monogamous, so Ms. Bad always waited for Mr. Bad to come back. Meanwhile, she felt loved by venting with other women.

With nurture, feminine men have learned to be monogamous and masculine women have learned to be polygamous. How do Mr. and Ms. Grey dance between monogamy and polygamy?

The Grey Dance of Love between Porn Sex and Tantric Sex

To stay in a monogamous relationship, you must have both kinds of sex—to dance between porn and Tantric sex.

Why? Men crave porn sex, while women crave Tantric sex. Porn is a masculine act of sex without emotions or feelings; it is purely physical. It focuses on physical pleasure.

Tantric sex is a feminine act of sex with emotions that are about connection and attachment. It is physical and emotional. It is about being present, breathing. It is about mindfully touching and feeling your partner. Tantra focuses on physical and emotional pleasure.

In Tantra, you have to connect first (feel first), and then start sexual intercourse.

On the Other Hand, if Couples Only Have Porn Sex, Women Will Fake Orgasm

As sexual educator Christina Antonyan says, *"A man is turned on by a woman's smile, moans, the way she moves, and her radiant energy. A woman is turned on by a man's depth of presence and his attentiveness to her. Making love is sensual, not just physical. It's not an exercise. It's an erotically pleasurable journey of discovery."*

The key to making Ms. Nice orgasm? Be physically and emotionally present before, during, and after sex. Be playful, teasing, and court her all the time. Remember that feminine energy works in progress and process. When you disrupt the process (of courting her), you will have to restart from the beginning. So, if you want Ms. Nice to be horny all the time, keep teasing her, keep flirting with her, and never stop. Remember that the longer the foreplay, the bigger her orgasm. The foreplay is not only sexual; use the power of touch to make her feel desired, attractive, sensual, and sexual. Which leads us to this:

Three Must-Dos to Create More Sex and Intimacy
1) Understand each other's sexual love maps.
2) Discuss sexual shame and rejection.
3) Plan sex occasionally; it creates anticipation and shows dedication to the relationship.

Since men connect through sex and women must connect emotionally before sex, we have different needs, and it is important to share how we feel and process them. Once you do that, you will find that it is much easier to rekindle your sparks and connect to forge a better relationship with your partner.

> **Tip 27**
> Vulnerability is the way to deepen intimacy. Control, which comes from the ego, is masculine, while vulnerability, which comes from connection, is feminine.

Twenty-one Tips to Rekindle a Tired Relationship [17]
We move toward the end of our analysis of rekindling your sparks with your partner with an extensive list of the steps you can take to ensure you are creating a healthy relationship. Here are some of my favorites:

1. Agree never to give up. If you don't want to do the work, it will be the same with the next relationship.
2. Fixing a relationship involves two people.
3. Make new promises, and begin with a first step.
4. Take immediate action.

---

17   Based on Tiffany Taylor

5. Remake the future; don't relive the past.

6. Work on yourself first—two broken people cannot fix each other.

7. Be honest.

8. Begin with a fresh start, and set a new relationship goal.

9. Recreate the good times; act like you were acting when you first fell in love.

10. Laugh and have fun (disconnect from daily life); no one said life had to be serious.

11. Use the five intellectual love languages; spend quality time together, give sincere gifts, show appreciation, show affection—the power of touch—and do chores.

12. Celebrate how long you have been together.

13. Be spontaneous (suggest something extravagant); acting ridiculous breaks down defenses.

14. Communicate and listen.

15. Tell your partner how much he or she means to you; tell them all the things they have done and said that you are grateful for.

16. Learn to trust again.

17. Go the extra mile.

18. Recall your happiest memories.

19. Tell them and show them how much you care. Give a hug for no reason. Kiss them. Be there for them.

20. Share your dreams, and share your joys.

21. Make eye contact.

Each of these actions is a powerful and meaningful way that you can bridge the gap and reconnect to a relationship that is fizzling and lacking the passion you so desire. Start with one or two of these and add on until you are regularly implementing each one into your love life.

Step Ten: The Keys to a Successful Relationship

A study by the National Bureau of Economic Research found that marriage contributes to overall happiness, but the partners who were best friends were also the happiest. There are many keys, but here are some of my favorites:

Fourteen Keys of Success for Couples to Remain Passionately in Love for the Long Run

1. Trust, respect, believe (in yourself, in your partner, and in your relationship), and love unconditionally.

2. Be grateful, and focus on what your partner does right.

3. Communicate through the eleven love languages; accept your differences, celebrate your similarities, and connect emotionally.

4. Set common goals, and dream big. Review and discuss your goals and dreams often; see if you can find a way to support each other to reach your personal goals as well.

5. Effort should be put in by both sides.

6. Refuse to play the blame game; both should take ownership of the problem and find a way to solve it together.

7. Create special rituals and shared moments to honor your connection; go to bed at the same time, walk hand in hand, hug each other after work, etc..

8. Reaffirm your commitment.

9. Be present, listen intently before replying, and cheer each other.

10. Have fun sharing new and challenging activities (physical or mental).

11. Spend time together; even doing chores together can bond you both.

12. Be physically affectionate (hugs, kisses, etc.), and laugh together.

13. Challenge each other, but remain considerate of each other.

14. Learn continuously about each other. Invest in each other. Reflect on how you and your partner usually interact and talk about how you impact each other.

Scientists studied marriages in the 1970s because of a very high and unprecedented rate of divorce. Six years after the research, the couples were divided into two groups; let's call them happy couples and unhappy couples. According to Dr. John Gottman, one of the research scientists, happy couples look for the things they are grateful for and appreciate in their partner and environment, and they build respect and appreciation. Unhappy partners, on the other hand, look for their partner's mistakes.

Ms. Nice and Ms. Friend tend to be disrespectful of their partner by focusing on criticizing them, and criticism is found to be the number one factor that tears couples apart, according to Dr. Gottman. Ms. Nice and Ms. Friend tend to focus on the negativity more than the positive traits of their partner, and with time they start creating their own scenarios. Mr. Nice and Mr. Friend tend to give the silent treatment and ignore their partner, which damages the relationship as well as makes them feel not valued. It becomes a loop because as they start to go back and forth between criticism and silent treatment, the bond gets weaker and weaker.

This happens because unhappy couples get stuck in stage two and then find themselves in the reverse polarity. The feminine man and the masculine woman are both feeling more irritated because neither are living in their core natural energies. This leads to a drop in the level of satisfaction, and because they are not at ease in their natural energies, they cannot connect. Friedrich Nietzsche, famed philosopher, cultural critic, poet, and philologist, reminds us that, *"It is not a lack of love, but a lack of friendship that makes unhappy marriages."* Here is how this looks in comparison:

Unhappy Couples	Happy Couples
Live their lives based on fear	Live their lives based on love
Resist unpleasant situations	Accept unpleasant situations
Live with negative emotions such as hate and doubt	Live with positive emotions such as kindness and forgiveness
Put their egos in front of the relationship	Put the relationship in front of their egos
Blame and criticize their partner	Praise and trust their partner
Ungrateful and focus on lack and problems	Grateful and focus on abundance and solutions
Complain and are never present	Find solutions, take responsibility, and are present
Focus on what they see (realistic)	Focus on what is possible (see beyond the current reality)
Are negative	Are positive

Tip 28

If you try to win the argument (your ego talking), you are losing because you are putting your relationship in jeopardy (you are not loving unconditionally). You are living in stage one or two rather than in stage three. When you are trying to be right or win an argument, that means that your partner will lose, which means you are working against each other instead of creating a win/win situation. You are in competition with your partner—with your enemy. This is not a relationship, and this is not how you grow together.

See the differences? They are not only substantial but are frankly two sides of the same coin. Happy couples literally do the opposite of what unhappy couples do. You simply take your bad practices and flip them to good ones. It can be difficult in practice, but with a little effort, you can find yourself turning your bad habits into good ones.

The Science behind a Happy Relationship [18]

It isn't a theory, as there is great science in supporting how to build a happy relationship.

1. Happy couples have five positive interactions for every negative one (the 5 to 1 ratio) versus couples who ultimately divorce who have just 0.8 happy encounters for every one negative interaction (the 0.8 to 1 ratio).

2. The determining factor in whether couples feel satisfied with the sex, romance, and passion in their marriage is, by 70 percent, the quality of their friendship with each other.

3. Happy couples talk more; people in the most successful marriages spend five more hours a week being together and talking.

4. Happy couples have a positive interaction every day. They give a compliment, show their appreciation for something big or small, relive a fun memory, and/or do something nice for their partner.

5. They make time for intimacy. The happiest couples have sex two to three times a week.

6. More sex = more joy. People are 55 percent more likely to report higher levels of happiness when they have sex every few days.

7. The once-a-week boost: Having sex once a week makes people 44 percent more likely to have positive feelings.

8. When it comes to strengthening your relationship, studies show that the most crucial factor is how you celebrate your partner's good news; you show enthusiasm, ask questions, congratulate your partner, and relive your experience with them.

9. Couples who have new experiences together report feeling more loving and supportive toward each other and more satisfied with their marriages.

---

18   Credits to Happify

10. The Michelangelo Effect: Couples in the happiest relationships bring out the best in each other. They help each other get closer to becoming their ideal selves.

11. Couples who were asked to recall a moment that involved shared laughter reported being more satisfied in their relationship than those prompted to recall positive moments in their relationship.

12. When happy couples fight, they tend to diffuse the tension by showing humor, expressing affection, and conceding on certain points that their partner makes. Unhappy couples tend to do the following when they fight: criticize, show contempt, roll their eyes, act defensively, resort to name-calling, and tune out.

13. Think positive. Couples who can put a positive spin on their marriage have a 94 percent chance of experiencing a happy future together.

Based on a twenty-year British study, marriage leads to a big happiness boost for two years on average. After that, couples' happiness levels tend to return to what they were before the engagement. This is simply because PEA (the love hormone) has gone, and all you need is to reboot it to raise the thermostat.

You can implement endless tips and tools to create a healthy relationship for you and your partner. Should each of you take even a few of these steps to heart, you'll likely find yourself living in a more connected, deep, and loving relationship.

Step Three: Emotional Chemistry

The final step you can take to rekindle the sparks of your relationship: Develop your emotional chemistry. Women leave relationships because men are not caring for their emotions. Men leave because women are not having sex with them. While women feel loved when talking about their emotions, men feel loved when having sex.

When Mr. Nice is not present and not listening to Ms. Nice's emotions, she thinks he is not making her his priority. Mr. Nice can be a great parent, always there for the family, but he is not providing Ms. Nice her basic need for love and being heard.

When Ms. Nice is not present and not having sex, Mr. Nice thinks that she is not making him her priority. Ms. Nice can be a great parent, always there for the family, but she is not providing Mr. Nice his basic need for love-having sex. Men and women leave because of a lack of emotional connection.

Twelve Ways to Reconnect: The Road to Intimacy

Intimacy is about vulnerability, communication, and physical closeness. If the problem is a lack of intimacy, Andrew G. Marshall indicates a lack of play is often the problem. He says play is important because it tackles the three ingredients of intimacy: *Good verbal communication* and *physical closeness* are obvious byproducts of play, and in the excitement of the moment there is also *vulnerability*—nobody stops to think how she or he might look or whether they are being ridiculous. Play also reconnects us to our childlike sense of creativity (which is good for boredom). With that in mind, let us tackle twelve ways to deepen our connection.

1. Validate each other.
2. Grab opportunities to talk.
3. Set aside quality talking time.
4. Confide a secret.
5. Touch your partner.
6. Share.
7. Set the scene.
8. Slow down your lovemaking.
9. Find new erogenous zones.
10. Skip intercourse.
11. Make initiation a shared responsibility.
12. Experiment.

> **Tip 29**
>
> If you are too grounded, it will look as though you are rational and she is emotional; then you are competing while she is trying to connect.

And my personal favorite connection rituals are:
- ✓ Five minutes of eye contact
- ✓ Twenty seconds of hugging every time I see my partner; after twenty seconds of hugging, oxytocin is released
- ✓ Creating our own special rituals

Shelly Bullard outlines five very intriguing connection rituals. Reflecting on how you and your partner react, have fighting rituals, and play games, ask your partner when you hurt them and share what you learned about how to deal with emotions through your families.

At the end of all of this, our goal is to develop a greater level of intimacy, as that increase has a powerful way to rekindle sparks and connect you to your partner. According to Gurit Birnbaum, a psychology professor at the Interdisciplinary Center (IDC), a study conducted on 100 couples who kept a diary for six weeks on their sexual desires as well as their partner's responsiveness showed the following: Partners who are responsive to each other outside the bedroom can maintain their sexual desire because they feel special and both think their partner is more valuable.

What turns off intimacy for feminine energy?

1. Feeling Unseen (Solution: Give Attention)
2. Feeling Unsafe/Not Trusted (Solution: Give Reassurance)
3. Feeling Misunderstood (Solution: Give Real Presence)

What turns off intimacy for masculine energy?

1. Being Criticized (Solution: Admire and Appreciate)

2. Feeling Closed (Solution: Be Open and Playful)

3. Feeling Controlled (Solution: Give Freedom and Love)

As you manage these issues, you begin to better connect with each other, which leads to a greater level of love and reduced anger and frustration.

Connection: Open Your Hearts and Be True to Each Other

The best way to open the heart of another is through a concerted effort to open your own heart. It is about authentic connection and loving yourself more so you can be loved more. [19] Three main barriers to an authentic connection are:

1. **When you can't relax into the moment.** Physical, mental, or emotional tension prevents you from relaxing with your partner, as does worrying about the future or being resentful about the past. You've got to explore what distracts you from relaxing and opening your heart with your partner if you want a deeper connection.

2. **Masks of self-protection.** If you want a deeper connection, you've got to allow yourself not only to be present but also to be seen, felt, and known, just as much as you want to truly see, feel, and know your partner. This takes courage and vulnerability, but it's the only way to create an authentic connection.

3. **Trying to "get" something from your partner.** People can feel it when you're trying to get something from them. When they do, they normally put a wall up to protect themselves. This can be really obvious or quite subtle. Neediness kills the connection, so be responsible for your own needs.

---

19   Ruediger Schache, *Magnetic Heart: 10 Secrets of Love, Attraction and Fulfillment* (Hunter House, 2014).

Avoid these dangerous behaviors so you can remain open and true to your partner. It is easy to get lost in these challenges, but if you want to live "happily ever after," then this is more than a mere suggestion.

Can Two People Really Stay in Love Forever?

True love grows fonder with time. The more time passes, the more love grows because of the shared experiences. And guess what? Science confirms it. A study conducted by researchers from Stony Brook University verified the validity of the claim of men and women still being madly in love (the participants were married for an average of twenty-one years). After being shown pictures of their partners, fMRI scans detected intense activity in the ventral tegmental area of their brains, which is the region that produces dopamine, and this specific region showed similar activity with participants who were newly in love (in the attraction phase).

This proved that passion or attraction could last. These same scans showed activity in the ventral pallidum, a brain region associated with feelings of long-term attachment that produces serotonin (associated with calmness and less obsession). Here is what anthropologist Helen Fisher and social psychologist Arthur Aron had to say about the results of the study:

"The real difference between early-stage and late-stage romantic love: You feel that deep attachment and that you want to be with the person, but you don't have that early, manic obsession of when you first fall in love if you don't hear from the person you cry. If you ask people around the world whether romantic love can last, they'll roll their eyes and say 'probably not,' and most textbooks say that too. We're proving them wrong."

Early stage romantic love (stage one) is mainly about physical chemistry (differences, mystery, and dopamine), while late-stage romantic love (stage three) is mainly about emotional chemistry (connection, deep attachment, and serotonin).

> **Tip 30**
> When couples tend to avoid taking risks in relationships (because they are so much invested in them), they stop expressing their real desires. They are afraid of sexual conversations and what their partner will think of them, but this leads to a lack of eroticism, which might lead to affairs. There is no big difference between happy couples and unhappy couples. Happy couples just work daily on their relationships, while unhappy couples take their relationships for granted.

Esther Perel says, *"Desire doesn't happen when you are too close or too far apart. It's when I'm looking at my partner from a comfortable distance, where this person that is already so familiar, so known, is momentarily once again somewhat mysterious, somewhat elusive, and in this space between me and the other lies the erotic élan (desire)."*

Understanding How Masculine and Feminine Energies Argue Differently to Better Solve Challenges

If we are ever to reduce conflict in order to increase connection, then it only makes sense to conclude this chapter by recognizing and then celebrating the differences in how masculine and feminine energies argue. Remember that masculine and feminine energies argue differently. While a couple believes they are arguing about the same issues, they are actually upset about very different things.

For example, when Ms. Nice argues with Mr. Nice about the cup left in the TV room, Mr. Nice automatically assumes she is accusing him and thinks that it is always his fault. If Ms. Nice weren't indirect (Ms. Nice was brought up as Ms. Bad, which is why when she is emotional she goes back to her feminine energy) and had instead pointed out that she is overwhelmed with household work and feels unsupported, Mr. Nice wouldn't have felt accused and cornered. If Ms. Nice wants the help of Mr. Nice, she should talk to Mr. Nice's *nature love language*, especially when they are both tired. If Mr. Nice wants the help of Ms. Nice, he should talk to Ms. Nice's *nature love language*.

According to Dr. John Gottman, more than 69 percent of the problems couples have never get solved; instead, the conflicts get managed. It's about finding strategies to overcome them, and if sometimes you can't find a compromise, you can always come to an agreement.

Arguments are not created to win over your partner, because then you have already lost. True, you won the argument, but you lost your partner. Is that what you want?

A stage one relationship is about the ego talking, so: Win/Lose.
A stage two relationship is about the ego talking, so: Lose/Win.
A stage three relationship is about love talking, so: Win/Win.

Men, don't enter the blame game, and, women, don't try to fix your men. Dr. David Niven says, *"Married couples who report they never argue with each other are 35 percent more likely to divorce within four years than are couples who report regularly disagreeing."* Arguing is very healthy. It shows that you are two individuals in a relationship, and it keeps the sparks alive; however, the key is HOW you argue. You must communicate very clearly to your partner how you feel in order to avoid resentment. You won't agree on everything, but you have to find ways to settle those disagreements. Disagreements can strengthen your connection or increase the separation between you both. It is okay to renegotiate and change agreements when they do not work. Also, when all else fails, rely on these three steps to resolve any argument:

1. Understand where your partner is coming from.

2. Validate your partner by showing him or her that you understand their viewpoint.

3. Come to an agreement and compromise.

Important Note: When we argue, it is not because of a communication issue, but rather it is a problem of lack of connection. Both partners are feeling disconnected and unloved, and it is through an argument that they try to reconnect and express their unmet needs or unmet feelings.

By becoming conscious of how you communicate and work on communicating better with each other, you will forge a stronger bond and will connect at a deeper and more satisfying level. Learn how to better talk to each other, because you were brought up to talk in one way and it is time to embrace the other way. Learn how your parents communicated with each other, and if you are replicating it (which is the most probable case), then change that if you are not satisfied. Involve your partner in your process of change by asking him or her how they see you express yourself, share your feelings, listen, and so on.

You are in a relationship, for goodness sake. Act like you are in one. Share, learn, and grow together. Discover each other. Better yet, discover how you can make each other feel better. I can't repeat it enough: A relationship is a journey and a process, not a destination and a fixed product.

Mr. and Ms. Nice, look at your differences as an opportunity to grow, and commit to learn from those differences. *Talk to each other, not at each other.* Don't ignore the differences, but embrace them and create strategies to deal with them before they happen.

Friend at Last Sight

As you progress through this process of reconnecting, you might just find yourself getting closer to the relationship you desire. As Mr. and Ms. Nice, learn how to reconnect with your nature energies, recommit to each other, develop special rituals, learn how to argue and express your emotions, and learn how to be vulnerable and intimate. Learn more about your differences, and embrace them because it is your differences that create the spark. Cherish your similarities, for it is your similarities that bring you closer. Connect your differences and your similarities by being vulnerable and intimate, because this is how you grow stronger together and develop a deeper connection.

Mr. Nice, rediscover your masculine side, reconnect with it, and show it to your partner. If you don't want to be tamed anymore and for Ms. Nice to cheat on you or just criticize you, then set strong bounderies for a start.

Ms. Nice, rediscover your feminine side, reconnect with it, and show it to your partner. If you don't want to end up alone and alienated from Mr.

Nice, then be more feminine and start praising him for the good things he does rather than bitching about the things he isn't doing. Be vulnerable, and drop your mask.

However, that is not enough. You both have to create special rituals and learn how to manage arguments. You have to learn how to love your partner's flaws. Moreover, remember that change takes time, so be patient and commit.

You have a lot of work to do to rediscover your physical chemistry to recreate the sparks, rediscover your intellectual chemistry to come closer to the middle, and discover your emotional chemistry to grow deeper in love. It is time to redefine your relationship and transform yourselves and your relationship dynamic. Remember that the honeymoon period can be reawakened—all is not lost. It is time for you to start the Grey Dance of Love.

CHAPTER 13
THE GREY THEORY

IN PART I, YOU DISCOVERED the secret formula for love and began to understand the formula in all its aspects. In Part II, you received a how-to, "step-by-step" guide that takes you from where you are to where you want to be. If you want to delve further into secret techniques and recipes that will help you implement relationship changes in a practical way and want to learn "The Love Secrets to Successfully Dance Like The Greys," then please visit www.greydanceoflove.com and claim the additional chapter free of charge. There you will find extensive resources, including a variety of targeted workbooks to help you through your own journey. Last but not least, it is now time to put together all that we have learned and start applying the principles in the Grey Dance of Love.

However, before you go, this chapter will close the journey by discussing the Grey Theory in all of its glory. Andrew G. Marshall, the author of *I Love You, but I'm Not in Love with You*, says, *"For a long-term relationship we need to find enough similarities with our partner to make a connection, yet we need enough difference to stop the relationship from stagnating. Often it is the friction of rubbing off each other's rough edges that provides the spark of passion."*

Now that you have a wonderfully intimate understanding of the right ingredients to rekindle, win, and keep your man's or woman's heart, it is time for you to start the Grey Dance of Love. James Michael Sama best described this tango when he said, *"Women don't want someone who sways too far in either direction. Women want a man who is adventurous but also stable. They want a man who is going to challenge her but also support her. Who is going to empower her but also protect her? Who is going to seduce her but also respect her? A man who is going to provide for her but also not take away her independence to do so herself. A man who is going to make her feel sexy, but also make her feel safe."*

You'll find yourself out of the game if you go to any of the extremes. If you're too intense, people might view you as a jerk or a bitch. On the opposite side of the coin, you'll find yourself friend-zoned and/or cheated upon if you're too friendly. So dance. Take one step toward being a lover and one step toward being a friend, and then reverse your steps to do it again and again. You lose when you stop dancing. The dance is not static. Rather, it is a movement. It is the bouncing of energy from the masculine pole to the feminine pole. By stopping the dance, you are stopping the flow of energy. To find and then keep lasting love, men should balance between being Mr. Bad (their nature side) and Mr. Friend (their nurture side), while women should balance between being Ms. Bad (their nature side) and Ms. Friend (their nurture side). Men and women should be Grey.

Mr. Grey and Ms. Grey are dancing in love. They are dancing between the attraction side and the friendship side. Whenever their relationship gets too serious, they spice it up, and whenever the relationship gets too intense, they dance toward the friendship side. They always dance in love by bringing the set point back to the equilibrium. **Imagine a relationship full of compassion, understanding, fun, and passion ALL THE TIME. That is the Grey Dance of Love.**

Remember:

Mr. and Ms. Bad (the *lovers*) create problems.

Mr. and Ms. Nice (from *lovers* to *friends*) have the entitlement mentality.

Mr. and Ms. Friend (the *friends*) don't know how to create attraction.

But, Mr. and Ms. Grey dance between outgrowing problems and creating solutions.

To win a heart, you need physical chemistry and short-term emotional chemistry.

To keep that heart, you need intellectual chemistry and long-term emotional chemistry.

Love is ours for the taking. It is not some foreign concept only available in fairytales. It is a magical dance that we should all enjoy together. However, you have to understand the nuances of the dance and be careful not to step on your partner's toes. We see that happen often, and it can occur when you try to force love with the wrong person. You'll never recognize the Grey Dance of Love in this waltz, as it will always fall short of a harmonious connection.

Are You Forcing Love?

Have you tried to be friends with someone by force? It doesn't work, right? (At least not right away, not until you have developed enough things in common.) Forcing love doesn't work either; it is like trying to force being friends with someone. You are either compatible, or you are not. You can, of course, develop common values and goals that will lead to you becoming friends; but this will take time.

When you dance, are you forcing it, or are you pushing and pulling your partner?

Dancing is about pushing and pulling, not forcing or controlling. When you use the equation to move from the friendship side to the attraction side, you and your partner are dancing; you are pushing each other and pulling each other. This is why the equation is not about controlling or forcing love but allowing love to mature in its most natural habitat.

Mr. Bad is forcing love. He is living on the attraction side, and whenever the relationship gets serious and real feelings start to creep in, he forces love by bringing the set point back to the attraction side. Ms. Bad is forcing love. She is living on the attraction side, and whenever the relationship gets serious and real feelings start to creep in, she forces love by bringing the set point back to the attraction side.

Mr. Friend and Mr. Nice are forcing love. They are living on the friendship side, and whenever the relationship gets uncomfortable or when they have to man up and be more adventurous, they force love by bringing the set point back to the friendship side. Ms. Friend and Ms. Nice are forcing love. They are living on the friendship side, and whenever the relationship gets uncomfortable or when they have to woman up and be more adventurous, they force love by bringing the set point back to the friendship side.

Mr. Grey and Ms. Grey are dancing in love. They are dancing between the attraction side and the friendship side. Whenever the relationship gets too serious, they spice it up, and whenever the relationship gets too intense, they dance toward the friendship side. They always dance in love by bringing the set point back to the equilibrium.

I would say that by being purely masculine or purely feminine, you are forcing love because you are not the real you. You force people to believe in a certain image of you that makes you uncomfortable.

I wonder who is forcing love now.

After all, we all need a certain safety and a certain unpredictability. Imagine dancing between safety and unpredictability. Imagine being safe in an unpredictable environment.

If your friend or partner loves you and you love them back, help them live or rediscover their nature energy and let them help you discover your nurture energy. Once both of you are bathing in your core energies and learn to develop your nurture energies, you will start dancing the most beautiful salsa you have ever seen. Moreover, once you do that, you can begin the process of finding the change you need to find to connect to the Grey Dance of Love meaningfully.

Are We Really Changing?

Change is an important part of life, and our sensitivity and awareness regarding change can prove to be a tremendous difference-maker. Should you strive to do the Grey Dance of Love, you'll find yourself transitioning and changing along the way. During your transitional period, keep your friendly qualities (if you are Mr. and Ms. Nice or Mr. and Ms. Friend), while you develop your lover qualities. Work toward the new while still celebrating the old. Similarly, keep your lover qualities (if you are Mr. and Ms. Bad), and develop your friendly qualities. Don't forego one for the other. The greatest win is in the middle. In other words, keep on playing the dance of polarity.

Remember that you are not changing yourself, just remodeling your under-developed love ingredient to reach your full potential. You are showing a repressed part of your character and discovering more knowledge, skill, and experience that you have inside you to become a sexier person.

Learning to be more masculine, feminine, or even playful is not chang-ing; it is not being inauthentic. You are embracing a skill you were born with but didn't develop, and then you are working to expand your current abilities. You might stumble, and people might even find you awkward or different at times. Even when that might occur, remember that it is not about them but about you. And because people are accustomed to a certain version of you, they may resist letting go of the old you and fear the change because they don't understand what is occurring in front of their very eyes. However, that is ultimately their problem and not yours. You are changing for the better to connect and find a lasting relationship. That should be celebrated and enjoyed.

With the ingredients of your love potion in your hands—and now that you have the secret recipe to mix the right ingredients with the right dosage to make your magical love potion and create the love that you want—it is time for you to start dancing.

A Final Word from the Greys

In the end, it's all about being Grey, like us. That leaves us with our four commandments to build great relationships.

1. We value growth over outcome.

2. We take ownership of our problems.

3. We are honest about our feelings.

4. We practice love.

Remember that we chose each other because we have a common destination—love. We knew that there would be times when our relationship would test us. This is why we accept and welcome fights and different viewpoints. They help us grow. We are not in a relationship to cater to our personal needs; we are mature enough to fulfill them ourselves. We are in a relationship to grow together and push each other further than we ever would have alone. We take ownership of our problems by approaching them with a positive mindset, unlike unhappy couples, who have a victim mentality and approach their problems with a negative mindset.

We ask ourselves questions such as, "What can I learn from the situation?" or "What is he/she trying to trigger in me?"

Unhappy couples ask different questions, such as, "What's in it for me?" or "How can I win and obtain what I want?"

We never sugarcoat problems or emotions. We are honest with our emotions, even when they hurt, because that is how we grow and trust our partners. We know that we all have wounds and limiting beliefs from our past lives, which our partners will test and sometimes trigger. We expect to be abandoned or rejected, and we face our emotions together by understanding them. We are not in a pleasing mindset but rather in the have-fun mindset. We don't care who is right; we prefer to work out our issues to improve the relationship. It is not me versus him or me versus her; rather, it's us versus the world.

We have a growth and abundance mentality, while unhappy couples have a stagnant and scarce mentality when it comes to love and relationships. We believe that a relationship is a journey of evolution rather than a destination, which is also why we understand that there is no peak all the time and that sometimes there are ups and downs. We don't want our partners to be or act in a certain way; we prefer to let them be and act as they please because that is unconditional love and that is what we are here to experience.

When you love yourself first, when you are passionate about your life first, when you are connected to yourself, then you can connect, love, and be passionate with your partner. It's about "being" love rather than "seeking" or "getting" love. Once we "became" love, we started learning and understanding the Love Formula to better communicate with each other.

Intellectual chemistry helps us be more appreciative of our similarities and love each other more.

Physical chemistry helps us be more understanding of our differences and accept each other just the way we are.

Emotional chemistry helps us connect with each other deeply.

We know that any one ingredient alone is powerless, but together they are the secret glue that binds us. We also understand that biology plays a part, a very big one, and that evolution has changed how we humans perceive love. We were born to procreate (biology) but evolution (most probably because we are living many more years) created romance and love (nurture) in order for us to enjoy our years (and nurture helped us understand each other more and be more compassionate). We also discovered that procreating alone doesn't work and that growing up with a friend doesn't work either. So we tried a NEW method. We tried combining both. We are best friends, and we are lovers.

We embraced our biology. We embraced the changes nurture gave us, and we created a bridge.

We both know that we have danced too much into the friendship side when we are too friendly and bored by our routine. When our triggers ring, we know it's time to rekindle the passion, and it's time for Mr. Grey to be more masculine and for Ms. Grey to be more feminine. And when polarity time comes, we know that fun is on the way. Writer Lisa Page says, *"The moment you feel that deep passion that magnetically attracts you to your partner, what you're FEELING is an arc of energy flowing between you."*

We will let you in on some of our secrets.

1. Make a commitment and a pact with each other.

2. Write a list of successful relationships every year.

3. Celebrate your anniversary in a special way every year.

4. Be adventurous, and have fun during sex.

5. Encourage each other to pursue his or her interests and passions.

6. Speak your truth.

7. Celebrate each other's growth and evolution.

8. Walk together.

9. Talk together.

10. Sleep naked.

11. Be lovey-dovey, and kiss passionately.

12. Love unconditionally, not despite the other's flaws, but because of them—they allow you to be imperfect too.

13. Say "I love you" every day.

We also discovered that to **attract** each other we have to dance with our biology, and to **keep** each other we have to dance with our nurture (or what society taught us). We discovered that we have to dance between nature, nurture, and connection to be together (attract and keep) and live our happy forever after.

We love Charles Darwin, and we strongly believe in his wise words and theory of evolution: *"It is not the strongest of the species that survives, nor the most intelligent that survives. It is the one that is most adaptable to **change**."*

The strongest species = Nature = Biology = Physical Chemistry

The most intelligent species = Nurture = Society = Intellectual Chemistry

The most adaptable to change species = Nature + Nurture + Connection = Physical Chemistry + Intellectual Chemistry + Emotional Chemistry

Even our physiology has adapted our biology to the new reality and shows us that we can no longer live in the past.

Authors Dr. Leslie Becker-Phelps and Megan Kaye stated in *Love: The Psychology of Attraction*, "*We've been through 2.5 million years of human evolution, and our brain size has tripled to cope with communication, tool-use, and love.*"

A Word from the Little Prince
Perhaps the Little Prince, who started our journey in this book, offers us the greatest treasures. In his own words:

> "*We only know the things that we tame. Men don't have time anymore to get to know anything. They buy ready-made stuff from merchants. But since there does not exist a friend merchant, men don't have friends anymore. If you want a friend, tame me,*" *said the Fox.*

> "*What should be done?*" *asked the Little Prince.*

> "*We must be patient,*" *answered the Fox.* "*You must first sit a little far from me. I will stare at you from the corner of my eye, and you won't say a thing. Language is a source of misunderstanding. But, every day, you can sit a little closer . . .*"

> *The Little Prince came back the next day.*

> "*It would have been better to come back at the same time. If you come, for example, at 4 o'clock in the afternoon, starting at 3 o'clock I will start to be happy. At 4 o'clock, already, I will become restless and will start to worry: I will discover the price of happiness. But if you come at any time, I won't know at what time to dress my heart . . . there must be rituals.*"

There are eight golden treasures inside this quote for men and women seeking love.

The first treasure: Love is built, and like everything that is built, it needs time.

The second treasure: You can't buy love. There are no shops that sell it. If you want love, you have to build it yourself, but remember that it takes two to tango. That is why people don't love anymore; they want a quick fix or love on the go. If you want love, learn to tame someone and be tamed.

The third treasure: Patience. It's about dancing back and forth between being a friend and being a lover. It's about integrating our nature with our nurture.

The fourth treasure: Do not push a lot too soon; build things gradually.

The fifth treasure: Language is a source of problems. Men speak with their penises first and their hearts second, while women speak with their hearts first and their vaginas second.

The sixth treasure: Set love habits and rituals.

The seventh treasure: Set expectations and bounderies. Feminine energy requires bounderies from the masculine energy to control the chaos instilled by the feminine energy.

The eighth treasure: Fulfill those expectations.

A Final Word

Consumed by today's hectic pace, we don't take the time to build relationships. We then wonder why we see an increase in divorces. We still believe that a relationship is just about having our own needs fulfilled (nature). We can no longer afford to live only in nature if we want to build magical relationships.

Divorce rates are at an all-time high, and they are mainly due to wanting the sparks and only the sparks. The irony: The sparks are the easiest thing to build and rebuild, anytime you want to work on them. You can recreate the love hormone PEA anytime you want. The friendship part is much more important to keep the relationship alive; of course, emotional chemistry plays its role as well. The friendship part combined with an emotional connection is what will lessen divorce rates. When you are friends and then build the sparks, I promise you that marriage rates will be skyrocketing.

Our biggest challenge: Men and women both believe they can do it by themselves. In that state of mind, no one wants to help the other succeed; this is their ego talking—stages one and two of relationships.

After choosing the right person, you can just let the relationship flow naturally. Whenever you believe there is not enough passion, add more sparks, and by that I mean for the man to go back to his core masculine energy and for the woman to go back to her core feminine energy. Also, be more playful. If you believe there is too much tension or fights, start to dance toward the friendship part of the formula.

This short story resonates very much with stages one and two of relationships:

> *"Once upon a time there was an island where all the feelings lived together. One day there was a storm in the sea, and the island was about to get drowned. Every feeling was scared, but Love made a boat to escape. Every feeling boarded the boat, and only one feeling was left. Love got down to see who it was. It was EGO. Love tried and tried, but ego wasn't moving. Meanwhile, the water was rising. Everyone asked Love to leave him and come in the boat, but Love was made to love. In the end, all the feelings escaped, and Love died with Ego on the island. The moral of the story is that Love dies because of EGO."*

We will only see a decrease in separation and divorce when we tame our egos. Everything will be much easier if and when both men and women put aside their egos and work on making their relationships work by triggering the sparks and embracing friendship by and through doing the dance. However, the question is: Are they both ready to do so?

Men and women today want fairytale romances while still believing destiny will control their outcomes. No one wants to work for the perfect relationship. But what if fairytale romances and destinies have been redefined? Men and women are expecting a world that no longer exists. They are still seeking someone who will save them.

Women still expect their men to swoon over them all the time, and men still expect their women to nurture them all the time. A relationship is not a destination but rather a beautiful journey. If nothing else, this book should have helped you better understand that.

To the women reading this book: When you are fighting and the tension is high, know that you have to be direct with your man, and tell him what you want from him. Tell him the plan and strategy from A to Z and stop the guessing games (only when the tension is really high). Accept men for who they are. They love sex because that's how nature created them. If you want to punish them by not having sex, they will punish you by not listening to you. You see, it goes both ways.

And to the men: First and foremost, listen (to acknowledge her). She fixes her problems by talking about them, and only then can you offer her a solution. If you insist on fixing her problem, then instead of giving her the answer, rephrase it as a question. She will think that she came up with the solution. [1] Accept women for who they are. They love to talk, especially about their emotions. That is how nature created them.

If you master the three ingredients of the Love Formula (first within yourself), they will guide you to ultimate and blissful love.

By mastering intellectual chemistry, you are making your partner your best friend, and that is a third of the requirement for a blissful relationship (nurture). By mastering physical chemistry, you are making your partner your complementary energy, and that is a third of the requirement for a blissful relationship (nature). By mastering emotional chemistry, you are integrating the dance between nature and nurture, and that is a third of the requirement for a magical relationship (nature and nurture integrated).

Nothing will stop us from living in a magical daily state of love when we master intellectual chemistry, emotional chemistry, and physical chemistry.

And now, after roaming across that ocean, searching for the pieces of your broken heart, you understand that it is you, and only you, who is in control

---

1   Carine Sarkis offered me this brilliant tip.

of your heart and that you should be its only guardian. That's the moment when you stop building walls, stop giving control of your heart to someone else, and reclaim it for your own. Keep it in a place where no one will ever reach it. Share parts of it when you believe it's necessary. For through your journey, you have picked up not only pebbles of wisdom, but you have also regained your masculinity or femininity, discovered your true self, and allowed yourself to be who you really are and not what society mistakenly makes you believe that you have to be. Step up your game, go and get the woman or man of your dreams, but make her/him work for it. Don't do all the work yourself.

Yes, we all want magic, and yes, we can all have magic. Magic is in our hands!

We have been told that love is a fairytale, and I showed you it could be.

We have been told that love is magical, and I showed you it could be.

Yet, we have also been told that love is not in our hands, and yet I showed you it should be.

I showed you how to have your fairytale and live in magic.

I showed you the home passion that awaits you once you develop all the ingredients of your love potion.

I showed you how to be happy.

I showed you how to be loving.

I showed you how to be passionate.

I showed you the Grey Dance of Love.

But now, my friend, it is up to you to fulfill your obligation and responsibility and just DANCE.

Wishing you a Happy Forever After.

PART III

Afterthoughts

SOMETIMES WE ARE NOT AWARE of how love impacts our lives and how we can impact the lives of others. I want to thank you for investing in this book and I want to applaud you for you have just helped a child. Your contribution just gave an education to a child through the Unstoppable Foundation. As per my promise, I will give $1 from the profits of this book to the Unstoppable Foundation. The only way to change the world is by raising awareness and this can only be done through education.

You can continue your journey and adventure to learn more about love, how to love, and how to be loved through *The Grey Dance of Love* workbooks, which are more interactive and topic specific, or contact us for a keynote and tailored workshop. My hope is that you will choose the right resources for you and share them. Love should be spread throughout the world, and the more we share, the more we illuminate the lives of others.

Unstoppable Foundation empowers lives through education so that communities never need charity again.

The Unstoppable Foundation is a non-profit humanitarian organization that moves communities in developing countries from surviving to thriving so that every person can realize their full potential. It is their vision that every child receives access to a quality education.

The Foundation takes a holistic approach to creating sustainable education by supporting community development through our Sponsor A Village (SAV) program, a proven 5-Pillar Development Model. SAV incorporates everything crucial to lifting communities out of poverty and removing obstacles to educating children by providing access to education, clean water and sanitation, healthcare, food and nutrition, and income training for parents.

To ensure students are able to gain employment in their community and increase the standard of living for themselves and their families, the Foundation awards full scholarships to qualifying graduates in the Maasai Mara region of Kenya. Scholars also complete the Unstoppable Leadership Academy, a two-year certificate program enabling students to achieve their full potential as leaders in their families, communities, and the world at-large. This high level education is the final piece to providing a full circle solution to transform this region of the world.

100% of donations to the Unstoppable Foundation fund our international programs.

To learn more about the Unstoppable Foundation, visit:
UnstoppableFoundation.org

Hearts to be Heard

Giving a Voice to Creativity!

Wouldn't you love to help the physically, spiritually, and mentally challenged?

Would you like to make a difference in a child's life?

Imagine giving them:
confidence; self-esteem; pride; and self-respect.
Perhaps a legacy that lives on.

You see, that's what we do.
We give a voice to the creativity in their hearts,
for those who would otherwise not be heard.

Join us by going to

HeartstobeHeard.com

Help us, help others.

Book References

Allen, James. *As a Man Thinketh*. Freeland Press, 2017.

Becker-Phelps, Leslie and Megan Kaye. *Love: The Psychology of Attraction: A Practical Guide to Successful Dating and a Happy Relationship*. DK, 2016.

Bell, Rob and Kristen Bell. *The Zimzum of Love: A New Way of Understanding Marriage*. HarperOne, 2016.

Black Belt Seduction. *Crash Course: Expert Answers to the Pick Up Artist's Most Commonly Asked Questions*, 2016.

Boggs, Mat. *The 5 Feminine Qualities High Value Men Find Irresistible*. Mat Boggs, 2014.

Boothman, Nicholas. *How to Make Someone Fall in Love with You in 90 Minutes or Less*. Workman Publishing Company, 2009.

Branson, Sir Richard. *Screw It, Let's Do It: Lessons in Life and Business*. Virgin Books, 2007.

Byrne, Rhonda. *The Magic*. Atria Books, 2012.

———. *The Power*. Simon and Schuster Ltd., 2010.

Carnegie, Dale. How to Develop Self-Confidence and Influence People by Public Speaking. Gallery Books, 2017.

Chengxiang, Song. *The Core Solution Report*.

Collins, Suzie and Otto. *The Relationship Attractor Factor*. Self-published ebook.

D'Cruz, Chris. *Finding "The One": Secrets to Finding True Love*. Self-published ebook.

———. *How to Get Women You Desire into Bed*. Self-published ebook.

———. *Red Hot Romance: Secrets to Igniting the Passion in Your Love Life*. Self-published ebook.

DeAngelis, Barbara. *Are You the One for Me? Knowing Who's Right & Avoiding Who's Wrong*. Harper Element, 2013.

———. *Secrets About Men Every Woman Should Know.* Harper Element, 2012.

de Saint-Exupéry, Antoine. *The Little Prince.* Mariner Books, 2000.

Dweck, Carol S. *Mindset: The New Psychology of Success.* Ballantine Books, 2007.

Dwoskin, Hale. *Wealth and Success*

Eker, Harv T. *Get Hardwired for Success.* Peak Potentials, 2012.

Ford, Arielle. *Wabi Sabi Love: The Ancient Art of Finding Perfect Love in Imperfect Relationships.* HarperElixir Reprint edition, 2013.

Gray, John, MD. *Mars and Venus Together Forever: Relationship Skills for Lasting Love in Committed Relationships.* Vermilion, 1996.

———. *Men Are from Mars, Women Are from Venus.* Harper Thorsons, 2015.

Hansen, Carolyn. T*he Wealthy Entrepreneur Mindset: How to Attain It, How to Develop It.* Kindle Edition, 2016.

Hay, Louise L. *The Power Is Within You.* Hay House, 1991.

———. *You Can Heal Your Life.* Hay House, 1984.

Hicks, Esther and Jerry. *Ask and It Is Given.* Hay House, 2004.

———. *The Astonishing Power of Emotions.* Hay House, 2008.

Ledwell, Natalie. *Never in Your Wildest Dreams: A Transformational Story to Tap into Your Hidden Gifts to Create a Life of Passion, Purpose, and Prosperity.* Sherpa Press, 2013.

Lorius, Cassandra. *Tantric Sex: Learn How to Use Your Sexual Energy.* Thorsons, 2000.

Maltz, Maxwell. *The New Psycho-Cybernetics.* Prentice Hall Press, 2002.

Marina, Rebecca. *10 Tips: How to Get People to Like You in 30 Seconds or Less.* CelebrationHealing.com, 2005.

Marshall, Andrew G. *I Love You, but I'm Not in Love with You: Seven Steps to Saving Your Relationship.* Bloomsbury Paperbacks, 2016.

McCraty, Rollin. *Science of the Heart: Exploring the Role of the Heart in Human Performance.* The HeartMath Institute, 2015.

Meet Your Sweet. *How to Be the Strong Man That Women Crave*—Slade Shaw.

———. *Inner Game Tactics: Interview with Carlos Xuma.*

Mohr, Barbel. *How to Make Declarations to the Universe.*

Nhat Hanh, Thich. *Cultivating the Mind of Love.* Parallax Press; 2nd edition, 2004.

Orban, Christine. *Petites Phrases Pour Traverser La Vie En Cas De Tempête . . . Et Par Beau Temps Aussi (French).* Albin Michel, 2007.

Pease, Allan and Barbara Pease. *The Body Language of Love.* Manjul Publishing House, 2012.

————. *The Mating Game: Why Men Want Sex & Women Need Love.* Orion, 2010.

Pilinski, Michael. *The Three Keys to Seducing Any Woman.* Self-published ebook.

Proctor, Bob. *You Were Born Rich.* LifeSuccess Productions, 1997.

Ruiz, Don Miguel. *The Four Agreements.* Amber-Allen Publishing, 1997.

————. *The Mastery of Love: A Practical Guide to the Art of Relationship.* Amber-Allen Publishing, 1999.

SalesForce. *20 Customer Service Best Practices.*

Schache, Ruediger. *Your Magnetic Heart: 10 Secrets of Love, Attraction and Fulfillment.* Hunter House, 2014.

Sharma, Robin. *The Leader Who Had No Title: A Modern Fable on Real Success in Business and in Life.* Simon and Schuster UK, 2010.

Stanway, Andrew. *Massage Secrets for Lovers: The Ultimate Guide to Intimate Arousal.* Da Capo, 2002.

Strauss, Neil. *Rules of the Game.* It Books, 2009.

Summers, Mia and Amy Waterman. *Conversation Chemistry.* Self-published ebook.

Tate, Brett. *The Professional Bachelor Dating Guide: How to Exploit Her Inner Psycho.* Cambridge Publishing, LLC, 2007.

Taylor, Tiffany. *The Single Man's Guide to Great Women: A Step-by-Step Guide to Help You Meet, Attract, and Date the Girl of Your Dreams.* Self-published ebook.

————. *Tiffany Tells All: The Attraction and Seduction Audio for Men*

Templar, Richard. *The Rules of Love: A Personal Code for Happier, More Fulfilling Relationships.* FT Press, 2013.

Vitale, Joe. *Spiritual Marketing.* AuthorHouse, 2002.

Westra, Christopher. *Realms of Joy: Time of Light.* I Create Reality, 2004.

Wilcox, Woody O. *Guy Gets Girl: A Guy's Guide to: Meeting and Greeting, Dating & Mating the Various Women That You Desire.* Self-published ebook.

Appendix II
TED Talks and YouTube Videos

Helen Fisher, "The Brain in Love," February 2008, TED Talk [video], https://www.ted.com/talks/helen_fisher_studies_the_brain_in_love.

Helen Fisher, "Why We Love, Why We Cheat," February 2006, TED Talk [video], https://www.ted.com/talks/helen_fisher_tells_us_why_we_love_cheat.

Arielle Ford, "Art of Love Relationship Series," 2016, YouTube series [video], https://www.youtube.com/watch?v=WI0H-6cusGk.

Hannah Fry, "The Mathematics of Love," April 2014, TED Talk [video], https://www.ted.com/talks/hannah_fry_the_mathematics_of_love.

Christian Pankhurst, "Night 3—Building Polarity and Sacred Sexuality," June 2013, YouTube [video], https://www.youtube.com/watch?v=QFQwdIoQWYY.

Esther Perel, "The Secret to Desire in a Long-term Relationship," February 2013, TED Talk [video], https://www.ted.com/talks/esther_perel_the_secret_to_desire_in_a_long_term_relationship.

REFERENCED ARTICLES

Aishwarya. "Stages of Love: Signs, You're Infatuated." *Like Love Quotes.* http://likelove-quotes.com/stages-love-signs-youre-infatuated/.

Albo, Bonny. "Why Can't I Create Chemistry?" *About Relationships* (April 30, 2016). http://dating.about.com/b/2010/02/15/why-cant-i-create-chemistry.htm.

Amante, Chase. "Sexual Tension: 7 Ways to Make Women Excited and Randy." *Girls Chase.* http:// www.girlschase.com/content/sexual-tension-7-ways-make-women-excited-and-randy.

Anthony, Whitney. "10 Ways That Happy Couples Argue Differently." *The Mind Unleashed* (April 7, 2015). https://themindunleashed.com/2015/04/10-ways-that-happy-couples-argue-differently.html.

Antonyan, Christina. "How 'Sexual Energy' Flows in Your Body." *Confident Lover* (January 8, 2015). http://www.confidentlovers.com/flow-sexual-energy-sexual-polarity/.

———. "3 Things You Don't Know About Nipple Orgasms." *Confident Lover* (November 20, 2014). http://www.confidentlovers.com/nipple-orgasms/.

———. "Penis Size—Is Your Penis the Right Size for Her Vagina?" *Confident Lover* (January 1, 2015). http://www.confidentlovers.com/does-size-really-matter/.

———. "How to Be the Best Lover She Ever Had." *Confident Lover* (July 2, 2015). http:// www.confidentlovers.com/how-to-be-the-best-lover-shes-ever-had-2/.

———. "Woman's 'Hidden' Hot Spots." *Confident Lover* (October 23, 2014). http://www.confidentlovers.com/womans-hot-spots/.

Barnes, Andrew. "How to Relate to the Opposite Sex—The Essential Guide." *Raw Attraction Magazine.* http://rawattractionmagazine.com/relationship-tantra/.

Bashedly, Anna. "This Is What It Means to Truly Love Her." *Idea Spots.* http://ideaspots.com/truly-love-her/.

Baumann, John and Micki. "Overview of the Masculine-Feminine Polarity." *Love Sedona.* http://www.lovesedona.com/02.htm.

Ben Shalom, Aleeza. "How to Create Chemistry." *Aish.com.* http://www.aish.com/d/w/How-to-Create-Chemistry.html.

Benson, Kyle. "The Top 3 Vulnerabilities That Ruin Your Relationship." *The Minds Journal.* http://themindsjournal.com/vulnerabilities-ruin-your-relationship/.

———. "3 Must Do's For Amazing Sex." *Kyle Benson.* https://kylebenson.net/3-must-dos-for-amazing-sex/.

———. "8 Profound Lessons Intimate Relationships Teach Us." *The Minds Journal.* https://themindsjournal.com/8-lessons-intimate-relationships-teach-us/.

Bratton, Susan. "Stealth Turn-Around Tricks." *Personal Life Media* (2011). http://members.personallifemedia.com/wp-content/uploads/2011/04/RHD-Stealth-Turn-AroundTricks.pdf.

———. "Polarity: How to Increase Your Masculine Energy for Feminine Attraction." *Personal Life Media* (November 12, 2012). http://personallifemedia.com/2012/11/polarity-how-to-increase-your-masculine-energy-for-feminine-attraction/.

BST. "Hunter Gatherer Brains Make Men and Women See Things Differently." *The Telegraph* (July 30, 2009). http://www.telegraph.co.uk/news/uknews/5934226/Huntergatherer-brains-make-men-and-women-see-things-differently.html.

Bullard, Shelly. "4 Qualities of a Conscious Relationship." *Shelly Bullard.* http://shellybullard.com/the-4-qualities-of-a-conscious-relationship/.

———. "4 Tantric Practices That Create Intimacy and Connection in Your Relationship." *Shelly Bullard.* http://shellybullard.com/4-tantric-practices-create-intimacy-connection-relationship/.

———. "Conscious Relationships." *G Jewelry* (October 13, 2015). http://gjewelry.blogspot.com.

———. "The Truth About Chemistry Between Two People." *Mind Body Green* (June 20, 2013). http://www.mindbodygreen.com/0-9984/the-truth-about-chemistrybetween-two-people.html.

Campbell, Kelly, PhD. "Relationship Chemistry: Can Science Explain Instant Connections?" *Psychology Today* (August 21, 2011). https://www.psychologytoday.com/us/blog/more-chemistry/201108/relationship-chemistry-can-science-explain-instant-connections.

Carmen, Katelyn. "How to Reset Your Wife When She's Falling Apart." *Family Share* (October 28, 2016). https://familyshare.com/26288/how-to-reset-your-wife-when-shes-falling-apart.

Cernovich, Mike. "Raise Testosterone, Lower Cortisol, and Look Taller." *Danger and Play* (June 23, 2014). http://www.dangerandplay.com/2014/06/23/raise-testosterone-lowercortisol-look-taller/.

Chernof, Angel. "20 Habits Happy Couples Have (But Never Talk About)." *Marc and Angel* (February 11, 2015). http://www.marcandangel.com/2015/02/11/20-habits-happy-couples-have/.

Christian, Melanie. "The Real Reason Why Women Lose Interest in Men." *The Minds Journal.* http://themindsjournal.com/why-women-lose-interest-in-men/.

Chubb, Tanaaz. "The Difference Between Soulmates and Life Partners." *The Minds Journal.* https://themindsjournal.com/the-difference-between-soulmates-and-life-partners/.

Christine3005. "Pandoras Box Vin DiCarlo." *Slideshare* (March 7, 2014). http://www.slideshare.net/Christine3005/pandoras-box-vin-dicarlo-32032029?related=1.

Clark, John Alex. "How to Use Psychology to Make Someone Fall (and Stay) in Love with You." *The Minds Journal.* http://themindsjournal.com/use-psychology-make-someone-fall-in-love/.

———. "The #1 Way to Create Chemistry without Saying a Word." *Dating Advice* (October 9, 2015). http://www.datingadvice.com/for-men/the-1-way-to-createchemistry-without-saying-a-word.

Clerke, Philipss. "Innocent Words That Turn Women On." *Slideshare* (October 13, 2013). http://www.slideshare.net/philipssclerke/make-any-girl-want-to-fuck.

Cola, Frankie. "How to Create Chemistry with a Girl—One Simple Conversation 'Trick' That Triples Your Chemistry with Women." *Slideshare* (March 21, 2015). http://www.slideshare.net/mrmojo13/chemistry-tension.

———. "How to Get a Girl to Chase You—8 Reasons You Should Be Sending Mixed Signals." *Slideshare* (November 18, 2015). http://www.slideshare.net/mrmojo13/how-to-get-a-girl-to-chase-you-8-reasons-you-should-be-sending-mixed-signals.

Coleman, Toni. "True Love and Chemistry: Finding Your Soul Mate." *The Sideroad*. http://www.sideroad.com/Relationships/love-and-chemistry-finding-your-soul-mate.html.

Conger, Cristen. "Love Potion No. 9: Top 5 Love Chemicals in the Brain." *Stuff Mom Never Told You.* http:// www.stuffmomnevertoldyou.com/blogs/5-love-chemicals-in-the-brain5.htm.

Connop, Cynthia. "Polarity, Sex and Self-love." *Living Love Blog* (December 18, 2015). http://livinglove.com.au/polarity-sex-and-self-love/.

———. "Warrior Tips for Men." *Living Love Blog* (February 2015). http://livinglove.com.au/wp-content/uploads/2015/02/Warrior-tips-for-men.pdf.

———. "Feminine Pleasure Plan Tips." *Living Love Blog* (January 2015). http://livinglove.com.au/wp-content/uploads/2015/01/Feminine-pleasure-plan-tips-e1362349174633.jpg.

ConradDrake. "Steven Peliari PDF Covert Hypnosis Rules of Persuasion." *Slideshare* (October 30, 2012). http://www.slideshare.net/ConradDrake/steven-peliari-pdf-covert-hypnosis-rules-of-persuasion.

Cooley, Grace. "Why Nice Guys Finish Last." *The Elephant Journal* (November 30, 2014). http:// www.elephantjournal.com/2014/11/why-nice-guys-finish-last/.

Cournia, Zoe. "The Chemistry of Love." *Life Is Chemistry*. https://lifeischemistry.com/tag/vasopressin/.

CovertHypnosis. "How to Conversational Hypnotic Words to Enchant Anyone." *Slideshare* (April 1, 2009). http://www.slideshare.net/CovertHypnosis/how-to-conversational-hypnotic-words-to-enchant-anyone.

Datu, Arvhie. "The DiCarlo Escalation Ladder." *Slideshare* (September 15, 2012). http://www.slideshare.net/vhie130501/16768511-vindicarloescalationladder.

Deane, Alban and Patrick Alban. "Serotonin Deficiency: Signs, Symptoms, Solutions." *Be Brain Fit.* https://bebrainfit.com/serotonin-deficiency/.

De Flandes, Juan. "Seduce Her with Words," *Slideshare* (June 20, 2008). http://www.slideshare.net/donjuandeflandes/seduce-her-with-words.

Deida, David. "The Play of Sexual Polarity and Its Effects on Relationship Choices." *Awaken* (January 24, 2013). http://www.awaken.com/2013/01/the-play-of-sexual-polarity-and-its-effects-on-relationship-choices/.

———. "David Deida on Sexual Polarity." *Integral Options Café* (March 21, 2008). http://integral-options.blogspot.com/2008/03/david-deida-on-sexual-polarity.html.

Dennert, Jake. "Words That Attract Women: Your Unfair Advantage over Rich, GoodLooking Guys. . ." *Slideshare* (March 3, 2012). http://www.slideshare.net/jakedennert/words-that-attract-women-your-unfair-advantage-over-rich-good-looking-guys.

Developed Man. "Why Chemistry Is Not Sexual Attraction." *Developed Man* (December 19, 2014). http://developedman.com/sexual-attraction/.

———. "The Truth About What Women Want (It's Wladimir Klitschko)." *Developed Man* (December 14, 2014). http://developedman.com/wladimir-klitschko/.

———. "Get out of Friend Zone—The Virtues of Lovers vs. Friends." *Developed Man* (September 17, 2013). http://developedman.com/get-out-of-friend-zone/.

Diamond, Jed. "Red Hot Sex and Real Lasting Love: Understanding the New Science of Desire." *Men Alive* (February 12, 2016). http://menalive.com/red-hot-sex-and-real-lasting-love-understanding-the-new-science-of-desire/.

———. "The One Thing Men Want More Than Sex." *Good Men* Project (February 17, 2017). https://goodmenproject.com/sex-relationships/the-one-thing-men-want-more-than-sex-wcz/.

———. "Testosterone: 10 Surprising Things Every Woman and Man Needs to Know." *Men Alive* (March 24, 2017). http://menalive.com/testosterone/.

DiCarlo, Vin. "How to Create Chemistry Between You and a Girl You Want." *Vin DiCarlo.* http://vindicarlo.com/how-to-create-chemistry-between-you-and-a-girl-you-want/.

DiDonato, Theresa E., PhD. "Do Nice Guys Really Finish Last?" *Psychology Today* (March 15, 2014). https://www.psychologytoday.com/blog/meet-catch-and-keep/201405/do-nice-guys-really-finish-last.

Doktor, Ray Dr. "What Is the Difference Between Love, Falling in Love, and Sexual Attraction?" *Ray Doktor.* http://raydoktor.com/what-is-the-difference-between-love-falling-in-love-and-sexual-attraction/.

Duncan, Adrian. "7 Stages of a Twin Flame Relationship." *Astrology Answers* (June 6, 2016). http://astrologyanswers.com/article/relationship-compatibility-stages-of-the-twin-flame-union/.

Dwivedi, Richa. "15 Tricks That Lead to a Long and Happy Relationship." *Witty Feed.* https://www.wittyfeed.com/story/32049/1/15-Tricks-That-Lead-To-A-Long-And-Happy-Relationship?i=2.

Edwards, Scott. "Love and the Brain." *Harvard Medical School.* http://neuro.hms.harvard.edu/harvard-mahoney-neuroscience-institute/brain-newsletter/and-brain-series/love-and-brain.

Eliyah. "The Healthy and Unhealthy Masculine and Feminine: An Easy Guide." *Eliyah* (October 17, 2016). https://www.eliyah.com.au/the-healthy-and-unhealthy-masculine-and-feminine-an-easy-guide/.

Enlightened Consciousness Staff. "Why Women Leave Men They Love—Every Man Needs to Know," *Enlightened Consciousness* (November 27, 2016). http://www.enlightenedconsciousness.com/why-women-leave-men-they-love-every-man-needs-to-know-1/.

Etsy. "Pressed Flowers Jewelry ARROW ARMOR pendant." *Etsy Jewelry.* https://www.etsy.com/listing/253581061/pressed-flowers-jewelry-arrow-armor?ref=shop_home_listings.

Everts, Sarah. "The Truth About Pheromones." *Smithsonian Magazine* (March 2012). http://www.smithsonianmag.com/science-Nature/the-truth-about-pheromones-100363955/.

Evolution: Male. "Sexual Polarity, Part 1." *Evolution: Male* (April 18, 2011). https://evolutionmale.wordpress.com/2011/04/18/sexual-polarity-part-1/.

———. "Take the Lead . . . It's Your Job." *Evolution: Male* (March 24, 2011). https://evolutionmale.wordpress.com/2011/03/24/take-the-lead . . . it's-your-job/.

———. "Why 'Nice Guys' Aren't Really Nice." *Evolution: Male* (March 6, 2011). https://evolutionmale.wordpress.com/2011/03/06/nice-guys-arent-really-nice/.

———. "Lessons About Women I Would Teach My Younger Self." *Evolution: Male* (July 31, 2012). https://evolutionmale.wordpress.com/2012/07/31/lessons/.

———. "Eye Contact Part 3: The Look of Love." *Evolution: Male* (August 22, 2011). https://evolutionmale.wordpress.com/2011/08/22/eye-contact-part-3-the-look-of-love/#more-94.

Felicity, Keith. "Your Looks Aren't to Blame for His Lack of Interest ... But Here Is What Is." *Digital Romance* (December 26, 2016). https://digitalromanceinc.com/dating/hislack-of-interest-your-looks-arent-blame/.

Fiore, Michael. "Why Men Lie to Women They Truly Do Love." *Michael C. Fiore* (January 13, 2017). http://michaelcfiore.com/men-lie-women-truly-love/.

Flanagan, Graham. "6 Scientifically Proven Features Men Find Attractive in Women." *Business Insider Australia* (May 16, 2015). https://www.businessinsider.com.au/scientifically-ways-women-attractive-2015-5.

Fleming, Ian. "James Bond (Personality and Traits)." *FANDOM.* http://jamesbond.wikia.com/wiki/James_Bond_(Personality_and_Traits).

Fletcher, Victoria. "Crazy in Love: What Happens in Your Brain When You Really Do Have Chemistry." *Daily Mail UK* (November 10, 2012). http://www.dailymail.co.uk/health/ article-2230969/Crazy-love-What-happens-brain-really-chemistry.html.

Geist, Lyn. "How Do We Fall in Love?" *Psycho to Go.* https://www.psych2go.net/fall-love-head/.

Gerzema, John. "Feminine Values Can Give Tomorrow's Leaders an Edge." *Harvard Business Review* (August 12, 2013). https://hbr.org/2013/08/research-male-leaders-should-think-more-like-women.

Gestalt Reality. "Archetypal Masculine and Feminine Forces—the Keys to Creation." *Rise Earth* (2016). http://www.riseearth.com/2016/06/archetypal-masculine-feminine-forces.html.

Gleason, Annie. "How to Add Spark and Create Chemistry." *Get a Love Life* (September 5, 2013). http://www.getalovelife.net/dating-blog/entry/chemistry/how-to-add-spark-and-create-chemistry.

Goldstein, Elisha. "How to Fall in Love and Uncover Happiness in 4 Minutes or Less." *Mindful* (March 6, 2015). http://www.mindful.org/how-to-fall-in-love-and-uncover-happiness-in-4-minutes-or-less.

Goulston, Dr. Mark. "Psychiatrist Reveals 10 Habits of Happy Couples (#7 Is A Must Do For Everyone)." *Simple Capacity* (January 10, 2017). https://simplecapacity.com/2017/01/10-habits-of-happy-couples/.

Gray, Jordan. "6 Connection Exercises for Couples to Build Intimacy." *Jordan Gray Consulting* (November 18, 2014). https://www.jordangrayconsulting.com/2014/11/6-connection-exercises-for-couples-to-build-intimacy/.

———. "10 Questions to Ask to Go Deep in Your Relationship." *Jordan Gray* (August 19, 2014). https://www.jordangrayconsulting.com/2014/08/questions-to-ask-to-go-deep-in-your-relationship/.

Gupta, Anil. "5 Questions to Instantly Change Your Family Relationships." *Mind Valley Academy.* http://blog.mindvalleyacademy.com/parenting-and-family/5-questions-instantly-transform-family-relationships.

Hall, Steve. "Why Couples Who Argue Love Each Other More." *Power of Positivity.* https://www.powerofpositivity.com/couples-argue-love/.

Happify. "Science Behind a Happy Relationship." *Happify.* http://my.happify.com/hd/the-science-behind-a-happy-relationship/.

Hatch, Stephen. "Feminine and Masculine Shape-Shifting: Experimenting with a Contemplative Essentialism." *Jesus Jazz and Buddhism.* http://www.jesusjazzbuddhism.org/feminine-and-masculine-shape-shifting-experimenting-with-contemplative-essentialism.html.

Hendricks, Katie and Gay Hendricks. "Create Real Intimacy by Changing This One Thing." *Hearts in True Harmony.* http://www.heartsintrueharmony.com/relationship-bliss/create-real-intimacy-by-changing-this-one-thing.html?s=11745.

———. "6 Important Changes You MUST Make If You Want to Find Love." *Your Tango* (January 25, 2016). http://www.yourtango.com/experts/katie-and-gay-hendricks/6-important-changes-to-make-ASAP-to-learn-how-to-find-love.

Hogan, Kathryn. "Why Nice Guys Stay Single." *The Minds Journal.* http://themindsjournal.com/why-nice-guys-stay-single/.

Hormone Health Network. "What Is Estrogen?" *Hormone Health Network.* http://www.hormone.org/hormones-and-health/hormones/estrogen.

Hypnosis Unlocked. "The 5 Most Powerful Hypnotic Seduction Techniques." *Slideshare* (July 18, 2013). https://www.slideshare.net/hypnosisunlocked/slideshare-the-5-most-powerful-hypnotic-seduction-techniques?qid=4f5d940d-57c0-4b79-8abb-523cee1b59a2&v=&b=&from_search=1http://www.slideshare.net/hypnosisunlocked/slideshare-the-5-mostpowerful-hypnotic-seduction-techniques?qid=a5157bd8-30fe-4979-891a-5adb06287 668andv=defaultandb=andfrom_search=1.

Indra. "Full Spectrum Bliss: The Secret to an Oxytocin-Based Sexual Connection." *Wake Up World* (September 28, 2015). http://wakeup-world.com/2015/09/28/full-spectrum-sex-the-secret-to-oxytocin-and-blissful-sexual-connection/.

———. "Sex, Love and Oxytocin—The Full Spectrum Connection." *Wake Up World* (April 24, 2015). http://wakeup-world.com/2015/04/29/sex-love-and-oxytocin-the-full-spectrum-connection/.

Instantfamily. "How to Increase Your Pheromones-Attract the Opposite Sex." *Hub Pages* (June 20, 2015). https://hubpages.com/relationships/How-to-Increase-Your-Pheromones.

Ioa. "An Alpha Female: The Best Girlfriend You'll Ever Have." *The Minds Journal.* http://themindsjournal.com/alpha-female-girlfriend/.

———. "The Reason Why We Lose Interest in People Who Show Too Much Interest in Us." *The Minds Journal.* http://themindsjournal.com/why-we-lose-interest-in-people/.

Jameson, Sean. "11 Signs of Sexual Attraction You Must Know." *Bad Girls Bible* (April 2, 2014). http://badgirlsbible.com/signs-of-sexual-attraction.

Johnson, Dr. Sue. "Where Does Love Go Wrong?" *Dr. Sue Johnson Creating Connections* (2013). http://www. drsuejohnson.com/where-does-love-go-wrong/.

Johnston, Trudy. "Understanding Masculine and Feminine Essence." *Sacred Women's Business* (March 4, 2016). http://www.sacredwomensbusiness.com/understanding-masculine-feminine-essence/.

Jones, Daniel. "The 36 Questions That Lead to Love." *New York Times* (January 9, 2015). https://www.nytimes.com/2015/01/11/fashion/no-37-big-wedding-or-small.html.

K., Apollonas. "The 3 Types of Friendships Defined by Aristotle 2400 Years Ago Are Still Valid Today." *Life Advancer.* http://www.lifeadvancer.com/types-of-friendships-aristotle-defined.

K., Sara Ann. "On Creating Chemistry: A Letter to My Single Friends." *Sara Ann K* (February 4, 2016). http://saraannk.com/2016/02/on-creating-chemistry-a-letter-to-my-single-friends/.

Kevin. "How to Avoid the Friend Zone by Being Sexual with Women." *Root of Attraction* (March 25, 2013). http://www.rootofattraction.com/how-to-avoid-the-friend-zone-bybeing-sexual-with-women/.

———. "Being Sexual with Women—Desire and Expression." *Root of Attraction* (April 23, 2011). http://www.rootofattraction.com/sexual-desire-and-expression/.

Kirschner, Dr. Diana. "Six Relationship Tips to Spark Chemistry with a Good Man." *Love in 90 Days.* http://lovein90days.com/six-tips-to-spark-chemistry-with-a-good-man/.

Knowles, Brenda. "Masculine, Feminine, Dominance and the Love Dance." *Brenda Knowles.* http://brendaknowles.com/masculine-feminine-dominance-and-the-love-dance/.

Knit. "Illegal Seduction Technique." *Slideshare* (January 2, 2013). http://www.slideshare. net/Knit/illegal-seduction-technique.

LadyLux. "The Secrets of Creating Chemistry." *LadyLux* (September 2, 2015). http://www. ladylux.com/articles/the-secrets-of-creating-chemistry.

Lalla, Annie. "5 Things He Must Feel to Fall in Love." *Annie Lalla.* http://annielalla.com/6-things-must-feel-fall-love/ .

———. "These Are the 5 Proven Things That Make a Man Fall in Love." *Medium* (February 13, 2014). https://medium.com/@MindvalleyAuthors/these-are-the-5proven-things-that-make-a-man-fall-in-love-271f113ca90c#.rfxu9ilus.

Last, Walter. "The Neurochemistry of Sex." *Health Science Spirit.* http://www.health-science-spirit.com/neurosex.html.

———. "Sexual Relationships." *Health Science Spirit.* http://www.health-science-spirit. com/sexrelation.html.

Lin, Vince. "Polarity/Sexual Polarity." *Pua Lingo* (August 12, 2009). http://www.pualingo. com/polarity/.

Lipton, Dr. Bruce and Dr. Deborah Sandella. "The Biology of Love." *Uplift Connect* (July 24, 2016). http://upliftconnect.com/the-biology-of-love/.

Livzy. "How to Know If Your Relationship with Someone Is Karmic, Soulmate or Twin Flame." *The Mind Journal.* http://themindsjournal.com/how-to-tell-if-a-relationship-is-karmic-soulmate-or-twin-flame/.

Loyola University Health System. "What Falling in Love Does to Your Heart and Brain." *ScienceDaily* (February 6, 2014). https://www.sciencedaily.com/releases/2014/02/140206155244.htm.

Macke, Emily. "Oxytocin, Vasopressin and a Tale of Two Voles." *The New View on Sex* (April 4, 2008). http://thenewviewonsex.blogspot.com/2008/04/oxytocin-vasopressin-and-tale-of-two.html.

Maniaci, Dr. Joylyn. "The Easy Button to Getting What You Want From Your Man." *Digital Romance* (December 28, 2016). https://digitalromanceinc.com/romance/getting-what-you-want-from-your-man-easy-button/.

Martin, Brandon. "What a Man Finds MAGNETICALLY Attractive." *Yintegrity.* http://yintegrity.com/saving-a-relationship/the-magnetism-that-draws-men-and-women-together-polarity.

Martin, Sharon. "10 Steps to Setting Healthy Bounderies." *Psych Central.* http://blogs.psychcentral.com/imperfect/2016/05/10-steps-to-setting-healthy-bounderies/.

Martinez, Silvia. "The Chemistry of Love." *Silviamar.* http://www.silviamar.com/Documents/love.htm.

Mcloughlin, Claire. "Science of Love—Cupid's Chemistry." *The Naked Scientists* (February 14, 2006). https://www.thenakedscientists.com/articles/features/science-love-cupids-chemistry.

Menzel, Elizabeth. "What Is Your Love Energy Really Attracting?" *The Good Men Project* (February 13, 2014). https://goodmenproject.com/author/elizabeth-menzel/.

Miller, Luke. "5 Non Sexual Ways to Be Intimate." *Truth Theory* (February 14, 2017). http:// truththeory.com/2017/02/14/5-non-sexual-ways-intimate/.

———. "What Happens to Your Body and Brain When You Fall in Love." *Truth Theory* (April 28, 2016). http://truththeory.com/2016/04/28/what-happens-to-your-body-and-brain-when-you-fall-in-love/.

mind GAG. "How to Flirt over Text." *Slideshare* (July12, 2014). http://www.slideshare.net/mindGAG/how-to-flirt-over-text-by-mind-gag.

Minds Journal. "If Your Partner Does Any of These 5 Things, Never Let Them Go." *The Minds Journal.* http://themindsjournal.com/if-your-partner-does/.

Mind Openerz. "21 Habits of Happy People." *Mind Openerz* (January 30, 2013). http://www.mindopenerz.com/21-habits-of-happy-people/.

Miss Solomon. "How to Get out of the Friend Zone." *The Dating Truth.* http://www.thedatingtruth.com/2015/06/how-to-get-out-of-the-friend-zone/.

Modern Man Blueprint. "Rekindle Your Intimacy by Discovering Your Masculinity." *Modern Man Blueprint* (April 26, 2015). http://www.modernmanblueprint.com/rekindle-your-intimacy-by-discovering-your-masculinity/.

Mogul. "Do Not Get Married Unless You Ask Your Partner These 15 Questions Or Else You'll Wish You Had." *Mogul.* https://onmogul.com/stories/do-not-get-married-unless-you-ask-your-partner-these-15-questions-or-else-you-ll-wish-you-had.

Morava, Matthew Larsen. "Right Where You Belong: Thoughts on Cultivating Vitality in Romantic Relationships." *Slideshare* (September 20, 2011). https:// www.slideshare.net/MMORAVA/healthy-relationships-9347352.

Naden, Liam. "Using the Law of Opposites to Create a Great Marriage." *Liam Naden* (April 7, 2014). http://liamnaden.com/using-the-law-of-opposites-to-create-a-great-marriage/.

Nguyen, Thai. "Hacking Into Your Happy Chemicals: Dopamine, Serotonin, Endorphins and Oxytocin." *Huffington Post* (October 20, 2014). http://www.huffingtonpost.com/thai-nguyen/hacking-into-your-happy-c_b_6007660.html.

Nickols, Sherri. "How You're Ruining Your Relationship." *Your Tango* (February 27, 2013). http://www.yourtango.com/experts/sherri-nickols/5-ways-living-your-masculine-energy-blocks-love-expert?page=1.

Noronha, Helen. "11 Little Things Men Secretly Adore About the Woman They Love." *The Minds Journal*. http://themindsjournal.com/men-adore-woman-love/.

Not Your Average Bro. "The Three Types of Chemistry You Need to Make Your Relationship Successful." *Not Your Average Bro* (November 13, 2014). http://notyouraveragebro.com/dating-tidbits-and-advice/the-three-types-of-chemistry-you-need-to-make-your-relationship-successful/.

Page, Lisa. "The Secret to Keeping Love, Passion and Connection Alive in a Long-term Relationship (Part 1 of 3)." *Digital Romance* (December 30, 2016). https://digitalromanceinc.com/romance/long-term-relationship-secret-keeping-love-passion-connection-alive-part-1-of-3/.

———. "The Secret to Keeping Love, Passion and Connection Alive in a Long-term Relationship (Part 2 of 3)." *Digital Romance* (January 6, 2017). https://digitalromanceinc.com/romance/long-term-relationship-secret-keeping-love-passion-connection-alive-part-2-of-3/.

———. "The Secret to Keeping Love, Passion and Connection Alive in a Long-term Relationship (Part 3 of 3)." *Digital Romance* (January 13, 2017). https://digitalromanceinc.com/romance/long-term-relationship-secret-keeping-love-passion-connection-alive-part-3-of-3/.

Patenaude, Monique. "The Right Kind of Intimacy Keeps Couples Feeling Sexy." *Futurity* (July 21, 2016). http://www.futurity.org/passion-sex-intimacy-1208202-2/.

Plett, Heather. "What It Really Means to Hold Space for Someone." *Uplift Connect* (September 1, 2018). http://upliftconnect.com/hold-space/.

Proffitt Howells, Shelli. "20 Ways to Make Your Wife Fall in Love with You—Again." *Family Share*. https://familyshare.com/1884/20-ways-to-make-your-wife-fall-in-love-with-you-again.

Psalm, Isadora. "How to Boost Testosterone and Last Longer In Bed." *Mind Valley*. http://blog.mindvalleyacademy.com/love-and-relationships/increase-testosterone-last-bed.

———. "Want Multiple Orgasms? Here Are 8 Simple Techniques." *Mind Valley*. http://blog.mindvalleyacademy.com/love-and-relationships/how-have-multiple-orgasms.

———. "All You Need To Know About Tantra (Infographic)." *Mind Valley*. http://www.mindvalleyacademy.com/blog/body/tantra-touch-infographic.

Rave, Liz. "Polarity 101: An Intro to Masculine and Feminine Dynamics." *The Art of Flirting* (January 16, 2012). http://www.artofflirting.com/polarity-101-an-intro-to-masculine-and-feminine-dynamics.

———. "It's Called Sexual TENSION for a Reason." *The Art of Flirting* (September 18, 2012). http://www.artofflirting.com/its-called-sexual-tension-for-a-reason.

———. "Leadership Part 1: Becoming the Masculine Leader that Women Are Looking For." *The Art of Flirting* (May 16, 2013). http://www.artofflirting.com/leadership-part-1-becoming-the-masculine-leader-that-women-are-looking-for.

———. "The Key to Fostering Sexual Tension." *The Art of Flirting* (October 27, 2014). http://www.artofflirting.com/the-key-to-fostering-sexual-tension.

———. "Why Women (Sometimes) Date Jerks." *The Art of Flirting* (August 7, 2013). http://www.artofflirting.com/why-women-sometimes-date-jerks.

———. "Leadership Part 2: How to Inspire His Strength through Being More Feminine." *The Art of Flirting* (May 23, 2013). http://www.artofflirting.com/leadership-part-2-how-to-inspire-his-strength-through-being-more-feminine.

———. "Polarity Principles, a.k.a. Rant on Gender Roles, Societal Pressures, and Achieving Sexual Fulfillment." *The Art of Flirting* (June 11, 2013). http://www.artofflirting.com/polarity-principles-a-k-a-rant-on-gender-roles-societal-pressures-andachieving-sexual-fulfillment.

———. "Reader Question: How Do I Handle Being in the 'Friend Zone'?" *The Art of Flirting* (June 21, 2013). http://www.artofflirting.com/reader-question-how-do-i-handle-being-in-the-friend-zone.

———. "Romance vs. Logic." *Getting Inside a Woman* (September 16, 2011). http://www.gettinginsideawoman.com/romance-vs-logic.

———. "I Just Don't Think of You That Way." *Getting Inside a Woman* (April 21, 2011). http://www.gettinginsideawoman.com/i-just-dont-think-of-you-that-way/.

———. "Animal Desire (a.k.a. Why Women Love Edward from Twilight)." *Getting Inside a Woman* (December 7, 2010). http://www.gettinginsideawoman.com/animal-desire-why-women-love-edward-cullen-from-twilight/.

———. "Why You're in the Friend Zone." *Getting Inside a Woman* (June 17, 2010). http://www.gettinginsideawoman.com/why-youre-in-the-friend-zone/.

———. "How to Flirt: With a Graph and an Equation." *The Art of Flirting* (October 18, 2012). http://www.artofflirting.com/how-to-flirt-with-a-graph-and-an-equation.

———. "How to Get Your (Much-Needed) Space." *Getting Inside a Woman* (November 2, 2011). http://www.gettinginsideawoman.com/how-to-get-your-much-needed-space/.

———. "3 Myths About Masculinity in Relationships." *Getting Inside a Woman* (August 26, 2011). http://www.gettinginsideawoman.com/3-myths-about-masculinity-in-relationships/.

———. "Searching for the Perfect Woman?" *Getting Inside a Woman* (August 12, 2011). http://www.gettinginsideawoman.com/searching-for-the-perfect-woman/.

Reader's Digest editor. "8 Natural Ways to Increase Endorphins Instantly." *Reader's Digest.* https:// www.rd.com/health/wellness/natural-endorphin-boosters/1/.

Relationship Rules. "A True Story That Will Bring Tears to Your Eyes—Choose Him or Her Everyday." *Relationship Rules* (January 31, 2016). http://www.relrules.com/true-story-choose-him-or-her-everyday/.

Relationship Rules. "18 Signs That Prove—HE Truly Loves You." *Relationship Rules* (March 28, 2018). http:// www.relrules.com/18-signs-that-prove-he-truly-loves-you/.

———. "8 Reason Why Giving a Chance to the 'Nice Guy' Can Be the Best Decision." *Relationship Rules* (July 25, 2016). http://www.relrules.com/dating-nice-guy-best-decision/.

———. "10 Signs Your Relationship Is a Healthy One That Will Last Forever." *Relationship Rules* (July 13, 2016). https://www.relrules.com/10-signs-your-relationship-is-a-healthy-one-that-will-last-forever/.

———. "8 Signs Your Relationship Is Worth Saving." *Relationship Rules* (August 4, 2018). http:// www.relrules.com/8-signs-your-relationship-is-worth-saving/.

————. "If Your Girl Does One of These 15 Things, Do Not Let Her Go." *Relationship Rules* (May 30, 2018). https://www.relrules.com/if-your-girl-does-one-of-these-15-things-do-not-let-her-go/.

————. "9 Signs You've Found Mr. Right." *Relationship Rules* (September 11, 2018). http://www.relrules.com/9-signs-youve-found-mr-right/4/.

Ricard, Alison. "10 Big Problems in a Relationship and How to Fix It." *Love Panky.* http://www.lovepanky.com/my-life/relationships/problems-in-a-relationship.

Robbins, Tony. "Watching Your Tone." *Tony Robbins.* https://www.tonyrobbins.com/love-relationships/watching-your-tone/.

Rogers, Kara. "Norepinephrine." *Encyclopædia Britannica.* https://www.britannica.com/science/norepinephrine.

Russell, Tracy. "How to Heal and Unite Your Inner Feminine and Masculine." *Cherie Roe Dirksen* (March 11, 2015). https://cherieroedirksen.com/2015/03/11/healing-and-integrating-your-inner-feminine-and-masculine/.

S., Valerie. "10 Signs You Have Found Your Soulmate." *Life Advancer.* http://www.lifeadvancer.com/10-signs-you-have-found-your-soulmate.

Salhi, Teresa. "Mistakes Women Make with Men." *Empower the Dream.* http://www.empowerthedream.com/mistakes-women-men/.

Salwaessa. "16 Unconventional Signs You've Found Your Soulmate." *The Minds Journal.* http://themindsjournal.com/unconventional-signs-soul mate/.

Santos, Glenn. "33 Ways to Increase Dopamine to Boost Your Productivity." *Endless* (March 15, 2018). http://helloendless.com/10-ways-to-increase-dopamine-to-boost-your-productivity/.

Satyapriya. "5 Qualities That Women Find Irresistible In Men." *Collectively Conscious.* http://collectivelyconscious.net/articles/5-qualities-that-women-find-irresistible-in-men/.

————. "Social Science Says Lasting Relationships Come Down to 2 Basic Traits." *Collectively Conscious.* http://collectivelyconscious.net/articles/social-science-says-lasting-relationships-come-down-to-2-basic-traits/.

————. "The Difference Between a Mature Relationship and an Immature Relationship." *Collectively Conscious.* http://collectivelyconscious.net/articles/the-difference-between-a-mature-relationship-and-an-immature-relationship/.

————. "7 Crazy Amazing Facts About the Clitoris." *Collectively Conscious* (October 20, 2015). http://collectivelyconscious.net/articles/7-crazy-amazing-facts-about-the-clitoris/.

————. "14 Ways to Create the Best Relationship of Your Life." *Collectively Conscious* (January 2, 2014). http://collectivelyconscious.net/articles/14-ways-to-create-the-bestrelationship-of-your-life/.

Saviuc, Luminita D. "6 Things You Should Know About True Love." *The Minds Journal.* https://themindsjournal.com/6-things-you-should-know-about-true-love/.

Self Hacked. "Norepinephrine: Good or Bad? (And Natural Ways to Increase It)." *Self Hacked* (June 23, 2017). https://selfhacked.com/2016/08/28/norepinephrine-stress-hormone/.

Shakti, Joanna. "5 Keys to Creating Chemistry." *Joanna Shakti's Blog* (August 4, 2013). https://ecstaticintimacy.com/5-keys-to-creating-chemistry/.

————. "The Masculine-Feminine Dance." *Joanna Shakti's Blog* (February 11, 2010). https://ecstaticintimacy.com/the-masculine-feminine-dance/.

Shvedova, Ksenia. "5 Meaningful Ways to Express Love That Make a Relationship Stronger." *Bright Side.* https://brightside.me/inspiration-relationships/5-meaningfulways-to-express-love-that-make-a-relationship-stronger-199305/.

Sinclair, Joel. "Relationships 101: The Masculine and Feminine Dance." *Joel Sinclair* (June 6, 2014). http://www.calgaryrelationshipcoach.com/2014/06/06/relationships-101-the-masculine-feminine-dance/.

Single Dating Diva. "The Impact of Instant Chemistry on Relationship Success." *Single Dating Diva.* https://singledatingdiva.com/2014/04/07/the-impact-of-instant-chemistry-on-relationship-success/.

Smith, Shannon. "How to Create Chemistry? ~ Masculine and Feminine Essence." *Shannon Roxy Smith.* http:// shannonrsmith.com/create-chemistry-masculine-feminine/.

Smith, Sylvia. "5 Marriage Secrets from Happily Married (A Long Time) Couples." *Finer Minds.* http://www.finerminds.com/love-relationships/marriage-secrets-happily-married-couples.

Staff at Like Love Quotes. "12 Things Happy Couples Talk About and Feel Closer." *Like Love Quotes.* http://likelovequotes.com/12-things-happy-couples-talk-about-and-feel-closer/.

———. "16 Reasons Why My Love Is Only for You." *Like Love Quotes.* http://likelovequotes.com/16-reasons-why-my-love-is-only-for-you/.

Starling, Josh. "21 Things Divorced Couples Say Would've Saved Their Marriage." *Inspire More* (January 8, 2017). http://www.inspiremore.com/21-things-couldve-saved-marriage/.

Terrazas, Janie. "Are You More Male or Female Brained In Your Relationship?" *Janie Terrazaz* (November 25, 2015). http://www.thelovecoaches.com/left-and-right-brain/.

Tessina, Tina B. "Love and Chemistry." *Tina B. Tessina* (2017). http://www.tinatessina.com/love-and-chemistry.html.

The Minds Journal. "Why Women Fall for the Bad Guys." *The Minds Journal.* http:// themindsjournal.com/women-fall-bad-guys/.

Toccaceli, Giordana. "When Your Partner Isn't Attracted to You Anymore." *Man Talks* (April 24, 2016). http://mantalks.com/when-your-partner-isnt-attracted-to-you-anymore/.

———. "How Masculine Men Protect Women's Feminine Energy." *Man Talks* (May 22, 2016). http://mantalks.com/masculine-men-protect-womens-feminine-energy/.

Tuartschwa. "Top 10 Vin Dicarlo Dating Tips," *Slideshare* (August 28, 2013). http://www.slideshare.net/tuartschwa/top-10-vin-dicarlo-dating-tips-j.

Urban, Tim. "How to Pick Your Life Partner—Part 1." *Wait But Why* (February 12, 2014). http://waitbutwhy.com/2014/02/pick-life-partner.html.

Valadez, Luis R. "Psychology Finally Reveals the Answer to Finding Your Soulmate." *Truth Theory* (November 15, 2014). http://truththeory.com/2014/11/15/psychology-finallyreveals-the-answer-to-finding-your-soulmate/.

W., Holly. "What's the Psychology Behind Why Women Fall for the Bad Guys." *Life Advancer.* http://www.lifeadvancer.com/why-women-fall-bad-guys.

———. "Psychology Finally Explains Why We Make the Same Mistakes in Our Relationships Over and Over." *Life Advancer.* https://www.lifeadvancer.com/make-same-mistakes-relationships/.

Wade, Renee. "6 Keys to Respecting a Masculine Man." *The Feminine Woman.* https://www.thefemininewoman.com/how-to-respect-a-man/.

———. "What Kind of Man Is Right for You?" *The Feminine Woman.* https://www.thefemininewoman.com/the-ideal-man-how-do-you-know-what-kind-of-man-is-right-for-you/.

———. "Surrendering to Masculine Energy." *The Feminine Woman.* https://www.thefemininewoman.com/surrendering-to-masculine-energy.

———. "5 Reasons Why Women Shouldn't Deprive Their Man of Sex." *The Feminine Woman.* https://www.thefemininewoman.com/5-reasons-why-women-shouldnt-deprive-their-man-of-sex/.

———. "Can You Really Expect Your Man to Be Monogamous?" *The Feminine Woman.* https://www.thefemininewoman.com/can-you-really-expect-a-man-to-be-monogamous/.

———. "Why Men Go Hot and Cold & 5 Things You Need to Do . . ." *The Feminine Woman.* https://www.thefemininewoman.com/why-men-go-hot-and-cold/.

———. "Feminine and Masculine Energy in Same-Sex Relationships." *The Feminine Woman.* https://www.thefemininewoman.com/feminine-and-masculine-energy-in-same-sex-relationships/.

———. "Surrendering to the Masculine Energy." *The Feminine Woman.* https://www.thefemininewoman.com/surrendering-to-masculine-energy/.

———. "Mistakes Women Make to Destroy Sexual Polarization with Men." *The Feminine Woman.* https://www.thefemininewoman.com/depolarization-mistakes-women-make/.

———. "How Most Women Reject Their Femininity & How You Can Stand Out from the Crowd." *The Feminine Woman.* https://www.thefemininewoman.com/how-most-women-reject-their-femininity-and-how-you-can-stand-out-from-the-crowd/.

———. "The Real Pain of When Men Pull Away & How to React in a High Value Way." *The Feminine Woman.* https://www.thefemininewoman.com/pain-of-when-men-pull-away/.

———. "Why Do Men Really Love Blowjobs?" *The Feminine Woman.* https://www.thefemininewoman.com/why-men-love-blow-jobs/.

Wade, Renee and D. Shen. "Not Knowing Where Your Relationship Is Going." *Shen Wade Media.* http://shenwademedia.com/offer/cc2offer/?utm_source=femwomblog&utm_medium=widget%20banner&utm_campaign=CC2&_ga=1.141558258.1568785838.1473160064.

Wanda881Davis. "How to Seduce Any Kind Of Woman Easily—Using 3 Confirmed Tips of Straightforward Seduction." *Slideshare* (February 27, 2012). http://www.slideshare.net/Wanda881Davis/how-to-seduce-any-kind-of-woman-easily-using-3-confirmedtips-of-straightforward-seduction.

Watkins, James. "How to Make Yourself Fall in Love—or Out of Love." *Ozy* (September 26, 2016). http://www.ozy.com/acumen/how-to-make-yourself-fall-in-love-or-out-oflove/71532.

Wayne, Corey. "Polarity & Attraction Secrets." *Corey Wayne: Life Is Relationships* (April 19, 2015). https://understandingrelationships.com/polarity-attraction-secrets/19523.

———. "What Women Are Attracted to in Men." *Corey Wayne: Life Is Relationships* (November 1, 2010). https://understandingrelationships.com/what-women-areattracted-to-in-men/688.

———. "How to 'Go with the Flow' with Women." *Corey Wayne: Life Is Relationships* (July 14, 2011). https://understandingrelationships.com/how-to-go-with-the-flowwith-women/2867.

———. "What Are We?" *Corey Wayne: Life Is Relationships* (January 16, 2014). https://understandingrelationships.com/what-are-we/16456.

———. "Jerks, Nice Guys & Assertive Men." *Corey Wayne: Life Is Relationships* (November 29, 2013). https://understandingrelationships.com/jerks-nice-guys-assertive-men/14709.

———. "Pickup & Date Questions That Build Attraction." *Corey Wayne: Life Is Relationships* (July 1, 2013). https://understandingrelationships.com/pickup-date-questions-that-build-attraction/13871.

———. "Women Want to Be in a Love Story." *Corey Wayne: Life Is Relationships* (November 4, 2010). https://understandingrelationships.com/women-want-to-be-in-alove-story/747.

———. "I Feel for You More As a Friend." *Corey Wayne: Life Is Relationships* (February 2, 2014). https://understandingrelationships.com/i-feel-for-you-more-as-a-friend/16531.

———. "How to Communicate with Women Effectively." *Corey Wayne: Life Is Relationships* (July 7, 2011). https://understandingrelationships.com/how-to-communicate-with-women-effectively/2667.

———. "Don't Complicate Things." *Corey Wayne: Life Is Relationships* (November 2, 2013). https://understandingrelationships.com/dont-complicate-things/14573.

———. "Why 'Nice Guys' Finish Last …" *Corey Wayne: Life Is Relationships* (November 29, 2011). https://understandingrelationships.com/why-nice-guys-finish-last/4822.

———. "Pay Attention to What a Woman Does, Not What She Says." *Corey Wayne: Life Is Relationships* (August 24, 2011). https://understandingrelationships.com/pay-attentionto-what-a-woman-does-not-what-she-says/3060.

———. "Women Want You at Your Best." *Corey Wayne: Life Is Relationships* (August 23, 2011). https://understandingrelationships.com/women-want-you-at-your-best/3044.

———. "10 Reasons Why Women Chase More." *Corey Wayne: Life Is Relationships* (October 3, 2016). https://understandingrelationships.com/10-reasons-why-women-chase-more/27330.

———. "Be a Gentleman, Not a Doormat." *Corey Wayne: Life Is Relationships* (November 18, 2011). https://understandingrelationships.com/be-a-gentleman-not-a-doormat/4485.

———. "A Swift Kick to Your Balls," *Corey Wayne: Life Is Relationships* (January 15, 2012). https://understandingrelationships.com/a-swift-kick-to-your-balls/5559.

———. "Be the Hero … Always." *Corey Wayne: Life Is Relationships* (November 23, 2011). https://understandingrelationships.com/be-the-hero-always/4698.

———. "Unbalanced Sexual Polarity." *Corey Wayne: Life Is Relationships* (December 5, 2015). https://understandingrelationships.com/unbalanced-sexual-polarity/24640.

Whitbourne, Susan Krauss, PhD. "11 Ways to Tell if Your Lover Loves You." *Psychology Today* (March 15, 2014). https://www.psychologytoday.com/us/blog/fulfillment-any-age/201403/11-ways-tell-if-your-lover-loves-you.

Wikipedia. "Estrogen." *Wikipedia English.* https://en.wikipedia.org/wiki/Estrogen.

Wikipedia. "Biological Basis of Love." *Wikipedia English.* https://en.wikipedia.org/wiki/Biological_basis_of_love.

Wilson, Jeff. "9 Signs You've Met Your True Soulmate." *The Minds Journal.* https://the-mindsjournal.com/9-signs-youve-met-true-soulmate/.

Xwayne. "Five Romantic Archetypes: Which One Are You?" *The Minds Journal.* https://themindsjournal.com/five-romantic-archetypes/3/.

Young, Simon N. "How to Increase Serotonin in the Human Brain without Drugs." *National Center for Biotechnology Information* (November 2007). https://www.ncbi.nlm.nih.gov/pmc/articles/PMC2077351/.

Zak, Paul J. "The Top 10 Ways to Boost Good Feelings." *Psychology Today* (November 7, 2013). https://www.psychologytoday.com/us/blog/the-moral-molecule/201311/the-top-10-ways-boost-good-feelings.

Ziogas, Lizzy. "The Dance of the Masculine & Feminine: How to Harmonize the Polarity of Our Relationships." *The Elephant Journal* (May 10, 2013). https://www.elephant-journal.com/2013/05/the-dance-of-the-masculine-feminine-how-to-harmonize-the-polarity-of-our-relationships-lizzy-ziogas/

"3 Tips for Dealing with Controlling Women." *Hot Alpha Female* (2012). http://hotalpha-female.com/2012/11/controllingwomen.html.

"4 Habits of Couples That Last." *Power of Positivity.* https://www.powerofpositivity.com/habits-of-couples-that-last/.

"6 Signs You're in a Relationship with Your Soulmate." *Power of Positivity.* https://www.powerofpositivity.com/soulmate-relationship-signs/.

"7 Important Things to Know Before Dating an Alpha Female." *The Usual Routine* (November 30, 2016). https://theusualroutine.com/2016/11/30/7-important-things-know-dating-alpha-female/.

"10 Pieces of Advice on How to Make Up After a Fight." *Bright Side.* https://brightside.me/inspiration-tips-and-tricks/10-pieces-of-advice-on-how-to-make-up-after-a-fight-252160/.

"10 Reasons People Fall Out of Love." *Power of Positivity.* https://www.powerofpositivity.com/people-fall-out-of-love/.

"10 Ways to Increase the Oxytocin in Your Body." *Power of Positivity.* https://www.powerof-positivity.com/increase-oxytocin-levels/.

"10 Ways to Supercharge Your Dopamine Levels to Never Feel Sad, Stressed or Depressed Again." *Simple Capacity.* https://simplecapacity.com/2016/10/supercharge-dopamine-levels-never-feel-sad-stressed-depressed/.

"13 Ways to Boost Your Oxytocin Levels (The Love Hormone)." *Sun Warrior* (February 2, 2017). https://sunwarrior.com/healthhub/13-ways-to-boost-your-oxytocin-levels-the-love-hormone.

"15 Celebrity Couples Who Prove That True Love Can Last Forever." *Bright Side.* https://brightside.me/wonder-people/15-celebrity-couples-who-prove-that-true-love-can-last-forever-207555/.

"16 Celebrity Couples Who Prove That Love Truly Can Last a Lifetime." *Bright Side.* https://brightside.me/article/15-celebrity-couples-who-prove-that-love-truly-can-lasta-lifetime-86455/.

"Are You More Astrologically Feminine or Masculine?" *South Florida Astrologer.* www.southfloridaastrologer.com/masculine--feminine-signs-are-you-more-masculine-or-feminine.html.

"Bringing Out 'The Feminine' in a Woman . . ." *Hot Alpha Female* (May 2013). http://hotalphafemale.com/2013/05/feminine-woman.html.

"Dating, Sex and the Masculine and Feminine Energies," *Dating to Relationship Advice.* http://www.datingtorelationshipadvice.com/DatingRelationshipTipsHelp/MasculineFeminine.html.

"Do Women Really Like Compliments?" *Hot Alpha Female* (February 2011). http://hotalphafemale.com/2011/02/do-women-really-like-compliments.html.

"Female Pheromones: 4 Ways to Use Your Feminine Charms." *Nexus Pheromones.* https://www.nexuspheromones.com/info/female-pheromones/.

"How to Get the One You Want . . . Or Not." *Hot Alpha Female* (2011). http://hotalphafemale.com/2011/06/how-to-get-the-one-you-want-or-not.html.

"How to Let More Love into Your Life." *I Soul Science* (June 2015). http://isoulscience.com/2015/06/how-to-let-more-love-into-your-life/.

"How to Tell She Is Emotionally Immature …" *Hot Alpha Female* (February 2011). http://hotalphafemale.com/2011/02/how-to-tell-she-is-emotionally-immature.html.

"Human Pheromones: The Science behind the Scent of Attraction." *Smart Publications.* http://www.smart-publications.com/articles/human-pheromones-the-science-behindthe-scent-of-attraction.

"I'm Only High Maintenance When You Don't Maintain Me …" *Hot Alpha Female* (January 2011). http://hotalphafemale.com/2011/01/im-only-high-maintenance-when-youdont-maintain-me.html.

"Keep Your Promise. Keep Her Interest." *Hot Alpha Female* (2013). http://hotalphafemale.com/2013/02/keep-your-promise.html.

"Little-Known Ways to Increase Your Natural Pheromone Levels." *Pheromone Authority.* http://www.pheromoneauthority.com/articles/increase-natural-pheromone-levels/.

"Masculine Attractions." *Alignment Technologies.* https://alignmenttechnologies.us/masculine-attractions.

"Masculine vs. Feminine Energy Crash Course." *Gurus Say.* https://www.gurussay.com/understanding-men/2014/3/masculine-feminine-energy-crash-course?rq=Masculine%20vs.%20Feminine%20Energy%20Crash%20Course.

"One Sentence Reminders Every Relationship Needs to Hear." *Power of Positivity.* https://www.powerofpositivity.com/one-sentence-reminders-every-relationship-needs-to-hear/.

"Research: Semen 'Is Good for Women's Health and Helps Fight Depression'." *Healing Life Is Natural* (July 22, 2016). http://healinglifeisnatural.com/research-semen-is-good-for-womens-health-and-helps-fight-depression/.

"Serotonin: What You Need to Know." *Health Line.* https://www.healthline.com/health/mental-health/serotonin.

"The Masculine Man and the Feminine Woman." *Hot Alpha Female* (March 2011). http://hotalphafemale.com/2011/03/the-masculine-man-and-the-feminine-woman.html.

"The Saga of Broken Men: The Three Reasons He Cannot Win Love." *The Minds Journal.* http://themindsjournal.com/the-saga-of-broken-men/.

"The Science of Love." *Your Amazing Brain.* http://www.youramazingbrain.org/lovesex/sciencelove.htm.

"The True Art of Flexible Persistence . . ." *Hot Alpha Female* (February 2012). http://hotal-phafemale.com/2011/02/the-true-art-of-flexible-persistence.html.

"Vasopressin (ADH): Its Role in Chronic Health Issues and How to Increase/Decrease It." *Self Hacked* (September 7, 2018). https://www.selfhacked.com/blog/need-know-vaso-pressin-role-chronic-health-issues/.

"What Keeps the Spark and Attraction Alive?" *Hot Alpha Female* (September 2011). http://hotalphafemale.com/2011/09/what-keeps-the-spark-and-attraction-alive.html.

"What She REALLY Means vs. What She Says." *Hot Alpha Female* (March 2013). http://hotalphafemale.com/2013/03/what-she-really-means.html.

"Why Women Leave Men They Love: What Every Man Needs to Know." *The Minds Journal.* http://themindsjournal.com/women-leave-men-love-every-man-needs-know/.

Note from the Publisher: Some of the articles had broken links at the time of the publishing of this book; as such, we opted to remove them.

MY THEORIES

The step-by-step guide to take you from where you are to where you want to be (structure and choice of content)

The Concept of Nature and Nurture in Relationships

The 8 Characters and the Relationship Character Types

The Emotional Love Connections

The Magical Love Formulas

The Love Cake

What Movies Taught Us

The 3 Scenarios

The Development of Relationships through each stage

The Evolution of relationship needs over time with Maslow's updated hierarchy of needs for relationships

The Positive, Negative, and Purpose of Each Relationship Stage

The 3 ingredients of the Magical Love Formula as well as the structure and choice of their content

The Eleven Love Connections

The Ingredients of Emotional Chemistry

Emotional Connection and Sexual Connection

Men Sexual Connection and Women Emotional Connection

Men Need Foreplay for Communication and Emotions

The Grey Theory

INDEX

Sternberg, Robert, 90
Strauss, Neil, 154, 235
stress hormone. *See* noradrenalin/
   norepinephrine
Strien, Jan van, 264–265
success, 191, 282–286
Superman power pose, 188, 232

T
Tailor, Tiffany, 98, 150
tantra, 279
tegmental area, 147, 290
tension. *See* sexual tension
Terrazas, Janie, 79
testosterone
   commitment and, 123
   levels in men and women, 123–124
   pheromones and, 126, 127
   recharging, 48, 75, 136
   role of, 122–123
   in stages of relationships, 74, 75
   Superman power pose and, 232
   triggering of, 122–123
tone of voice, 231, 233, 235–236
trust
   importance in relationships, 201
   in loving communication, 105
   male vs. female definitions of, 207–208
   non sexual ways to build and deepen,
      115–116
   during sex, 114
twin flame stage, 72

U
unconditional love
   in balance stage of relationships, 72
   freedom for partner to be or act as they
      please as, 301
   in friendships, 244
   putting ego aside in, 185, 186, 247, 284
   for self, 192–193
unhappy couples. *See* happy vs. unhappy
   couples
Unstoppable Foundation, 311

V
vagina
   biological nature of, 100
   energy flow and, 105, 108
   intercourse as connection, 141
   as passive and receptive, 105
   passivity and receptivity of, 105
   pheromones secreted from, 127
vasopressin, 137
venting, 45, 107, 158, 279
victim roles, fixed mindset and, 87
visualization, 189
voice. *See* tone of voice
vulnerability
   in arguments, 260, 264
   intimacy and, 242, 280, 287, 293
   sex and, 107
   of women, 172, 173, 213, 220

W
Wabi Sabi Love (Ford), 274, 275
Wade, Renee, 108–109, 269, 278
Walk of Light, 311
Wall, Sally N., 91
Walsh, Neale Donald, 71
Waters, Everett, 91
Wayne, Corey, 162, 197
The Well, 54
Wilcox, Woody, 152–153
Wile, Daniel, 185
women. *See also* Emotional Chemistry;
   Feminine Energy; femininity; vagina;
   women's needs vs. women's wants
   attraction to Mr. Bad, 33, 151–153,
      157, 161–162, 208
   creation of intimacy and connection
      by, 240–241
   defeminization of, 69
   emotional connection, 111
   emotional connection by, 104–109
   emotional needs of, 158–159
   foreplay, importance for, 105, 113–114
   irresistible qualities in men, 115
   Masculine Energy in, 39, 152, 160,
      163, 205
   mistakes made by, 103–104

ACKNOWLEDGMENTS

I WOULD LIKE TO RECOGNIZE each and every person who contributed directly as well as indirectly to the completion of this book.

First, I thank the Creator of all that is, the Light, Nefertiti, King Ahiram and Jupiter for their help and unlimited support throughout this journey.

Next, I thank my editors. I witnessed the Grey Dance of Editing through my *feminine energy* editor, Sandy Draper, and my *masculine energy* editor, Justin Spizman. I thank them both for their exceptional work that went beyond my expectations. Sandy and Justin turned an 800-page manuscript into the masterpiece you are holding now. I would also like to thank my proofreader, Sean Sabo. Despite his short time schedule, he managed to offer valuable recommendations. I would like to thank my designer (illustrations and characters), Zhivko Zelev, for his outstanding work; you are a brilliant mind reader and followed my brief for the character designs in exceptional fashion, sometimes even surpassing it. My cover is breathtaking, and it is all thanks to you, Amjad Shahzad; Nailia Minnebaeva, thank you for your final touches that added even more magic. Darlene Swanson of Van-garde Imagery marvelously crafted the typesetting and interior design of my book; thank you. Maria Sosnowski, you did a wonderful job as my indexer; thank you.

I would also like to thank the fantastic team that has been helping me bring the vision of my company to life, for without them, I wouldn't be here. Banafsheh Akhlagi, for her wonderful advice, and her deep care.

Bruce Cryer, for his great introductions. Nailia Minnebaeva, for her artistic genius. Rajie Kabli, for her great videographic talent. You are all pure gems. Each of you, with your own talent and personality, have contributed so much already, and I feel that this is just the beginning for us to spread some much needed love in the world.

Special thanks to the fantastic individuals and teams who helped bring this book to your hands—namely, Peggy McColl (the book writing program), Judy O'Beirn (Hasmark Publishing), Jackie Lapin (radio), Penny Sanseviery (AME), JoTo PR, Made for Success Publishing, Austin Netzley (2x), Joseph Alexander, Mark Dawson, Tina Dietz, Charbel Moarbes, and Ralph Sfeir and Suheil Najjar of Barb Agency.

Furthermore, I would like to recognize my teachers and colleagues of Grenoble Graduate School of Business: Dr. Jikyeong Kang, Dr. Alison Pierce, Dr. Michelle Mielly, Dina Antonios, Nora Berbery, Joanna Tamraz, and Vijay Shankar. From the Lebanese American University: Dr. Bassem Maamari, Dr. Leyla Mesarra, and Tony Moukarzel.

In addition, I would like to thank Rhonda Byrne, author of *The Secret*, and Bob Proctor, my "intellectual" mentor (Bob Proctor Coaching Program), for giving me the motivation necessary to start my personal development journey. Bob, you changed my life like night to day. Seven years later, I am still using your coaching program. It is a masterpiece. I would like to thank Jana Sharaf, my "spiritual" mentor, for her unconditional love and support. You taught me much more than you can imagine, and I am forever grateful to have you in my life.

Thank you, Tony Robbins—*Unlimited Power* and your motivational YouTube videos are simply phenomenal; Brian Tracy, your books and audios are simply wonderful. You give us very practical information that we can use on the spot! I particularly love your speech on self-confidence!; Robin Sharma, author of *The Monk Who Sold His Ferrari* and *The Leader Who Had No Title*, I love your storytelling style!; Esther and Jerry Hicks, I love all your books and all your work!; Louise L. Hay, you have filled my life with pure love. You taught me what self-love is—thank you; Dr. Bruce Lipton, I love your research on biology and how we can change our

DNA; Zig Ziglar, I love your tone of voice, and I look forward to modeling it someday; Jack Canfield, your success principles are magical!; John Assaraf, NeuroGym is one of the best tools I have used, and I will continue to use it. I love your genius concepts!; Vishen Lakhiani—Mindvalley, oh Mindvalley, a pure gem! I keep on learning, thank you!; T. Harv Eker, I love your book, *The Millionaire Mind*, and your "financial thermostat" concept; Brendon Burchard, author of *The Millionaire Messenger* and *The Charge*, your magnificent energy in your YouTube videos is inspirational. This is just the beginning! I look forward to starting your other programs. You are simply outstanding!; Glenn Harrold and Andrew Johnson, your hypnosis programs are simply wonderful!; Les Brown, Michael Jordan, Oprah Winfrey, Sir Richard Branson, and Muhammad Ali, your quotes and principle have been a true inspiration to never give up, for without all of you, I wouldn't have continued when times were tough.

I would like to thank Dr. John Gray, Dr. John Gottman, Dr. Helen Fisher, Dr. Leslie Becker-Phelps, Megan Kaye, Allan and Barbara Pease, David Deida, Neil Strauss, Renee Wade, Corey Wayne, Dr. Gary Chapman, Liz Rave, Jennifer Nielsen (*Hot Alpha Female*), Shelly Bullard, Nicholas Boothman, Andrew G. Marshall, Barbara De Angelis, Tiffany Taylor, Gerald Rogers, *Evolution: Male*, Carol S. Dweck, Christina Antonyan, Jed Diamond, Tracy Russel, Don Miguel Ruiz, Kathryn Hogan, Michael Pilinski, Heather Plett, Arielle Ford, Psalm Isadora, Semir Zeki, James Michael Sama, Annie Lalla, Susie and Otto Collins, Rob and Kristen Bell, Black Belt Seduction, Amy Cuddy, Michael Ellsberg, Kyle Benson, Giordana Toccaceli, Dr. Sue Johnson, Susan Bratton, Dr. Gail Slatz, Drs. Gay and Katie Hendricks, Hannah Fry, Daniel O' Leary, Angel Chernoff, Jordan Gray, Arthur Aron, Esther Perel, Tim Urban, Dr. Robert Sternberg, Chris D Cruz, Slade Shaw, Mia Summers, Amy Waterman, Cassandra Lorius, and many more in the relationship industry, for without all of you, this book could not have been written. Your work is pure genius.

Finally, I would like to thank my friends and family for their support daily. Through the bad times and good times, I know I can always count on them.

And a very special thanks to Elie Aoun, Carine Sarkis, Maïa Barghout, Sandra Naoum, Rebecca Chalach, Nayla, Randa Eid, Johanna Kazan, Laura Choueiri, Charles Abou Yakzan, Wissam Sabbagha, Elie Matta, and "My Ladies". Thank you, Michel Arystaghes, Tony Arystaghes, Gina Arystaghes, Tony Araman, Andrea Araman, and Philippe Araman for your feedback and very special support. Thank you to my sister for being such a unique bundle of love with such a big heart. Thank you to my mother for your love and support, which you are sharing in your own way. Thank you to my father, who is one of the first to believe in me and my project of spreading love in the world and backed me up. And last but not least, my ex-best friend, thank you.

ABOUT THE AUTHOR

By DANCING BETWEEN HIS HEART and his mind, George Araman has a fifty-year vision of spreading some much needed love around the world … so get ready for the Relationship Entrepreneur.

George was blessed to have been friend-zoned by his ex-best friend, as this allowed him to discover his life's purpose. Since then, he has dedicated himself to researching, experimenting, and writing. He wrote *The Grey Dance of Love* to show singles, friend-zoned individuals, and couples how to create sparks and how to be and grow in a magical relationship.

George believes that all the world's problems can be solved if we never give up. His message to you: "Your greatest treasure lies in your greatest struggle. If you never give up, even life itself will want to help you and make everything possible for you."

He plans on traveling around the world with his life partner and have sex on top of the Eight Wonders of the World. He has already seen more than thirty cities in Europe, Asia, and the Middle East, and he has been exposed to twenty-six different nationalities.

George is a proud member of Loudspeakers Toastmasters Club. He is also an avid reader of personal development books.

Meet George and discover your Relationship Character Type at
www.greydanceoflove.com.

www.ingramcontent.com/pod-product-compliance
Lightning Source LLC
LaVergne TN
LVHW091246080426
835510LV00007B/141